O My America!

O My America!

SIX WOMEN

AND THEIR

SECOND ACTS

IN A

NEW WORLD

Sara Wheeler

FARRAR, STRAUS AND GIROUX / NEW YORK

Farrar, Straus and Giroux
18 West 18th Street, New York 10011

Grateful acknowledgment is made to Bodleian Library Publishing, University of
Oxford, for permission to reprint quotations from Zoë Klippert (ed.),
An Englishwoman in California: The Letters of Catherine Hubback, 1871–76, 2010.

End-of-chapter illustrations of bird, toad, greyhound, ferret, and duck courtesy of
Shutterstock.com.

Library of Congress Cataloging-in-Publication Data
Wheeler, Sara.
    O my America! : six women and their second acts in a new world /
Sara Wheeler. — First American edition.
        pages   cm
    "Originally published, in somewhat different form, in 2013 by Jonathan
Cape, Great Britain, as O my America! : second acts in a New World"—
T.p. verso.
    Includes bibliographical references and index.
    ISBN 978-0-374-29881-4 (hardcover) — ISBN 978-1-4668-3690-7 (e-book)
    1. British—United States—History—19th century.   2. Women
travelers—United States—History—19th century.   3. Women travelers—
United States—Biography.   4. United States—Social conditions—19th
century.   I. Title.

E184.B7 W45 2013
973.9—dc23

                                                              2013007572

Designed by Abby Kagan
Map by Jane Randfield

www.fsgbooks.com
www.twitter.com/fsgbooks • www.facebook.com/fsgbooks

1   3   5   7   9   10   8   6   4   2

O my America! my new-found-land,
My kingdome, safeliest when with one man man'd,
My Myne of precious stones: My Emperie,
How blest am I in this discovering thee!

—JOHN DONNE

CONTENTS

Author's Note   xi
List of Illustrations   xiii
Map   xviii

Introduction   3

1. Merely Telling the Truth   13
   Fanny Trollope Goes to Ohio

2. Brave New World   62
   Fanny Kemble Goes to Georgia

3. A Great Embryo Poet   124
   Harriet Martineau Goes to Massachusetts and Kentucky

4. Is This America?   160
   Rebecca Burlend Goes to Illinois

5. Above Love and Hate   179
   Isabella Bird Goes to Colorado

6. No There There   207
   Catherine Hubback Goes to California

Epilogue   237

CONTENTS

Notes   249
Select Bibliography   269
Acknowledgments   273
Index   275

AUTHOR'S NOTE

The use of first names in biographical writing is deplorable—how can I refer to a woman I never met as "Fanny"? Successive drafts of this book, however, revealed surnames to be hopelessly confusing. It was nonsense to write of Mr. and Mrs. Burlend as "John and Burlend" in an effort to retain consistency. So I apologize for resorting to first names. Having reluctantly made that decision, I faced the problem of a superfluity of Fannys, and have opted for clarity over consistency where required. I must appeal to the reader's understanding.

LIST OF ILLUSTRATIONS

A portrait of Fanny Kemble by Thomas Sully, 1833.
(Pennsylvania Academy of the Fine Arts, Philadelphia)   6

When Fanny Trollope's *Domestic Manners of the Americans*
appeared in 1832, Americans were outraged. This
lithograph depicts Fanny as a fat grotesque, her artist
friend Auguste-Jean-Jacques Hervieu with a brush in his
mouth, and Thomas Trollope in front of a stag's head, so
he appears to sport cuckold's horns. (National Museum of
American History, Smithsonian Institution, Harry T.
Peters Collection)   14

An unkind caricature of Fanny Trollope published in
America in 1832. (Image courtesy of Pat Pflieger)   16

William Faulkner and his wife outside their home, Rowan
Oak, in Oxford, Mississippi, in 1955. (© Bettmann/Corbis)   28

John James Audubon's Golden Eagle with rabbit, 1833.
(State Historical Society of North Dakota)   40

Fanny Trollope's Bazaar in Cincinnati. A disastrous
project. (Cincinnati Museum Center)   49

The author in Pleasureville, Kentucky. (Author
photograph)   51

An engraving of Fanny Kemble from a painting by Sir
Thomas Lawrence, 1873. (The Granger Collection,
New York)   66

Mount Auburn Cemetery, Boston. Underneath the
corkscrew branches of a star magnolia, in October 1833
Pierce Butler asked Fanny Kemble to marry him.
(Author photograph)   74

Fanny Kemble's house on Butler Island, Georgia.
(Lenox Library Association, Fanny Kemble Collection)   86

The first transcontinental telephone call, made at the Jekyll
Island Club, Georgia, on January 2, 1915. Theodore N. Vail
holds the phone, William Rockefeller sits next to him with
an earpiece clamped to his ear and J. P. Morgan stands
gormlessly behind him. (AT&T Archives and History
Center)   92

Horseshoe crabs—the ones Kemble called land crabs—
abandoned these hinged shells on the beach on
Cumberland Island, Georgia. (Author photograph)   94

The Georgia Historical Society erected this metal sign
commemorating Fanny Kemble on land near Darien that
was once the Butler rice plantation. The wording suggests
she influenced the outcome of the Civil War. (It also gets
the length of her stay wrong, inadvertently extending it by
a year.) (Courtesy of Ed Jackson)   96

The only existing photograph of Fanny Kemble and Pierce
Butler, taken in about 1840. Note the liveried slave.
(Hargrett Rare Book and Manuscript Library/University
of Georgia Libraries)   98

Fanny Kemble's house The Perch, in Lenox in the
Berkshires. (Lenox Library Association, Fanny Kemble
Collection)   103

A *Punch* cartoon published on November 16, 1861. Mr. Bull,
representing Britain, arrives at the American Cotton Store
to find a Yankee and a Southerner brawling. "Oh!"
exclaims Bull. "If you two like fighting better than
business, I shall deal at the other shop." A merchant from
the Indian Cotton Depot rubs his hands in the background.
(*Punch* Limited)   105

During the Civil War photography was deployed for
propaganda purposes for the first time. Each side, both in
Britain and America, used Mathew Brady's 1863 image of
a corpse on the battlefield after Gettysburg. (Keya Morgan
Collection, Lincolnimages.com)   108

Al Capp's *Li'l Abner*, the thirties cartoon strip with a
backwoods Southern hero and 60 million readers.
(© Capp Enterprises, Inc.)   117

Fanny Kemble in about 1879. (Getty Images)   121

Harriet Martineau, undated. (© British Library Board/
Robana/TopFoto)   126

Laurel Lake, Kentucky, 2011. (Author photograph)   140

Biblical Mini-Golf: one of the attractions on the road to
Mammoth Caves from Cave City, Kentucky. (Author
photograph)   141

Harriet Martineau suggested that cricket might bring the
American character up to British standard. (Getty Images)   147

Mesmerism, which was much like hypnotism, was hugely
popular in mid-Victorian England. Harriet Martineau and

Fanny Trollope were both temporarily in its thrall.
(Science Photo Library)   152

The Knoll, the house Harriet Martineau built in the Lake
District. The author with Angela Hart, current owner of
The Knoll. (Author photograph)   153

Bethel Methodist Episcopal Pioneer Church, Pike County,
Illinois. After it was built in 1843, on Sundays Rebecca
Burlend walked there across the Illinois River valley
carrying her shoes and stockings. (Phil Husband, Fort
Wayne, Indiana)   175

Rebecca Burlend, about 1868, photographed in Pike
County, Illinois. (Bethel Church Reunion, 1995)   177

William "Butch" Burlend in 2012 at the graves of his great-
great-great-grandparents Rebecca and John Burlend in the
grounds of Bethel Methodist Episcopal Pioneer Church,
Pike County, Illinois. (Author photograph)   178

Isabella Bird photographed in San Francisco in 1873.
(The Lyman Museum)   183

Isabella Bird's home in Estes Park in the Colorado
Rockies. It rested on six legs above a skunk's lair, and she
called it Queen Anne Mansion. (Greeley Museums,
Colorado)   188

Buffalo Bill Cody, ultimate showman of the Old West.
(Time and Life Pictures/Getty Images)   193

The photographer G. D. Morse shot this portrait of
Catherine Hubback in his studio in Montgomery Street,
San Francisco, in 1871. Photography was a craze.
(Jane Austen Memorial Trust)   207

On May 10, 1869, laborers of the western Central Pacific
Railroad and the eastern Union Pacific Railroad met at
Promontory Summit in Utah. There railway magnate
Leland Stanford drove in a golden spike that linked both
halves of the Transcontinental Railroad. (The Bancroft
Library, University of California at Berkeley)   215

Eadweard Muybridge was the first person to capture
motion on film, 1878. (The National Archives)   226

Muybridge sought to express the fragility and smallness of
humanity. Self-portrait, Yosemite, 1872. (California
Historical Society)   229

Muybridge's thirteen-plate, seventeen-foot panorama of
San Francisco, now hanging in the banqueting room of
the The Big Four restaurant in the Huntingdon Hotel in
San Francisco. The author skulks alongside. (Author
photograph)   231

The author outside the former jail in Coloma, California.
A nugget spotted in the tailrace of a sawmill at Coloma in
1848 kicked off the Gold Rush. Catherine Hubback visited
in 1874. (Author photograph)   238

Norma Jean Baker, soon to be known as Marilyn Monroe,
was crowned Artichoke Queen of Castroville, California,
in 1948. (California Artichoke Advisory Board)   241

Pigeon Point Lighthouse, California. (Author photograph)   245

O My America!

INTRODUCTION

Thirty-five years ago I went to America after quitting my job as a Parisian shopgirl, changing francs into dollars and touring the United States on a Greyhound bus. Everything about America thrilled me, from the tumult of Rush Week in Tuscaloosa, Alabama, to the stupor of the Dakotan badlands. I still like the country today, as half the world gets on with its cordial loathing. In the course of a writing life I have traveled across twenty-seven states, and I feel at home both on the coasts and in the agreeable Fattytowns of the interior. And I owe my career to the hospitality of Americans on the frontier. They appointed me writer-in-residence at their base at the South Pole, and the book I wrote about that episode has kept me going in more ways than one. Ever since that Antarctic experience, when I was exposed to Americans in intimate conditions, I have wanted to write a book about their country. When a window opened and I had time to think more about it, I was approaching fifty—that treacherous female age. As I cast around for subjects and themes, I chanced upon Fanny Trollope.

Of all the hundreds of books Britons have disgorged about their American experiences, Fanny's captured my imagination— and not just because the author's name was an event in itself. (She was Anthony's mother.) *Domestic Manners of the Americans*, a smash bestseller on both sides of the pond, turned out to be a traveler's account of the republic halfway through its journey from Independence to Civil War—Fanny arrived fifty-four years after the Boston Tea Party and 182 years before the Republican Tea Party. Furthermore, she was a Bristolian of modest origins—someone just like me. I warmed to the personality that leaped off the page, and to the author's blend of topographical description, social commentary and waspish humor.

Fanny was forty-nine when she took off for Ohio. Like her, I knew a little about the conflicting demands of motherhood, economics and sanity. I had been tethered to a succession of books and children for many years, fearful of everything—not being taken seriously, not earning enough money, not building enough Legos. Not so much a caged bird, more a migratory one off course, endlessly gliding on the thermals. Often I felt like two separate people: writer, and domestic slave. Ahead of me the Frumpy Years stretched out like a downhill catwalk. Fifty is a tough age, as I have indicated. Role models are scarce for women contemplating a second act. Fanny was living proof that there is life after fertility, and in the course of the thermal-gliding I set out to discover if any other women had reinvented themselves in America, land of new starts. Looking back, it seems like the six characters in this book dropped out of the skies on to my desk. Born within half a century of one another, each of them followed the frontier west until the rails joined the coasts and made a nation. In their books and journals they wrote about eating oysters, making soap from pig gut and groping for a portmanteau in the freezing pre-dawn darkness of a boarding house. They describe a line of slaves vanishing in the mists of the Carolinas, and the way the oars of Mississippi flatboats bend like straws in the current. They saw how America was shaping up and wrote it down while navigating the shark-infested waters of their own lives. I decided to follow in their footsteps and think of myself as one person again. I hoped they might enable me to write the book I had always wanted to write, unconstrained by genre, or by anything at all. If not now, when?

Of course, the six women who stand up in these pages are quite different one from the other, both in personality and in the light they shine on an emerging America. The battle to be themselves in a man's world as late middle age loomed united them in my eyes, and I hope it will in yours. I have told their stories more or less chronologically, and the reader must forgive dashes of historical overlap. I focused on the process of reinvention, or at least reintegration, as that was the unifying strand. As far as possible I organized the material around that central theme; it was my guiding principle. That said, I did not choose these particular characters in order to prove a theory. It was a more instinctive selection, based on feelings of sympathy and empathetic mockery. As with all biographical subjects, I set out thinking I was going to possess my girls. But in the end they possessed me. Most of them nurtured a visceral, unexplained desire to get out of the front door—to leave that place called home behind—and so do I. In their various ways they restlessly reached out for a new sense of identity, and their stories illuminated briefly, like a Zippo flare, the dark gulf between appearance and reality. So little is ever said about the last gray chapters of female lives. I wanted to take a look at that experience as an interested observer. As it turned out, the three years I spent working on *O My America!* revealed a land as exotic as any youthful Xanadu.

The year after Trollope left America, her namesake Fanny Kemble stepped off a square-rigged clipper in a still stifling New York. This Fanny was a glamorous actress, the equivalent of a Hollywood star before the Victorians covered up the bosoms of Regency England. Touring as Juliet, she fell in love with the owner of two plantations in the Georgia Sea Islands—a swampy, miasmic region where the slaves flailed by hand, as they did in biblical times. The lovers married, and Kemble took her place among the tidewater aristocracy. But the plantations were not Tara. This was a role Kemble could not play. Star-crossed doesn't begin to describe the union. Her personal story is more dramatic than the scenes she acted out on the boards, and in this book Kemble reveals something of the terrible complexity of slavery.

"I am afraid she is not likely to like me much," Kemble confided to a friend when the English radical Harriet Martineau appeared on her own two-year tour of Jacksonian America. Harriet was a popularizing political economist, among the first of that species, and a particular kind of professional spinster who made a Faustian pact with a world that did not belong to women: she would pretend not to be a woman at all. Harriet's multitudinous books and pamphlets sold by the million. (I find them almost unreadable, a symptom, no doubt, of a weak intellect and an inability to engage with political economy, the concepts of which rarely seem to bear any relation to reality.) Like Fanny Kemble, Harriet loved America, and America loved her. On the day she arrived in D.C., 600 callers in stovepipe hats left cards in the parlor of her boarding house, and she later dined with the lanky president. My fourth subject, Rebecca Burlend, would have taken a loaf of bread over supper with the top man. When she crossed the Atlantic with five children she was almost forty, and had never traveled more than ten miles from her Yorkshire village. Installed in a log cabin in the Illinois River valley, Rebecca and her husband wore the same clothes for two years and plowed the black earth by hand because they had no oxen. Then there was Isabella Bird, who in her forties rose from an Edinburgh sickbed and went careering through Colorado on horseback, bedding down with the dudes and chancers roaming the West. "Travellers," Bird wrote, "are privileged to do the most improper things with perfect propriety." My sentiments exactly. Finally, Catherine Hubback, Jane Austen's niece. She had eight novels and three adult children to her name when at the age of fifty-two she rode the rails from New York to San Francisco, stopping at lonely station eating houses and shivering through the Wyoming hills dreaming of her husband locked in a far-off asylum. The golden spike that had just linked both halves of the Transcontinental Railroad signaled that the first chapter of the country's modern history had closed. So the train, the machine that did the most to transform the nineteenth-century United States, brought this book to a logical end. Like the others, Catherine reinvented herself. It was already morning again in America.

I am in awe of the physical hardships these women endured to get to the New World. For almost two months, and breastfeeding, Rebecca cooked for seven over a shared fire on the steerage deck of a sailing ship. Her cramped quarters were lit by a semi-pellucid porthole in the ceiling and an oil lamp that swung wildly with every dip of the waves. The women lived on the cusp of sail and steam. Although the SS *Savannah*, a steamship, crossed the Atlantic in 1819, the vessel relied heavily on auxiliary sail, and safe, all-steam commercial crossings were decades away. On arrival, the women had no idea what they would find. "America . . . is," Fanny Trollope remembered, "hardly better known than Fairy Land," and she used a plural verb for the United States. Cincinnati, where she settled, was the frontier, an open space of reckless entrepreneurial energy and whiskey-sodden schemes. America overall was thinly populated, exotic and provincial. When Isabella lay down to sleep in Truckee in northern California, her drunken roommates discussed chopped-up human bodies in sacks. The first standard time system had not yet been introduced, and the dusty railroad stations where Catherine bought tins of bacon still had two clocks: one for local solar time, and one for railroad time.

All these women had grown up with the entrenched idea that life was more or less over for a woman at fifty—on the streets of Cincinnati, strangers addressed Fanny Trollope as "Old Woman"—yet they struggled to prove that their lives were not over. Notions of personal identity, reinvention and redemption recur in various guises throughout these pages, giving the lie to my hero F. Scott Fitzgerald's bitter assertion that there are no second acts in American lives. In addition, the women all, to one extent or another, perceived America and in particular the frontier as both Eden and *tabula rasa*. It represented an inner land from which they fashioned their second acts. And they were deeply engaged in the vexed relations between the old country and the new. The question of national identity also looms large in this book.

O My America! explores these themes within the framework of a dynamic and shifting half-century of U.S. history. The concept of the West was only just taking shape; response to the frontier crystalized into the notion of Manifest Destiny; the most progressive country in the world risked losing everything because of an addiction to slavery. When Fanny Trollope sailed into the Gulf of Mexico the Navaho had not yet taken their Long Walk, the Sioux had not frozen to death after the Battle of the Black Hills and the Natchez living with the Cherokee had not followed the Trail of

Tears to Oklahoma. The white man did not yet even have a monopoly on cruelty. Comanche braves terrorized a Britain-sized slice of modern Texas, New Mexico and Oklahoma, dispossessing peaceful Pueblo Indians by torturing males, gang-raping females and introducing slavery. But from the 1840s, American settlers raised persecution and subjugation to a new level. "Although we are in different boats," said an Onandaga chief, "you in your boat and we in our canoe, we share the same river of life." The white man replied, "We own all the boats." That was the end.

I tracked my subjects from the Mississippi to the cinder cones of the Mayacamas at the tail end of the Cascades. On each trip I took a carpet bag and two maps: one current, and whichever one it was that the women would have had. You would see me on a levee or in a parking lot, hunched over two flapping maps weighed down at the corners by stones, one hand locating where Harriet's coach crashed on a splodge of sage green marked *Apache country*, the other finding the spot amid a spaghetti of highways on the Rand McNally. I followed my team up the Mississippi and down the Altamaha where millions of gallons of fresh water pour from the piedmont into the salt marsh. I haunted the former boarding houses of New York's Hudson Street and walked over the Nahant sand in the peaty winter light of Massachusetts. Catherine Hubback saw the Pigeon Point Lighthouse being built, and I stayed in it and lay awake in my bunk listening to shattering California surf. With Harriet I explored the Mammoth Caves of Kentucky, though she had a better time of it than I did. Sometimes I took my children like some of the women had, and it helped me understand the compromises they made. I went as far as I could along roads literal and metaphorical until, on good days, currents of electricity ran between us and it was no longer them and me. Their experiences revealed so many Americas. Who would have imagined eating calamari and chips at the end of the municipal wharf in Santa Cruz, listening to sea lions bark under the stanchions in Monterey Bay? Or that the buttes of chaparral around

Big Thompson gulch could blaze so red you see why the Spaniards named the region Colorado? On a segment of the Continental Divide where the air smelled of juniper, the Pacific drainage basin briefly lay east of its Atlantic counterpart. The past took on a physical presence when I looked out at a mountain slope or a building that was exactly as it had been when they were there. In the archives, an original letter or journal—something they had touched—had a peculiar alchemy, as if it brought the writer into the room.

Certain characters cropped up regularly and knitted the stories together. I could scarcely get through a day without crossing paths with Alexis de Tocqueville, high priest of European tourists, or running into Henry James, John Audubon and his fish eagles, or Dickens. (Americans were crazy about Dickens. In 1841 fans lined the New York wharves yelling, "Did Little Nell live?" at sailors on the mail boats who had read the latest installment of *The Old Curiosity Shop*.) Writing and reading pop up all the way through *O My America!*. Contact with the U.S. stimulated each of my subjects to write. At fifty-two Fanny Kemble produced the monumental *Journal of a Residence on a Georgian Plantation*, a powerful first-hand indictment of slavery as well as an exposition of one woman's fight to resolve the dilemmas and difficulties of being herself. Besides being authors, five of the six women were passionate readers—it was something we had in common. I researched *O My America!* in part by reading American fiction, and the process uncovered so many magical books it is a wonder this one ever got written. Who could stand on the levee road north of Vicksburg and not think about Faulkner, or loll in a cane chair in the Yazoo–Mississippi Delta and not feel the presence of Eudora Welty? Perhaps it is not surprising that writers inhabited these pages from the start. They stalked the stories like ghosts in a gallery. Some of them contributed to the American national journey by revealing, through their books, the choices available to a young country, and the consequences of those choices. At the time of writing, the demise of the book is predicted daily, and I hope the authors that gave me so much pleasure as I looked for the story I wanted to tell were not singing a literary swan song. One has the sense of the world shifting again, as it did in the period when my subjects were wrestling with their own manuscripts.

In short, this is a book about how middle-aged women respond when life puts the boot in, told against the period in which America was establishing both its borders and its identity. After so many years writing about explorers with frozen beards, spending my life with women proved a joy. My subjects spoke to me across the years, voices from what was once the distant shore of middle age, where women cease to exist. How suddenly it had come close. All biographers have hidden impulses and in some sense I was looking for clues—how to forge forward myself into that colorless land of barren women. I was going through a gloomy phase when I began thinking about this book: the shadow of late middle age, my children needing me less, me needing them more, the wheel turning. Writing *O My America!* liberated me. Through it all, on the road and at my desk, my characters were the best company a writer could hope for: spirited, intelligent, funny and inconsistent. I thought I was the luckiest author in the world to have found them. They were sometimes incontinently human—throwing tantrums, being bossy, running away—and that was when I loved them most, though I did not side with them, just as I try not to side with myself. My goal was always "the complete sympathy of complete detachment." There was poetry in the girls' moral dramas, and they made me realize what an unending adventure it is to be human; that is the larger argument that spools through *O My America!* Women like those depicted in these pages exist everywhere—I see their faces every day on the Tube. I had more fun writing this book than all my previous books put together, and if I can impart a fraction of that enjoyment to the reader, I will not have entirely failed to honor the spirit of these six noble individuals who refused to give up. My working title was *No Surrender*. After all, dying comes to us all in the end. Living is the trick.

1

MERELY TELLING THE TRUTH

Fanny Trollope Goes to Ohio

Fanny Trollope was broke when she turned fifty, and on intimate terms with pig manure. She had made the three-month trek to Cincinnati, she said, "to hatch golden eggs for my son." The frontier might have glittered, but not all of it was gold—Cincinnati turned out to be one big stinky pig factory (Easterners knew it as "Porkopolis," if they knew it at all). After three years Fanny slunk home with a suitcase of smashed-up dreams and three children incubating tuberculosis. Then she wrote *Domestic Manners of the Americans*. The voice that sings from its pages speaks with the inflections of another age, but it is Fanny's voice: stylish and pithy, elegant, sardonic and witty. The author refused to acknowledge any taboo, complaining about the way American museum curators covered up the penes of the statues. There is something true at the heart of *Domestic Manners*. It is a story of disillusion, of seeking and not finding, of the gap between expectation and reality.

The book appeared on both sides of the Atlantic on March 19, 1832, when Fanny was fifty-three. A British subaltern in New York reported, "The Tariff and Bank Bill were alike forgotten . . . At every corner of the street, at the door of every petty retailer of information for the people, a large placard met the eye with, 'For sale here, with plates, *Domestic Manners of the Americans*, by Mrs. Trollope.' At every table d'hôte, on board of every steamboat, in every stagecoach, and in all societies, the first question was 'Have you read Mrs Trollope?' The more it was abused the more rapidly did the printers issue new editions." In Britain the book whizzed through multiple reprints within weeks, and when Fanny's son Anthony produced his first novel, his roguish publisher placed adverts naming the author as *MRS*. Trollope. The family finances were at last secure, and Fanny's harrowing American experience brought her freedom in the long run. No wonder she laughed at the personal attacks pouring from the United States. A lithograph was published depicting a fat grotesque (her), a mysterious young artist friend with a brush in his mouth, and her husband in front of a stag's head sporting cuckold's horns. A waxwork in New York represented Fanny as a goblin, and a traveling menagerie in Maine advertised "an exact likeness of the celebrated Mrs. Trollope" in which she appeared puffing on a pipe. "Trollopize" became a verb that meant "to abuse the American nation." "No other author of the present day," wrote a critic, "has been so much admired, and so much abused." On and on it went, for years. The author "Nil Admirari" published a verse epic called *The Trollopiad* about a band of pompous gentlemen travelers observing the United States.

Later, Fanny picked up one fan in America: Mark Twain. In his own maudlin middle years he took a library of European commentators on a nostalgic Mississippi voyage, and on the last page of his copy of *Domestic Manners* noted, in his sprawling hand, "Of all these tourists, I like Dame Trollope best." She was, said the master stretcher-teller, "merely telling the truth." He recognized in her his own unquenchable gusto for life. Meanwhile, in Britain, invitations tumbled through the letterbox. Fanny rented a flat in a top London square and hurried between parties. "Lady Louisa Stewart," she gushed to her son Tom, "told me that I had quite put English out of fashion, and that every one was talking Yankee talk." The young Dickens praised her. "I am convinced," he wrote, "that there is no writer who has so well and so accurately (I need not add entertainingly) described America." Tory papers loved *Domestic Manners* while Whigs and Radicals noted that the author's background was not quite up to scratch. Britons can never escape their origins. In Anthony Trollope's novel *Is He Popenjoy?*, the Dean of Brotherton's father is a former groom. "The man looked like a gentleman," the author says of the Dean, "but still there was the smell of the stable." In *Domestic Manners*, Fanny insists that there *should* be a stable smell, so that one knew where one was—the alternative was a social free-for-all of the American kind. She needn't have worried. When the book came out, the cultural elite showed that hierarchies were alive and well in Britain. They resented the author of *Domestic Manners* for entering their territory. The poet Robert Browning announced that Fanny was vulgar and pushy.

Over the next few years, following the appearance of *Domestic Manners*, Fanny nursed her tubercular offspring with one hand and dashed out novels with the other, "So that," as Anthony put it, "there might be a decent roof for the children to die under." When there was nobody left alive to nurse, Fanny swanned round the great capitals: Prince Metternich escorted her into dinner and the last king of France held a ball in her honor. It was one of the most dramatic reinventions of all time. She loved life, and never gave up on it. "Of all the people I have known," Anthony wrote, "my mother was the most joyous, or at any rate, the most capable of joy."

Mrs. Frances Trollope,

She was born Frances Milton in Bristol halfway through the long reign of George III, the Hanoverian known as The King Who Lost America. Like me, she was descended from generations of hardy West Country stock. Her father was a parson and her grand-father a distiller, and she grew up on a street that runs between Clifton Hill and York Place, close to the Hot Wells spa where the slavers' wives took the waters. As a young woman Fanny moved to London to keep house for her brother in a dirty red-brick terrace sheathed in fog, and when she was thirty she married Thomas Trollope, a tow-headed barrister with a penchant for reckless schemes. Choleric (according to a colleague he was "industrious and disputatious in equal measure") and an original Casaubon, Thomas was compiling an ecclesiastical dictionary and practicing law in what Anthony described as "dingy, almost suicidal chambers at No. 23 Old Square, Lincoln's Inn." At home at 16 Keppel Street the couple shared a ruinous sense of entitlement that led to the purchase of French marquetry desks, grand pianos and glazed wallpaper, and they maintained a minimum staff of half a dozen. During the first decade of their marriage they produced seven children and regularly leaped over the back wall to escape a creditor. "My father," wrote Tom, their eldest, "was a poor man, and his establishment [the chambers] altogether on a modest footing. But it never would have occurred to him or to my mother that they could get on without a manservant in livery." When Thomas senior's law practice finally petered out, the family abandoned London for Harrow on the Hill, five miles outside the city, first renting a farmhouse, then leasing land to build a larger home with French windows, a lawn and a commodious parlour. Thomas was determined to set up as a gentleman farmer. The project, Anthony said, was to be the grave of all his father's hopes, ambitions and prosperity. Calomel prescribed for sick headaches raised Thomas' cantankerous outbursts to new heights (no wonder—it is mercurous chloride). "He is a good, honourable man," Fanny confided to a friend, "but his temper is dreadful—every year increases his irritability—and also its lamentable effects upon the children." Two of the seven children died: one a baby, the other, the beloved Arthur, at the age of twelve. Fanny, undiminished, held the family together. Thomas was, according to Tom, "a highly respected but not a popular or well-beloved man. Worst of all, alas! he was not popular in his own house . . . My mother's disposition, on the other hand, was of the most genial, cheerful, happy, *enjoué* nature imaginable. All our happiest hours were spent with her; and to any one of us tête-à-tête with her was preferable to any other disposal of a holiday hour." He said she "carried sunshine." Fanny marched her brood through London's smoking gaslights and yellow fogs to watch *Hamlet* or *Doctor Faustus*, and once queued for four hours to see Mrs. Siddons play Lady Macbeth. She enjoyed dancing, hiking and throwing parties, and above all was a passionate reader: unfinished books lay about the house like partly eaten sandwiches. Fanny considered herself a progressive radical, and knew many of the freethinkers floating round the capital in the 1820s. The Harrow farmhouse became a refuge for liberals seeking a temporary berth.

When the red-haired writer and social reformer Fanny Wright appeared dressed in Grecian robes, she dazzled Fanny, and introduced her to the idea of America. Tall and lithe with milky skin and a substantial inheritance, the Scots-born Wright had visited the States twice and was passionate about that country's potential as a utopian democracy free from the conservative conventions of the Old World. She was close to the septuagenarian General Lafayette, the aristocrat who had served in the American War of Independence. (Washington said Lafayette was the only Frenchman he liked.) Wright had even accompanied the old soldier to America on his triumphal return tour in 1824; some said she had joined him in his bed. She stayed in America for two years, visiting Economy, a commune near Pittsburgh, and the Wabash River bottomland in Indiana where the Welsh industrialist Robert Owen had founded New Harmony, a communitarian experiment in which money was banned. Socialism, rationalism, women's rights, free love—Wright was for it all. Convinced that she could prove the equality of the races, she had bought 200 acres on Tennessee's Wolf River to establish a cooperative community where black and white would live in peace and harmony. When she met Fanny Trollope in Harrow, she had left her sister Camilla in charge at her commune, which she called Nashoba (Chickasaw for wolf), and had returned to Europe to recruit candidates willing to join her in the Tennessee co-op. Fanny was like a ripe plum, just right for picking. Thomas had just moved the family into a semi-derelict outbuilding and installed tenants in the main farmhouse. The accommodation, Anthony remembered, "always seemed to be in danger of falling into the neighbouring horse pond. As it crept downwards from house to stables, from stables to barns, from barns to cowsheds, and from cowsheds to dung heap, one could hardly tell where one began and the other ended." No wonder Fanny became obsessed with Wright. She confided to a friend, "Fanny Wright is at once all that woman should be . . . I feel greatly inclined to say where her country is, there shall be my country. The more I see of her, the more I feel convinced that *all* her notions are right." Tennessee was Fanny's last best hope.

People did not expect menopausal women to reinvent themselves. "I can scarcely believe," one acquaintance wrote to another, "that Mrs. T is actually on her way, and Trollope in his old age alone in London." "Will wonders never cease?" wrote another. It was indeed a wonder, and I admired it. I didn't know what home meant until I had children, and I can barely imagine the courage required to uproot as Fanny did. When I became a mother, I worried that I would never be truly free to take off again. I know it's heretical to say it. At the time it felt heretical to feel it. I was forty-one when I had my second son, and I asked myself if, once he and his brother were gone, it would be too late.

As for Fanny's children: twelve-year-old Anthony and seventeen-year-old Tom, boarders at Hampshire's Winchester College, were to stay in England. Fanny took the other three with her—the feckless sixteen-year-old Henry, who was to teach Latin, fencing and dancing at Nashoba; Cecilia, who was eleven; and Emily, nine. Two servants agreed to take a chance with the party, and so did Auguste-Jean-Jacques Hervieu, a thirty-five-year-old French artist with a heroic moustache and republican views unappreciated by the authorities of his homeland. Hervieu was in search of a family: his father, a colonel in Napoleon's army, had perished on the outskirts of Moscow. The Trollopes had unofficially adopted him, installing him as drawing master at the farmhouse, and as an artist they held him in high regard. Hervieu was, Fanny said, "among the many young Frenchmen who have been exiled for wishing for more freedom than the Bourbon fools and knaves allowed . . . if I have any knowledge of what is meant by the phrase, a man of genius, I conceive it to belong to him."

The sailing ship *Edward* reached the mouth of the Mississippi in December 1827. "The first indication of our approach to land," Fanny wrote, "was the appearance of this mighty river pouring forth its muddy mass of waters." Flights of pelicans thrilled her, and so did alligators, which she called crocodiles. Trunks of mighty trees uprooted by a hurricane span in the current "like the fragment of a world in ruins." Bristolians are accustomed to narrow, placid rivers like the Avon, which subsides to a trickle twice a day, and Fanny's description of the Mississippi as it decants into the Gulf of Mexico displays a touch of the Gothic. "Only one object rears itself above the eddying waters," she wrote. "The mast of a vessel long since wrecked in attempting to cross the [sand] bar, a dismal witness of the destruction that has been, and a boding prophet of that which is to come." Above all she was amazed at the flatness of the shores and the ferocity of the river, "looking so mighty, and so unsubdued all the time, that I could not help fancying she would some day take the matter into her own hands again, and if so, farewell to New Orleans."

The party found lodgings on Canal Street early in the evening, as the nabobs were talking on their second-floor verandas. Below, crowds drifted towards the Vieux Carré and its Franco-Spanish houses of yellow adobe or stuccoed brick, the hinges on the gates a yard long, and on past the white walls of the St. Charles Hotel, where planters danced in the Salle de Condé. New Orleans was the fifth-largest city in the nation and the unofficial capital of the South. West African freemen, Europeans and Creoles traded with Atakapa hunters bringing alligators they had speared through the eye, and with shaggy French-speaking Acadians who rode into town to barter sugar for tin pots. Twenty-four years after the Louisiana Purchase—the biggest land sale in history, and one that doubled the size of the U.S.—the city had already established its place in American geomythology: sexy, hot and slightly dangerous. When Fanny arrived the sugar elite had just appeared from the plantations for a three-month spree. Shopkeepers beckoned chatelaines who craved everything French, from yards of Parisian lace to cases of Sauternes, and the city imported so much Limoges china that an entrepreneurial Limousin had shipped in a team of potters and set up production near a clay pit. But the people of New Orleans didn't want that. The dinner service had to be made in France. (The thing was to go full circle. When I was living in Paris in the 1970s, older people still said, *"Mais c'est l'Amérique!"* to describe something luxuriously desirable.) Fanny liked it all, but when she entered a milliner's shop, another customer introduced her to the milliner—a shopgirl—and the two enjoyed an "intellectual" conversation. It was "the first symptom of American equality that I perceived," Fanny wrote. The incident was to reverberate throughout her American sojourn. In New Orleans she kept an open mind, noting the division between "two distinct sets of people": the white Creole, and the mixed-race Quadroon. The latter she admired. They were, she wrote, "exquisitely beautiful, graceful, gentle and amiable." She herself was short and stumpy with a wide, toad-like face, and her protruding blue-grey eyes held a gaze with masculine authority. Her waist had thickened and she had lost the taut curves of her youth, with the result that her torso resembled a tube. She dressed badly, and according to an American observer walked "with those Colossian strides unattainable by any but Englishwomen." There was something of the grotesque about her, or at least of the rackety Regency. A West Country burr—almost Barsetshire—added a fatal final touch.

In July 2010 the New Orleans sky was enamel in the morning, and slabs heaved along the sidewalk. The Big Easy is a hundred years younger than Boston but soaked in suggestion, from the decayed scent of tupelo that drifts through Coliseum Square to the live oaks that arch over the St. Charles Avenue streetcar. I was using, like Fanny, a print of David Vance's 1825 cartographic engraving, which I carried rolled up in a cardboard tube. Marigny appeared as a forest of palmettos and Spanish moss that Vance called *drowned woods*. The Marigny night still smelled of the swamp, and the daytime sky held the watery reflection of the Mississippi. The novelist Richard Ford once lived in New Orleans. It was a place, he wrote, "where the firm ground ceases and the unsound footing begins. A certain kind of person likes such a place. A certain kind of person wants to go there and never leave." You had to enjoy living close to the edge; to feel the current pulling, and to grasp what Fanny had called "the fragment of a world in ruins." It was the opposite of sinking into suburbia. You felt the tension, even now. In a Bywater park I joined a public crawfish boil. People talked about hurricanes as if they were family members. "After Rita was here . . ." they said, or, "When Ike arrived . . ."

A friend had passed on a contact—an employee of the state legislature who had stayed throughout Katrina, despite Mayor Ray Nagin's mandatory evacuation. We met for Sunday brunch at Surrey's on Magazine Street. John was a young lawyer with four generations of relatives in the St. Louis Cemetery. It was not yet hurricane season, but I noticed, through the office windows, that people had installed satellite weather sites as their home page. Did they live in fear of the next one? John shrugged. "You grow up with an awareness of it being part of life. My grandmother used to say that as a girl, through the parlour window she watched ships sailing past higher than our house." After we had eaten, John drove me over to the Lower Ninth, the downriver ward devastated when Katrina broke the levees on both the Industrial Canal and the Mississippi River Gulf Outlet. On the way, he reeled off advice about food, a New Orleans preoccupation. My notebook records

Central Grocery muffalettas, fried oyster po-boys from anywhere, red beans and rice on Mondays. The Lower Ninth was a harlequin of plots from which clean-up teams had removed the debris of the worst destruction, leaving hollowed-out homes cross-hatched with numbers listing the body count, stigmata of the first rescuers. It was thirty-six degrees, and a lowering cloud pressed the humid air down on tracts of spindly grass. Katrina created the biggest storm surge ever recorded in the U.S.: a woman reported a giant sea turtle swimming through her kitchen while she sat on the counter waiting to be rescued. For the first time, as the disaster played itself out, Europeans watched television images revealing the poverty endemic in parts of America. It was not "Farewell to New Orleans," as Fanny had predicted, but it was apocalyptic enough. Residents of the Lower Ninth had painted *Do Not Demolish* on their walls before they fled. "There were about 5,300 homes in the Lower Ninth before Katrina," John said, "and every single one was flooded or wrecked. We reckon about 1,200 have been rebuilt. Geography meant the area was the worst hit, but economics means it's not recovering. Katrina revealed just what a divided city this still is, just like it's always been." On the front door of one house—uninhabited and collapsing—someone had daubed, in another color under *Do Not Demolish, Eddie come to Superdome.* Almost a Katrina haiku.

Before leaving New Orleans and heading up the Mississippi, I read the newspapers she had read. The mottled originals were stored in a 1915 beaux arts archive in the French Quarter. When I went there, music was always pounding out of some window or door nearby, often from more than one, nobody seeming to mind competing beats. I thought of her as I walked the same streets. The sun never let up, and the colors of the camelback houses throbbed. She had left two children behind, and so had I (mine were thirteen and eight)—though I had absented myself for three weeks, as opposed to three years. Astonishingly, in later life Fanny's abandoned infants never blamed her. On the contrary, they took trouble to praise her as a mother. That gave me some small comfort.

As I indicated earlier, I had not yet resolved the tensions between motherhood and other parts of my life. Note that I do not say "career," as being a writer cannot be said to be a career. It is what one is, for better or, as is more often the case, worse. I remember feeling sick when a well-meaning neighbor said, "It must be so hard concentrating on your work when yelping boys downstairs want to build bricks." The truth was rather different. It was hard to concentrate on the bricks. Work was always on my mind, on a continuous loop. I've never admitted that before. I felt ashamed—as if no other mother felt as I did. Beached there in New Orleans, in lucid moments I knew it was all right to leave my children for three weeks; they were no longer toddling, they were in the care of a loving father, and they did not need both of us all the time. The fear was displacement, I think, for a more generalized anxiety, one that did not yet have a name.

In the archive, which was air-conditioned to igloo-standard, I touched a page of a newspaper from December 1827. Almost all the papers appeared in both French and English. *L'Abeille*, on sale for one piastre, printed the shipping schedules from Liverpool, Le Havre and Bayou Sara alongside ads punting crepe ballgowns from Europe and beaver hats from New York. Wet nurses advertised services, and Dr. William Hudson's Drugstore and Medical Repository on the corner of Conti and Chartres offered a certain cure for baldness. News from the rest of the world was cursory: in three lines the Allied naval force triumphed at the Battle of Navarino, only to be overpowered by the announcement of a forthcoming sale of jars of jam.

On January 1, 1828, Fanny and her group left New Orleans for Tennessee on the paddle steamer *Belvedere*. Along the reaches of the wharves, columns of smoke rose from the pirogues and timber rafts nosed in alongside tobacco barges from Ohio and Indiana broadhorns piled high with hoop poles and pumpkins. Tinted rings of water formed rills on the towheads and leadsmen shouted, "Mark twain!" (pilots needed twelve feet of water to float, and a twain, being two fathoms, indicated safe water). Beyond the river, across thousands of acres of freshly cut cane and the tracery of seasonal bayous, slave gangs burned pyramids of fibrous sugar stalks called *bagasse*, and smoke formed a canopy in the sky. At times the plantations themselves vanished, and you could not see the rib of the embankment. After a cluster of shacks called Baton Rouge, named for a red cypress that marked the boundary between tribal hunting grounds, the river narrowed and began its passage between two thousand-mile vegetable walls that parted only for fueling woodyards. There were no women besides Fanny and Wright on the *Belvedere*, and the men all claimed to hold military rank. But when they sat down for supper, Fanny wrote, "The total want of all the usual courtesies at table, the voracious rapidity with which the viands were seized and devoured, the strange uncouth phrases and pronunciation; the loathsome spitting, from the contamination of which it was absolutely impossible to protect our dresses; the frightful manner of feeding with their knives, till the whole blade seemed to enter into the mouth; and the still more frightful manner of cleaning the teeth afterwards with a pocket knife, soon forced us to feel that we were not surrounded by the generals, colonels and majors of the old world." She concluded, "Let no one who wishes to receive agreeable impressions of American manners, commence their travels in a Mississippi steam boat; for myself, it is with all sincerity I declare, that I would infinitely prefer sharing the apartment of a party of well-conditioned pigs to being confined to its cabin." Everything turned on appearance, performance and a sense of triumph, and the American faux-generals, on hearing an English accent, were, according to Fanny, quick to dismiss the tired formality of the Old World, favoring praise of the egalitarianism that replaced it west of the Atlantic.

The water cuts the banks of the lower river into deep horseshoe curves in Louisiana, a navigational hazard in the days before government snag boats pulled the Mississippi's teeth. At night Fanny sat on the gallery that ran round the cabins, watching the glare from the furnaces illuminate, like a bloodied lightning flash, the floating riverstores that traveled without lanterns. But flat is never beautiful to one who has looked every day over the Avon Gorge, that epic 300-foot limestone slash that runs down west Bristol. It is a swooping view, the layered rock scoured by warm uplifts and colonized by honewort and Bristol onion, and it prejudices one against the plains. (I know. I thought I was going out of my mind in Kansas.) Mississippi had already become the twentieth state but less than 5 percent of the fertile delta land had been cleared and swamp was still the dominant feature of the landscape. Cast adrift between the flatlands, Fanny longed for a bluff on "that wearisome level line."

By ten I had cleared Baton Rouge. The sky was cloudless, and the Louisiana shore glowed in misty sunshine. North of Vicksburg (the city appeared on Vance's map as Walnut Hills) I picked up Mississippi 1 at Mayersville. The fields dissolved into pea-green soup, the spawny surface of the swamp holed with stumps and sweetbay magnolia. One expected a dinosaur to surge through the black gum, sending spumey flumes up hundreds of meters. When the ground solidified, levee and road diverged around the flamingo legs of a water tower, and thousands of acres of corn rolled ahead. Densely packed, ten-foot stems shot out leaves broad as flags. There was something impressive in the plants' implacable determination to swell in every direction. It did not surprise me to learn that there are three crops a year in the Delta. Three crops a night would not have surprised me. The Mississippi Delta is regularly cited as the distilled essence of the Deep South—the last Dixie stronghold. Properly the Yazoo–Mississippi Delta, its alluvial plain extends 200 miles from Vicksburg to Memphis, and the host of a local radio show boasted that the blues were born at the Tut-wiler railhead. The highway crept west across the lowlands, gun racks rattling on passing pickups. Outside Greenville, a funeral cortège blocked the road, and a row of construction workers stood with hard hats covering their hearts, the air around them spangled with corn dust. In the brakes, painted houses nestled among rowan oaks, netted windows black blanks. A chunky white man piloted a mower across a long lawn. The air drooped. The radio jock had a studio guest who had come on to demonstrate that raising federal income tax was unbiblical. The light died on the highway before Clarksdale.

Rowan Oak in Oxford, an hour from Clarksdale, was the home of William Faulkner. The novelist's central theme lay at the heart of my women's stories: the importance of the fight to be freely oneself. In homage to a master, I made a detour to Oxford. The flat green land-sea that rolled back from the levee as the Honda barreled north provided a vivid backdrop for *Old Man*, Faulkner's novella set in 1927, the year of the Great Flood. The Mississippi plays the title role. I learned more about the South from Faulkner than from anyone, or at least about that small area of northeastern Mississippi which inspired him—what he called his "postage-stamp world." Inside his handsome house, sunshine flooded in through well-proportioned windows and the silence of the woods came with it, barring the confidential oak creak of my own footfall. Cedars cast lacy patterns on the kitchen tiles and over the hollowed keys of Faulkner's Underwood Universal Portable. It was such a perfect writer's house that one wondered why Faulkner drank so much. From the cool of his rear study, he ran the domestic world that provided a foil to his internal creativity. He smoked hams in a brick smokehouse, kept a cow in a timber barn and petted Tempy, his favorite horse, in stables on the west side of his paddock. Walking among the sweet shrub of his maze, Faulkner composed the famous acceptance speech he made in Stockholm in 1950 when he collected his Nobel Prize. "I believe," he said, "that man will not merely endure, he will prevail." Although the evidence that man as a species will endure is weaker than it was when Faulkner stepped up to the podium, his belief in personal endurance resonates as one observes one's own crises zipping by. Faulkner was obsessed with the truth of history. "The past is never dead," he wrote in *Requiem for a Nun*. "It's not even past." He struggled to use the material of his own background to reach a reconciliation with life and the certainty of death, sidestepping fear of oblivion, at least in part, by creating literature. But in the shadows Faulkner glimpsed the annihilation to come, no matter how many masterpieces he created. It was enough to drive anyone to drink.

On the backroads to Tennessee, a country beat edged out the blues, both competing with volleys of static when the road dipped beneath the levee. Twiddling the dial, I found a station plugging a Christian Fun Day at Wolf River Mall in Germantown, a glossy Memphis suburb. At the same time, a purple and yellow hand-painted sign welcomed me to Jonestown in Coahoma County. Lopsided tin-roofed houses on cinder blocks lined the road between vacant lots strewn with litter. The metal double doors of the single grocery store looked as if they had been shot at. Closer inspection revealed that they had. Alongside the doors, half a dozen teenagers squatted among tires and broken-down white goods. There was none of Faulkner's prevailing spirit here. Jonestown bumps along at the bottom of every single health and education table while topping out in the unemployment and crime stakes. According to government figures, more than 57 percent of children live below the poverty line—and this on the most fertile agricultural land on the planet. Ninety-three percent of Jonestown residents are African American. Fanny had expressed shock at the housing conditions of agricultural workers in 1828. She predicted that once America had dealt with its inequalities, it would grow strong. It grew strong anyway—beefier than Fanny could have imagined—but the inequalities remained. The Delta is the poorest region of the poorest state, its startling juxtaposition of white affluence and black poverty the most enduring legacy of the Old South. As for Germantown, I drove through it later. It was a gleaming white mini-city of strip malls, multistory churches and enclaves of housing developments and manicured estates—not quite the communitarian paradise Wright envisaged.

Rain was falling when Fanny arrived in Memphis. According to Vance's map, there had been little in the way of settlements since Natchez, 260 miles downriver. A large splodge of mustard yellow simply noted *Chickasaw Country*. Fanny lost her shoes and gloves in the climb up the bank to the inn. "The house was new," she recalled, "and in what appeared to me a very comfortless condition, but I was new then to Western America." Steamers had not yet displaced smaller craft on the middle Mississippi and Memphis was known as "flatboat town," crowded with valley farmers preparing to float produce to river markets. Bears roamed between cabins, and there was no school, doctor, bank or brothel. The permanent residents were mostly poor Irish and German river-workers. A smallpox epidemic had just disposed of many, and yellow fever was on the prowl. Visitors from President Andrew Jackson to Davy Crockett convened at the inn, and every man in town ate his supper there too. On Fanny's first night the proprietor set a table for fifty, and the company dined on hard venison and peach sauce as rain hammered on the tin roof.

Nashoba was twelve miles from Memphis in territory hunted by the Choctaw, people who still danced the eagle tail dance under moonlight.* "It required some miles of experience," Fanny noted during the carriage journey, "to convince us that each stump would not be our last, crashing into trees and sinking into swamp." But green parrots made her feel she was in "a new world." The U.S. played an Edenic role in the European imagination, and the "New World" moniker suited utopians. As early as 1609 a vessel heading to Virginia to relieve the embattled colony brought a boatload of separatists called Brownists and Familists, both radical sects with communitarian yearnings. More than two centuries later, Goethe was writing *Amerika, du hast es besser,* and a hundred years again after that, Auden, in "New Year Letter," celebrated the immensity and freedom of the U.S. after the crabbed confinement of Europe. But European radicals of Fanny's generation really pounced. The spirit of the French Revolution had fostered a fresh communitarian spirit. The Romantics were in its thrall: Coleridge and Southey planned paradise on the banks of the Susquehanna River and Mary Wollstonecraft and her lover discussed founding a farm in some western territory of the U.S., released from the bounds of class, religion and frowsty institutions such as monarchy, marriage and money. This post-revolutionary generation dreamed of turning ideals into a way of life, and where better than in the shin-

---

*Two years later, the Indian Removal Act sent the Choctaw to Oklahoma and they never danced in Tennessee again.

ing new republic itself?* New England transcendentalists had the same idea. Their prototype Edens were founded on noble, politically sound principles almost always hijacked by dubious theorising and crackpottery. (As were the earlier ones. The ship on its way to Virginia in 1609 foundered off the coast of Bermuda. Deciding to make the most of it, the sectarians settled—Bermuda after all was a ready-made Utopia with no indigenous people in the way. But they squabbled over what paradise should look like, and started shooting one another.) In nineteenth-century Edens, new ideas on health and hygiene flourished—Louisa May Alcott's father Bronson, a tremendous windbag who founded a utopian farm in Massachusetts, recommended sex without thrusting. Others extended the remit of vegetarianism by allowing the consumption of "aspiring" vegetables such as tomatoes and banishing "downwards" specimens like carrots. Alcott believed it was wrong to "oppress" oxen by making them plow, a policy which made farming tricky. Many communards believed happiness was wrong. The Shakers shot themselves in their communally owned feet by banning sex altogether, as did Thoreau, who allowed nobody else into his private Utopia.

Ohio and Indiana were popular settings for these excruciating experiments as they lacked the hierarchies and elites of Eastern states, and so did Tennessee, which Wright had selected for her own experiment in cooperative living and loving. She had bought forty slaves, and, as soon as agricultural profits equated their purchase price, planned to free them and repeat the cycle. During her absence in Europe the project had not advanced toward this goal. It had retreated in the opposite direction. Buildings were in stages of disintegration, sanitation was non-existent and everyone was ill. In addition, the site was malarial and there was hardly any food. The slaves wanted to go back to proper slavery. "Desolation

---

*There were dissenting voices. Dickens produced an anti-Eden in *Martin Chuzzlewit*.

was the only feeling," wrote the horrified Fanny shortly after arriving. "Mother," asked Emily at the end of the first day, "when can we go to Nashoba?" "This is Nashoba," said Mother. She and her daughters shared a bedroom with Wright, and rain splattered through the rafters on to the cots. Falling out of love is sad. "The Fanny Wright of Nashoba," Fanny admitted in a description of the commune that was never published, "in dress, looks and manner, bore no more resemblance to the Miss Wright I had known and admired in London and Paris than her log cabin did to the Tuileries or Buckingham Palace." Privately, she wrote to a friend, "the brain fever which attacked her [Wright] last year has affected her intellect." But Fanny had a forgiving spirit. "I can never forget her many admirable qualities," she told the same friend, "and I certainly do not believe that it was her intention to deceive me, when she gave such a description of her Nashoba, as induced us to fix upon it as a residence for a year or two, during which, from motives of economy, we had decided upon residing abroad." Now, this was handsome. Wright had very nearly wrecked Fanny's life with her crazed scheme, and Fanny forgave her. She instinctually let go of negative feelings, which was no small gift. It was the key to her sunny disposition.

Now she was in a fix. After ten days of hell, Fanny prevailed upon the Nashoba trustees to advance her cash to return to Memphis. After that Wright battled on, but the dream had died. In December 1829 she freed the slaves and left Nashoba. She subsequently married a Frenchman, had a child, divorced and embarked on a lecture tour around America, pontificating about "the nature of true knowledge." According to Fanny she was "the advocate of opinions that make millions shudder, and some half score admire." Yet in some ways Wright was ahead of her time. Public sentiment was ready for emancipation, at least in some quarters, but could not yet tolerate racial equality.

Fanny and her beleaguered group reached Memphis again on

January 26. Six days later, they boarded the *Criterion* for Cincinnati, which she called "the metropolis of the West." Fanny had heard, she said, "on every side, that of all the known places on 'the globe called earth,' Cincinnati was the most favorable for a young man to settle." She planned to set Henry up in business, though she had not yet formed any idea of what that business might be. At Fort Johnson, the steamer left the Mississippi and breasted the muddy waters of the Ohio. After so long between uninhabited flatlands, Fanny was thrilled by the bluffs and rolling grasslands of the Kentucky shore, and relieved to see evidence of human habitation as well as hills. A glance at the 1825 map reveals just how important the Ohio was: the wiggling line through Vance's pastels thickens with settlements from Illinois to Virginia. When the *Criterion* moored at Louisville to drop off a pilot who had guided her through the Falls, Fanny disembarked for a walk close to the mill on First Street where George Keats, the poet's brother, was prospering in the lumber trade. "Louisville," she wrote, "is a considerable town, prettily situated on the Kentucky, or south side of the Ohio; we spent some hours in seeing all it had to show; and had I not been told that a bad fever often rages there during the warm season, I should have liked to pass some months there." Keats and his wife represented another type of pioneer: they had no interest in utopias or democracy. They wanted to chop the forest down and sell it. And they did. It was pioneer territory all right. Fanny found the inns along the Louisville wharf packed with drinking, swearing tobacco-chewers and the gambling room of a tavern on Main Street was open twenty-four hours. Men, when they fought, deployed the popular practice of "gouging," which involved scraping out one's opponent's eyeball till it dangled on his cheek, or, better still, pulling the organ off to take home and display on the mantelpiece. Keats, who had built a house at the head of the Falls, was close to becoming one of the wealthiest citizens of Louisville. But he lost everything in the Panic of 1837 and died in 1841 aged forty-one.

The *Criterion* proceeded to the teeming Cincinnati docks. "I have seen fifteen steamboats lying there at once," Fanny wrote, "and still half the wharf was unoccupied." The party struggled to a hotel on Front Street, dodging dock pilings and cracked hogsheads. Exhausted, they ordered tea to be sent up. As they drank it, hotelier Joe Cromwell hammered on the door.

"Are any of you ill?" he asked.

"No, thank you sir, we are quite well," Fanny replied through the door.

"Then madam, I must tell you, that I cannot accommodate you on these terms; we have no family tea-drinkings here, and you must live either with me or my wife, or not at all in my house." The speech was delivered, according to Fanny, "with an air of authority that almost precluded reply, but I ventured a sort of apologistic hint, that we were strangers and unaccustomed to the manners of the country."

"Our manners are very good manners," yelled Cromwell, despotic as his namesake, "and we don't wish any changes from England."

The conviction that America was more evolved than the Old Country was to become a leitmotif of Fanny's Ohioan adventures. "American weakness on the subject," she noted, "amounts to imbecility." If she challenged an opinion, her interlocutor dismissed her as a nonentity. Other nations, Fanny concluded, were "thin-skinned, but the citizens of the Union have, apparently, no skins at all; they wince if a breeze blows over them." She had no sense of historical context. It was only twenty-two years since Lewis and Clark, halfway through only the third recorded transcontinental crossing, sent a live prairie dog in a box to the White House, where Jefferson opened it with caution. The Western United States had no past, at least for the white man. No wonder people were anxious.

She found a three-story brick house to rent on Hollingworth Row off Race Street, but it had no drains—there was no municipal sewerage system despite a rising population of 28,000. Cincinnati had grown twelvefold in twenty years and the absence of drains was an indication of its makeshift status. Streets changed overnight as frame houses were wheeled to new locations. When Fanny inquired about garbage collection, the landlord revealed that was the job of the pigs roaming freely through the streets. Cincinnati exported almost a million dollars' worth of pork products a year. Streams ran with porcine blood, jawbones and tails littered the fields and Fanny said that if she walked up Main Street, "the chances were five hundred to one against my reaching the shady side without brushing by a snout fresh dripping from the kennel." She said she would have liked Cincinnati much better "if the people had not dealt so very largely in hogs." Besides piggy smells, after heavy rain followed by sun, the soil crumbled to dust and swathes of red cumulonimbus filled the streets, where the clouds mingled with timber dust. "Though I do not quite sympathise," Fanny wrote, "with those who consider Cincinnati as one of the wonders of the earth, I certainly think it a city of extraordinary size and importance, when it is remembered that thirty years ago the aboriginal forest occupied the ground where it stands; and every month appears to extend its limits and wealth." In three decades Cincinnati had grown into the first real inland American city and a vibrant manufacturing center.* Dockyards built steamboats, mills ground flour and fifty-four foundries cast iron, while

---

*In the same three decades the number of post offices in the U.S. rose from 195 to 7,651. The period covered in this book marked the golden age of the post just as it witnessed the flowering of photography. Before the introduction of the Penny Post in Britain in 1840, sending a letter cost the average worker a week's wages. With the arrival of the Penny Black and Two Penny Blue—the first adhesive stamps in the world—Fanny received ten mail deliveries a day. In the U.S. during the Civil War two decades later, a postal system for the first time enabled troops to remain in regular contact with their families. The railway, in part, was responsible for this transformative development. In Fanny's childhood, a mail coach traveled overnight from London to Bristol. Within a decade, the service had vanished. More about the railway later.

the firm of Read and Watson crafted clocks with mechanical wooden parts, there being a shortage of brass. Cincinnati exemplified the whole country's transformation from an essentially agricultural economy into an industrialised nation. It was the frontier, a zone of reckless entrepreneurialism. Every newspaper carried an advertisement for a new invention, from a candle with a tubular wick to a steam-powered carriage. Fanny loved the frontier energy. "I am delighted with this place," she wrote to a friend. But delight swiftly curdled. She found American society crude. "The 'simple' manner of living in Western America," she wrote, "was more distasteful to me from its levelling effects on the manners of the people, than from the personal privations that it rendered necessary; and yet, till I was without them, I was in no degree aware of the many pleasurable sensations derived from the little elegancies and refinements enjoyed by the middle classes in Europe . . . All animal wants are supplied profusely in Cincinnati, and at a very easy rate; but alas! these go but a little way in the history of a day's enjoyment. The total and universal want of manners, both in males and females, is so remarkable, that I was constantly endeavouring to account for it."

She was expecting her husband. "Is your father ill? Is he dead?" she wrote to the two sons left at home when Thomas failed to appear. The manservant had left, having secured a job in Memphis, but Fanny still had the maid. New staff proved elusive, "for it is more than petty treason to the Republic to call a free citizen a *servant*." One young woman left Fanny's employ "because I refused to lend her money enough to buy a silk dress for a ball." Fanny had no money to lend. Henry advertised Latin lessons in a newspaper ("By an improved method of teaching, now getting into general use in Europe . . . Fifty cents an hour") but demand for the classics turned out to be slow on the frontier. Soon they were reliant on Hervieu. After the debacle at the commune he had pursued a lucrative trade as a portrait painter in Nashville, but the settlement was so small that he had soon painted everyone. Now he joined Fanny and the children in Cincinnati, bringing his dollars. "It is more than a month," she wrote home bitterly, "since we have had a mouthful of food that he has not paid for." Until the end, which was to be bitter indeed, Hervieu never forgot Fanny's loyalty and support when he was a lonely French refugee.

When Henry fell ill, his mother shifted the ménage to the health-restoring countryside. She rented Gano Lodge, a timber cottage in its own field in Mohawk, at that time beyond the city limits and accessible via rope bridges over the basin marshes. "Our manner of life," she wrote after the move, "was infinitely more to my taste than before; it gave us all the privileges of rusticity, which was fully as incompatible with a residence in a little town of Western America as with a residence in London. We lived on terms of primeval intimacy with our cow, for if we lay down on our lawn she did not scruple to take a sniff at the book we were reading, but then she gave us her own sweet breath in return." Fanny took marathon hikes in pursuit of millepore and fossils, "crunching knee deep through aboriginal leaves" while fighting off mosquitoes, locusts and hornets. She said she used the forest "as an extra drawing-room." In the first drawing room, unannounced neighbors arrived on social visits and annoyed her by sitting in silence (the right to show up anywhere at any time Fanny took as a negative symptom of republican equality). But when a neighbor did talk that too annoyed her, because he or she inevitably harped on the failures of the Old Country. The English could not speak English; Britons were fake democrats, pretending to save the world but pursuing their own interests; Americans had a more refined linguistic sensibility. A man reputed to be a scholar told her, "Shakespeare, madam, is obscene, and, thank God, we are sufficiently advanced to have found it out." She said, "The want of warmth . . . upon all subjects which do not immediately touch on their own concerns is universal, and has a most paralyzing effect upon conversation . . . [America] may, I think, be compared to a young bride . . . —the honeymoon is not over yet;—when it is, America will, perhaps, learn more coquetry." Perhaps. She did not understand that the War of Independence had been defined in part by the appeal of a separate American identity. Reflecting later on his mother's views, even Tom, her most loyal defender, wrote that it was surely unreasonable to complain at Americans' "puffed-up patriotism" when one considered that at the time it was a "cardinal article of an Englishman's faith, that every Englishman could thrash three Frenchmen." And Fanny did make friends in Mohawk. "I must not venture," she wrote, "to linger among the cottages that surrounded us; but before I quit them I must record the pleasing recollection of one or two neighbours of more companionable rank, from whom I received so much friendly attention, and such unfailing kindness, in all my little domestic embarrassments, that I shall never recall the memory of Mohawk, without paying an affectionate tribute to these far distant friends."

Cincinnati supported nineteen newspapers and its Western Museum was one of the first scientific institutions in the country. In 1818, John James Audubon worked there. The thirty-three-year-old Audubon was a characteristically energetic and versatile first-generation American who exemplified the pioneer spirit in art, and the frontier awakened the genius within, as it did eventually within Fanny. Both, in the unlikely setting of Porkopolis, brewed books that took on international lives of their own. A skilled outdoorsman, Audubon could navigate his flatboat through broken ice up the Mississippi, reconnoitre the Louisiana backwoods and shoot his own dinner. He was a friend of the Osage and the Shawnee and learned their skills. He had reinvented himself in America—no longer a Haitian refugee or French émigré, he perceived the republic as a canvas against which he could become what he wanted to be. As a young man, he had moved to

Cincinnati and got a job painting backgrounds for display cases at the Western Museum before taking up work as a portraitist. Audubon was the first great American artist. While re-creating the habitat of stuffed bears, he conceived his life's work. He was going to paint every bird in North America, life-size, and publish the results in bound volumes. As the wild turkey was the largest bird, he began with that, as it would determine the size of the books (double elephant folio, as it turned out). Audubon and his wife, Lucy, dedicated their lives to this monumental task. Out collecting, Audubon regularly walked a hundred miles, often wading ankle-deep in cold water. Rats ate his pictures, his businesses collapsed and creditors hammered on the door, if there was a door. In Kentucky, when his sawmill business failed, he lodged with George Keats. Once, he went to debtors' prison. When he was painting, he used wire to twist his birds into lifelike poses—so a male passenger pigeon leans upwards to pass food into the beak of his mate reaching down from the branch above. Before Audubon, birds on the page were static. His wild turkey, glancing behind to see what's coming, looks as if he is about to fly up from between the covers. As he was amassing his paintings, Audubon collected advance subscriptions. No printer in America could create such an ambitious set of books so the artist took his hand-colored prints to Britain and oversaw production of etched and engraved copper plates, each thirty-nine by twenty-six inches. The five-volume *Birds of America* appeared between 1827 and 1838, with a separate five-volume accompanying text that Darwin was to quote three times in his *The Origin of Species*. Audubon's *Birds of America* stands among the masterpieces of world art as well as being a landmark in that country's coming of age. The pictures form a narrative: the birds hunting and nest building, tending their young and seeing off interlopers. Critics accuse him of anthropomorphism, but Audubon found meaning in the natural world and translated what he saw into human emotion—one sees naked violence in the uplifted face of the golden eagle as it lofts a live white rabbit over the mountains.*

When Fanny said she didn't think everyone should be eligible to be president, people rounded on her. She made resolutions to keep her mouth shut. But the resolve never held. Her friend Timothy Flint, editor of the *Western Monthly*, one of the first literary magazines that side of the Alleghenies, said she was "voluble as a French woman and . . . a first-rate talker," though he also considered her "a person of uncommon cleverness." Observing her progressing toad-like through the streets in a foot-tall hooped green bonnet and a plaid cloak that trailed in the mud, Flint described her as

---

*One hundred and nineteen sets of first editions survive. In 2010, one sold for over $11 million. The Cincinnati Public Library holds a set. One Monday morning, in the Rare Books Room, I watched a curator pull on white gloves, unlock a glass cabinet, and turn a page of the volume on display. A security guard stood at his side while a hallowed silence settled over the carmine head of a western tanager.

"singularly unladylike in her appearance and robust and mas-culine in her habits." The adjective "masculine" recurs. Yet Fanny criticized the women of Cincinnati for being flat-chested. She found most of them prudish and claimed one fainted when she heard the word "corset."

She was convinced that the famous American equality "lev-elled people downwards." Spitting in public drove her berserk, as did the chomping of foot-long watermelon slices. Fanny put poor manners down to the "universal pursuit of money." Complaining that she never heard "that most un-American phrase, 'I thank you,'" Fanny said that in the United States only getting ahead mattered. Like Dickens later on, she complained that Americans were too concerned about money. Yet a glance at the Victorian novels of Britain reveals an obsession with cash. *A Christmas Carol* is an allegory of the relationship between capitalism and charity. Anthony Trollope's *The Way We Live Now* is all about money, and his other novels are populated with characters calculating how much they are worth, or moneylenders preying on impoverished clerks. Thackeray's books reveal an acute awareness of how money is spent and lost. "Ours is a ready money society," George Os-borne says in *Vanity Fair*. Later, Gissing wrote about the emotional consequences of money's absence. You ask yourself what Fanny and Boz were moaning about.

More understandably, collective blindness to the double stan-dards of a society supposedly composed of equals also sent Fanny into paroxysms of fury. "You will see them with one hand," she said of her Kentucky neighbors, "hoisting the cap of liberty, and with the other flogging their slaves." The existence of slaves invali-dated the trumpeted American democracy. Ohio was not a slave state, but it bordered one, and Cincinnati newspapers bristled with notices about runaway slaves, each carefully identified: "She had a burn on one of her legs"; "She had arched toes"; "She was in the habit of selling cakes." Fanny hated slavery and equality with similar passion. She was appalled when servants and shopgirls behaved as if they were her equals, and like many European visitors noted with distaste that American servants *shared their employer's dining table.* "When she found she was to dine in the kitchen," Fanny wrote of one short-lived maid, "she turned up her pretty lip, and said, 'I guess that's 'cause you don't think I'm good enough to eat with you.'" Indeed it was. "You'll find that won't do here," the maid ended the conversation. To someone like Fanny, brought up in the stratified society of late Georgian England, dining alongside one's servant was like running naked through the streets. In Fanny's interior world, people were born in immutable tiers. "Queer effect," she noted in her Ohioan journal, "of hearing that one's friend's cousin is a shoemaker or a baker or a sailmaker." Discovering the exotic private life of another servant girl, Fanny concluded, "This adventure frightened me so heartily, that, notwithstanding I had the dread of cooking my own dinner before my eyes, I would not take any more young ladies into my family without receiving some slight sketch of their former history." As for the communal table: the custom lived on in the interior long after it died out on the East Coast. Sherwood Anderson complains about it in *Winesburg, Ohio*, a portrait of regional life based on the author's own experience growing up in Clyde in the 1880s. ("In Winesburg," Anderson writes, "servants were hard to get. The woman who wanted help in her housework employed a 'hired girl' who insisted on sitting at the table with the family.") The author had lived on the coasts for many years when he wrote *Winesburg* and the book is a reaction to the provincialism of his childhood: exactly the characteristics that irritated Fanny. He captures the fleeting, small-town moment of those years and pins it to the page like a lepidopterist. Anderson went for the flash of lightning that revealed a life without changing it—the silent moment in the Ohio cornfield when two inarticulate men almost connect, or a conversation flaring and dying at the stove in the back of a freezing dry-goods store. At his best, Anderson is one of the best. Hemingway admired him, and so did Faulkner and Thomas Wolfe, though all his disciples deserted him in the end, as did his readers. He ended up forgotten, living in New Orleans, and died after swallowing a toothpick.

When Fanny visited a "wild and lonely farm," she admired the pluck of the early homesteaders, though with misgivings:

> I think it the best specimen I saw of the backwoods independence, of which so much is said in America. These people were indeed independent, Robinson Crusoe was hardly more so, and they eat and drink abundantly; but yet it seemed to me there was something awful and almost unnatural in their loneliness. No village bell ever summoned them to prayer . . . When they die, no spot sacred by ancient reverence will receive their bodies . . . the husband or the father will dig the pit that is to hold them . . . and the wind that whispers through the boughs will be their only requiem. But then they pay neither taxes nor tithes, are never expected to pull off a hat or to make a curtsy, and will live and die without hearing or uttering the dreadful words, "God save the King."

Meanwhile, Cincinnati prospered. In March 1829, the first vessel breasted the Miami Canal from the Queen City to Dayton. When the *Advertiser* solicited subscribers for the Lexington and Ohio Railroad, investors fell over themselves in the race to spend. The evident availability of disposable income gave Fanny an idea. No people she had ever come across "appeared to live so much without amusement as the Cincinnatians. Billiards are forbidden by law," she complained, "so are cards. To sell a pack of cards in Ohio subjects the seller to a penalty of fifty dollars . . . Cincinnati has not many lions to boast." Fanny had noted the public appetite for spectacle—the papers constantly advertised performances by pirouetting dogs or trapeze artists. The exhibition galleries at the

Western Museum were often empty, so she shrewdly approached the curator, Joseph Dorfeuille. Drawing on shows she had seen at London's Vauxhall Gardens, Fanny sketched out a series of "talking panoramas" in which actors appeared as living exhibits. Hervieu, as artistic collaborator, co-opted the lanky young Hiram Powers, a Vermont-born mechanical genius who went on to become the most celebrated American sculptor of the nineteenth century. He was to make wax models. Dorfeuille agreed to Fanny's scheme, and in April 1828, *The Invisible Girl* opened at the museum. Twelve visitors at a time paid to ask an oracle three questions in a room lit with colored images. Henry played the oracle, at last making use of his Latin (at least between the questions: he delivered his answers in English). In an adjacent Magic Chamber, spectral figures danced on the walls. It was a quality show by frontier standards, and Cincinnatians loved it—*The Invisible Girl* ran for eight weeks. The next spectacle, *The Infernal Regions*, featured moving waxworks and "Horrid groans and terrible shrieks in every direction"—a depiction of hell Fanny stole from Dante (she even translated some of *The Inferno* to include in the script) and a far cry from the pieties of the Pilgrim Fathers. The public loved that too, and Dorfeuille installed an electric fence to keep the crowds back. *The Infernal Regions* ran for an extraordinary thirty-nine years. Fanny had money at last. For all her complaints about American fondness for cash above beauty, she found herself in permanent pursuit of lucre. "Perhaps they are right," she wrote of her neighbors. "In Europe we see fortunes crippled by a passion for statues, or for pictures, or for books, or for gems; for all and every of the artificial wants that give grace to life, and tend to make man forget that he is a thing of clay. They are wiser in their generation on the other side of the Atlantic; I rarely saw anything that led to such oblivion there." It was only partly ironic.

The public loved the shows almost as much as they enjoyed arguing over the imminent presidential election, and Fanny was amused to discover that Americans thought they had invented the democratic process. "We do these things openly here; you mince matters more, I expect," a neighbor remarked to her during the hustings. British suffrage might have been limited, but a democratic system had been evolving since the Great Councils that followed the Norman Conquest in 1066. That—the eleventh century—was a fertile period for the Acoma Pueblo in what is now New Mexico, but Washington, D.C., remained the lonely home of a few wandering Nacotchtank dreaming of beaver pelts. When Fanny settled in Cincinnati, Andrew Jackson was fighting it out for the second time against incumbent John Quincy Adams, and the *Advertiser* was batting for Jackson while its rival the *Gazette* came out for Adams. Most voters supported the boy from the Carolina backwoods with a bullet in his chest, and in October, in the biggest political meeting ever held in the city, 1,200 Jacksonians crushed into the candlelit theater to hear bombastic attacks on East Coast elitism. The process was only open to some. Before Fanny left Cincinnati, the newly crowned Jackson, a slaveholder whose quiffed likeness still goggles from the twenty-dollar bill, introduced his Indian Removal Act, which, in a hotly contested field, was one of the most rebarbative pieces of legislation ever passed. Elections apart, only the Fourth of July raised the citizens of Cincinnati from the single-minded pursuit of gain. "To me," Fanny wrote, "the dreary coldness and want of enthusiasm in American manners is one of their greatest defects, and I therefore hailed the demonstrations of general feeling which this day elicits with real pleasure. On the Fourth of July the hearts of the people seem to awaken from a 364 days' sleep; they appear high spirited, gay, animated, social, generous, or at least liberal in expense; and would they but refrain from spitting on that hallowed day, I should say that on the Fourth of July, at least, they appeared to be an amiable people."

Thomas Trollope had finally arrived in September 1828,

bringing the eldest son—his snub-nosed, shy namesake, known as Tom, who had grown into a gentle giant. Anthony remained alone in England, his school bills unpaid. "My boyhood," the latter wrote in his autobiography, "was, I think, as unhappy as that of a young gentleman could well be." His account of those years is almost unbearable in its misery. "I feel convinced in my mind," he wrote, "that I have been flogged more than any human being alive." He waited until she was dead till he said it, but she must have known. God knows how she stood it. Thomas and Tom were to stay for six months. Back at home the domestic treasury was in terminal decline, but in the Ohio forest buckeyes flamed, and when cold winds blew in from the plains, the family took up drawing-room dramas, or wrapped up for skating and moonlit sleigh rides. Fanny threw a party, inviting a hundred guests and installing a small orchestra. The hosts staged *The Merry Wives of Windsor*, and Henry, suitably drunk as Falstaff, went on with a pillow up his shirt. "Looking back at those Cincinnati days," Tom wrote in old age, "I have to say that I liked Americans."

Encouraged by the success of *The Infernal Regions*, toward the end of 1828 Fanny conceived the ambitious idea for a cultural entertainment center where the sexes could mingle as they did at the Hot Wells spa in Bristol, at Almack's Assembly Rooms in London's St. James', or at Vauxhall Gardens. Vauxhall was the most famous pleasure garden in Europe, open to anyone who could afford the shilling entrance fee, and it had just enjoyed its most profitable decade. Anthony Trollope once danced all night in the ballroom after walking fourteen miles from Harrow, and when the sun rose, he walked back. At Vauxhall an orchestra played on the upper floor of a rococo octagon, singers crooned from balconies and for the first time the middle classes ate in public, enjoying wafer-thin slices of ham, potted pigeon and arrack punch after viewing the latest stunt: a cat arrived by parachute, poor thing, and a horse went up under a hot air balloon, its hooves nailed to a wooden platform. The Gardens were popular with lovers—Keats

(John, not George) wrote the sonnet, "To a Lady Seen for a Few Moments at Vauxhall," and the Dark Walk at one end was the scene of more transactional romance. Before Fanny left England, the Gardens had begun to specialize in illuminations. Besides fireworks and crackerjacks, thousands of train-oil lights hung on trees (Vauxhall was "a wilderness of lamps," according to the young Wordsworth, though the Dark Walk remained unlit, for the sake of propriety, and business) and dramatic panoramas like the Western Museum tableaux represented the eruption of Vesuvius. Fanny believed she could sprinkle some Vauxhall fairy dust on the frontier. On January 20, 1829, she and Thomas purchased a plot close to the river for $1,665, almost exactly the sum she had received on her father's death. When he returned to Harrow, Thomas was to forward funds to complete the project. He suggested the inclusion of retail space. "This frightened me," Fanny wrote to a friend later, "as I knew we none of us understood anything of buying and selling." Thomas insisted that the goods he was going to send would be certain to generate handsome profits. Decades later, Anthony wrote of his father, "The touch of his hand seemed to create failure. He embarked on one hopeless enterprise after another, spending on each all the money he could at the time command. His temper was so bad that he estranged every one of his family, and yet I believe that he would have given his heart's blood for any of us. His life as I knew it was one long tragedy."

Construction of the Bazaar turned into a Dantean purgatory, like the talking panorama. Located on the industrial south side of Third Street, the site nestled among engine manufacturers and steam paper mills and smelled like the neighboring brewery. Thomas and Tom had left, leaving Fanny to manage the project. Every worker's insistence that he was equal to everyone else revealed the speed of democracy in action, and in the bitter winter months mortar froze before it was applied. The snow fell and fell and ice hardened on the mud puddles on Third Street, but no money appeared from Harrow. Fanny had instructed her husband not to spend more than 150 pounds on the retail goods. When the shipment arrived, customs duties exceeded the selling price. In addition, it was all trash. Fanny declared she had "4,000 dollars" worth of the most trumpery goods that probably ever were shipped." She ran out of money, completing the building on credit. In March 1829, with things at their worst, Fanny turned fifty. Failing eyesight, night sweats, unplanned micturition, forgetfulness, deafness, weight gain, a hairy chin—and gravity.

She had designed the building herself. The limestone frontage, inspired by the basilica of St. Athanase in Egypt, comprised three outsize arabesque windows and a battlement. The south face, an ersatz Apollinopolis, featured columns rising three stories to a twenty-four-foot rotunda. Fanny had lived her whole life under George III and the Bazaar reflected the Regency love of the flamboyant and exotic, reprising characteristics of contemporary buildings at home—Brighton's Royal Pavilion, the second Theatre Royal in Covent Garden, the Burlington Arcade, and especially the Turkish Tent and rotunda at Vauxhall. In England the style had evolved organically. On the American frontier, according to one resident, the Bazaar "could scarcely have been more out of place had it been tossed on the earth by some volcano in the moon." Americans favored neoclassical architecture, and Grecian restraint set the tone. Fanny had gone for the opposite effect, shaking up allusion, Orientalism and Georgian beau monde charade. As for the 3,800-square-foot interior: above the Exchange Coffee House and basement bar, the first floor had the shop, two rows of columns and a salon serving oysters and sherbets. On the second floor, Hervieu had painted the ballroom to look like the Alhambra, with *trompe l'oeil* columns, niches, and false windows filled in with Spanish landscapes. A staircase spiraling through four floors ended in the rotunda, which had been fitted out with panoramic screens. Cincinnati's first gaslights were to illuminate proceedings.

THE BAZAAR.

At the grand opening nobody wanted to buy ices or coffee, or waste time looking at pictures, and visitors considered the prices of the bric-a-brac a joke. The gas pipes eructated with vile-smelling smoke and Fanny had to bring in whale-oil lamps, which made their own contribution to the stink. A week later, the contractor engaged to repair the pipes absconded with the advanced cash. Fanny held a musical evening of songs and recitation. The entrance ticket was one dollar, tea and coffee included. "These species of amusement, so popular of late years, both in Paris and London," read the advert in the *Gazette*, "have not hitherto been introduced in America, and it is hoped the present attempt will be favourably received." It was not. Americans on the frontier were too busy to sit on their bottoms eating sherbets or humming along to operettas. Rescue schemes collapsed one after the other: Fanny tried to rent space to merchants and offered the Great Room for dinners, and Hervieu staged a weekly musical evening. When six drunks from a passing steamer were the only attendees, he called it off. The Bazaar would have been ambitious even without the retail fiasco. In the end creditors seized everything. Trollope's Folly, as residents dubbed the Bazaar, revealed a lack of commercial acumen, the worst crime in frontier America. On January 22, 1830, auctioneers moved in to sell piles of vases, watch cases, candlesticks, coral necklaces and gilt clocks. Unable to pay the rent, Fanny and her entourage had to give up Gano Lodge. But they could not leave Cincinnati until March, as the Ohio was frozen. Trading the parlor carpet for rent, they boarded with a neighbor, and Hervieu bought them all one meal a day. Creditors had even taken their beds, so through a hard Ohio winter, with the temperature down to three degrees below, Fanny and the two girls shared a small cot while Henry and Hervieu slept on the kitchen floor. Fanny contracted malaria and Henry fell seriously ill with an unknown malady. It was a desperate time.

At Pleasureville Pool Hall on Main Street, the owner was flipping cheeseburgers. *No fries*, said a sign, *—no frier*. A winking television on a hinge in the corner made no impact on the room. Under the high ceilings, islands of light picked out the pool tables even at two in the afternoon. Outside, one streetlight was on, the weak beam absorbed in the oven-like sunshine, and deserted sidewalks shimmered in 99 percent humidity. All the other shops had closed down—even the video store had succumbed. The Kentucky-born owner joined me for a triangle between frying burgers. "How's business?" I asked. "Fair," he said. He was sixty-three and had worked at the pool hall since he was ten, and recently had bought the enterprise from his uncle. It was hard to imagine anyone buying it from him. The hall was almost part of the past— about to slip into history and oblivion, swept away by a homogenizing tide of malls. But it wasn't quite the past yet. The thwack of balls on baize still reverberated around the cavernous room and the ceiling fans went through their lugubrious motions even though the hall was air-conditioned. One had the sense of continuity—touching hands with the long list of travelers to have roamed the bluegrass, even back to Fanny.

Two days later, I crossed the Ohio. In a parking lot in downtown Cincinnati, I posted dollar bills through a metal slit; a homely, unpoliced, non-metropolitan system of a piece with the old-fashioned tone of the quiet streets, brownstone walk-ups and fire escape ziggurats. A firmly worded sign noting the consequences of non-payment, with reference to by-laws and legislative procedures, exemplified the beady-eyed provincialism for which the

Queen City is infamous. (In 1990 the director of the Contemporary Arts Center was indicted on obscenity charges for putting on a Robert Mapplethorpe exhibition.) The fiberglass pigs in tutus outside the Cincinnati Ballet on Central Parkway were protesting too much, and little had changed over the last half-century in the subterranean Hathaway's diner beneath the Carew Tower. The Cincinnati coney dogs tasted great all the same—or perhaps because of the sleepy, stately charm that made the city hard to dislike. The frontier swagger of the 1820s disappeared in a generation as America rolled west, leaving Cincinnati in peace. Mark Twain said he would come here for the apocalypse, because Cincinnati was always twenty years behind the times. A lot of it had come to a standstill. In Mohawk, where Fanny had tramped through the forest looking for fossils, Sam's Meats and Eats had closed its doors forever and most of the nineteenth-century townhouses were boarded up, or for rent, or both. This, like Jonestown, represented another side of the American dream. People sat on plastic chairs on the sidewalks, fleeing the pressure-cooker of walk-ups without air-conditioning. Vines had coiled round overhead power cables that swagged from sidewalk maples. From the top of a hill I could see the two cones of the Proctor and Gamble building, known as Dolly Parton Towers, and the annunciatory glow of the moving newsband around the Great American Ballpark, home of the Cincinnati Reds. The cetacean puffs of steam were gone from the Ohio, and so was the Bazaar. After Fanny left America, the Presbyterian Society took it over, handing it on to the Ohio Mechanics' Institute. Subsequent businesses included a brothel and a hospital for Civil War soldiers, and in 1881 a developer tore it down to make way for an apartment block. On low ground a few hundred yards from the river, the concrete struts of Highway 77 encased any remnants of arabesques, battlements and dreams under a tide of roaring cars.

Fanny returned to Harrow with a rough draft of a book in three inky notebooks. This, now, was the only hope of financial salvation. The Scottish naval officer Basil Hall's *Travels in North America* had just gone through three rapid printings and Fanny judged that the reading public wanted to know more about the independent nation that had sprung from what had been, to most Britons, an uninteresting colony. And they did. America in the end delivered what Fanny had set sail to find—financial security. So it was the promised land after all.

What is *Domestic Manners*? It is a vivid, funny, idiosyncratic and deeply selective portrait of America written in prose with serrated edges. Fanny sailed from England a liberal and returned a conservative, and the transformation gave her book its tensile strength. From the start, she skews the evidence in an attempt to prove that equality is an antidote to improvement, and that handing state power to the populace leads to a breakdown of social control. Fanny was suspicious both of Jefferson's insistence that all men are born equal, and of the Jacksonian concept of popular democracy. "Were I an English legislator," she wrote, "instead of sending sedition to the tower, I would send her to make a tour of the U.S. I had a little leaning towards sedition myself when I set out, but before I had half completed my tour I was quite cured." A country needs a hierarchy, she believed, as a body needs a skeleton. "In the social system of Mr. Jefferson," she wrote, "the darling, 'I'm as good as you' would soon take the place of the law and Gospel." She dealt with Jefferson by referring to his numerous offspring by a slave (his long-term mistress Sally Hemings). In her prose and in her life Fanny moved with eighteenth-century ease from battlefield to boudoir. She is associated with the Victorians, but really she was raised in the world of rakes and Hogarthian vulgarity, unafraid of either in print or life. And America was not the only problem when she was writing *Domestic Manners*. The Reform Bill and the possibility of the first significant extension of voting rights in English history dominated the political agenda at home. The issue was so contentious that working Britons had been hanged and thousands deported to Australia; in Bristol, Fanny's hometown, rioters burned down the bishop's palace. Convinced by her American experiences that the masses should be denied power, Fanny hoped, through *Domestic Manners of the Americans*, to boost the Conservative cause.*

Fanny's central theme—the consequences of investing the power of the state in the hands of the populace—lay at the heart of Alexis de Tocqueville's investigations. Now the sacerdotal European commentator on the United States, Tocqueville had sailed over to Jacksonian America to compile a report on the prison system. He ended up writing a meditation on the nature of democracy that remains in print after 160 years, though that is not as long as *Domestic Manners*.

Tocqueville's people were ultra-royalists shacked up in a chateau on the Cotentin peninsula in Normandy. Many had heard the snick of the guillotine, and Tocqueville wept when he watched the last Bourbon king fleeing Versailles in a coach with the bossed royal emblem shrouded. What, he wondered, would replace the old forms of the social contract? Like many in Europe, he saw America as an experiment which might answer that question. Tocqueville set off in 1831 in the company of his friend Gustave de Beaumont: their three-masted schooner *Le Havre* passed Fanny's ship in mid-Atlantic. Both men were twenty-five-year-old assistant magistrates with patrician good looks. They toured for nine months, and took a steamboat down the Mississippi from Memphis to New Orleans, calling the latter "*le Midi*." Cincinnati, they noted in letters and journals, was unfettered by the blue-blooded traditions of the East. "This is a society," Tocqueville wrote of the nascent city, "that as yet has no bonds, political, hierarchical, social or religious, in which each individual is on his own

*Her fears for the leveling effects of democracy were unfounded. In 2012, in the group of the twenty most advanced democracies as defined by the Organization for Economic Cooperation and Development, America had the greatest inequality of incomes and the lowest social mobility.

because it suits him to be, without concerning himself with his neighbour, a democracy without limit or moderation." The whole place seemed to embody the essence of the new country and as such was crucial to Tocqueville's perceptions of American democracy. "The entire society [in Cincinnati]," he wrote in a notebook, "is a factory!" He told his mother that society appeared in big letters there, like a children's book—you could read America. Unlike the troubled country of his birth, and even unlike the East Coast of the U.S., Cincinnati was a place without a past. Tocqueville liked everything American except slavery and the forced resettlement of Indians—though these were sizeable issues. Unlike Fanny, he came to believe that the development of democracy was inevitable ("God-given") while at the same time harboring deep reservations about its institutionalisation. He warned, with foresight, that the new system was likely to produce fresh forms of tyranny, because too much equality could lead to materialism and individualism. Tocqueville did share certain Trollopian complaints. He too noted an unpleasant obsession with wealth. "The more deeply one goes into the American national character," he wrote, "the more one sees that they value everything on earth in response to this sole question: How much is it worth?" The notion of American rapacity persisted. Henry James, in *The American Scene*, made the point that Americans have no respect for the old unless there is money in it. Even in the 1990s, when the American writer Bill Bryson toured Britain by train, he expressed frustration at his fellow passengers' unwillingness to talk. It was all so different in America, wrote Bryson. There one only had to extend one's hand and ask, "How much money did you make last year?"

"The people here seem to be stinking with national conceit," Tocqueville wrote to his mother three days after disembarking from the *Le Havre*. Americans were so convinced of their superiority as "the only religious, enlightened and free people," that they almost believed themselves "a distinct species of mankind." But he came to recognize that what looked like vanity was insecurity, one aspect of the "restless spirit" that was the essence of Jacksonian America. The difference between Tocqueville and Fanny Trollope turns on this point. His was the more flexible mind; he was an intellectual, and in America experience informed his intellect. She was an empiricist, content to base broad judgements on a short spell of personal experience colored by her own shortcomings and prejudice. He took the nuanced view, displaying a largesse that came naturally to a wealthy *boulevardier* who went to so many balls in America that he wrote home for two dozen pairs of yellow kid gloves. *Democracy in America* might be more quoted than read but Tocqueville's reputation as a thinker has never been higher. He has become a prophet for all seasons, continually reinterpreted as the zeitgeist shifts, and the complexity of his analysis has made it possible for ideologues of every persuasion to claim him for their team.

She tried to dissuade Anthony from the writing business. "We Trollopes," Fanny told her son, "are far too much given to pen and ink as it is." Their output was indeed biblically vast. After *Domestic Manners*, Fanny published thirty-four triple-decker novels and six travel narratives, and by the time she put down her pen, she had racked up well over a hundred volumes. The bear-like Tom wrote in excess of sixty books, from tomes on Italian politics to histories, most of them bad; he worked from eight till two every day, standing at a lectern smoking cigars. His first wife produced translations and rather good poetry before expiring of TB in 1865, and his second, another Frances (sister of Dickens' mistress Nellie Ternan), churned out a dozen novels and a biography of Fanny, her mother-in-law, whom she had never met. Cecilia caught them up with a high-church novel. Between them they had almost every literary genre covered. Anthony clocked up a mere fifty books. Like Fanny, he places the crucial importance of marriage at the center of all his novels, but with an awful lot more subtlety and sophistication (he also enjoyed a more successful marriage than his mother). To a certain extent her novels are unevolved ancestral prototypes of his.

Fanny's novels are bright, coarse and not very good. "Oh . . . that ladies would make puddings and mend stockings!" wrote Thackeray in a review of an early one. Many reprise the themes of the American book. *Michael Armstrong, The Factory Boy*, which appeared in monthly shilling parts, publicizes the plight of 200,000 children, some as young as five, working at looms in the north of England in the 1830s, deprived of light, beaten awake by foremen with long sticks called billy rollers and so malnourished they resembled dwarves. It was slavery by another name. A reactionary Tory she might have been, but Fanny was quick to speak out against injustice, whether in Lancashire factories, Kentucky plantations or Cherokee enforced camps. In addition, although she did not champion female suffrage, she never stopped fighting for the right of women to control their destinies. The novels are crowded with strong women who win through. She was in many ways a pioneer, in that the education and the position of women were a central preoccupation, and she often spoke up, through her characters, on behalf of women whom society judged to be foolish or wayward. One reviewer called her "a bluestocking who travels in seven-leagued boots."

While the books poured out, Henry and both the girls who had accompanied Fanny to America developed full-blown TB. "A sadder household never was held together," Anthony remembered. "They were all dying, except my mother, who would sit up night after night nursing the dying ones and writing novels the while." She often worked through the night, sustained by laudanum and green tea; at other times she rose at four and worked till someone else woke or needed nursing. Then they did die: first Henry, aged twenty-three, then Emily, aged eighteen, then Cecilia, aged thirty-three.

The worst had actually happened. The deepest dread; the unspoken fear that lurks behind the joy of parenthood. Having a child entails almost too much risk: creating the most profound love, which can at any time be taken away. It so terrified me that I didn't dare do it until I was thirty-seven. It was not so much fear of the child dying. It was fear that he or she might be damaged and unhappy. In my case this was an understandable consequence of experience. My only sibling, Mathew, fourteen months my junior, has been profoundly brain damaged since he was a baby, and for large chunks of his life incapable of finding happiness. It's not that you love them less: the problem is that you love them more.

Of the seven children she had borne, only Anthony and Tom were still alive. The choleric Thomas also expired, at the age of sixty-one; he had reached F for Funeral in his ecclesiastical encyclopedia. "The doctor's vials and the ink-bottle held equal places in my mother's rooms," Anthony wrote years later. "I have written many novels under many circumstances; but I doubt much whether I could write one when my whole heart was by the bedside of a dying son." Talk about being two separate people. Yet was she? She had certainly done better than I had in that department. Even when the skies grew very black indeed, Fanny accepted the things that couldn't be changed. Unlike Faulkner, she never had to reconcile herself to the annihilation to come. Death, for her, was part of life.

I sensed there was something for me to learn here. What was it that I found so hard to accept? Entering the next phase, and letting all or most of that mothering business go? Becoming myself again? There was such obscurity swirling round that next "phase." In my grandmother's youth in the 1920s, let alone in Fanny's era, many in the medical profession perceived the menopause as a disaster. Doctors tried to reactivate menstruation by opening tissues of blood, in addition to the deployment of God knows what other more than useless interventions. In 1917, the Irish writer George Moore published a novel in which the narrator peremptorily announces, "At fifty a woman's life is really over." The heroine herself believes, "A woman dies twice, and in a very few years it is borne in upon us that our mouths are no longer fit for kisses." She is forty-five. Whole industries still devote themselves to the pursuit of eternal youth. The message that a woman in her fifties must strive not to show her age is deeply embedded in contemporary Western culture, as if we were all, we would-be crones, screaming desperately, *"Don't let me get old!"* (Reading the popular press, you would think that women of fifty and over do not exist, bar the odd prime minister or secretary of state carrying on like honorary men.) Elsewhere in these pages I made fun of Fanny Trollope's drooping bosom and the other physical indignities she faced on entering her sixth decade. But none of those things made her less of a woman. Our culture and hers say that they did. One would think nothing lay over the hill of the climacteric (a friendlier word than "menopause," I think) except gloomy decrepitude: twilight before death. "Old Woman" was not a friendly term when a Cincinnati neighbor used it to address Fanny Trollope 185 years ago. Little has changed. But if we don't like ourselves as we are, who will?

Anthony's portraits of his mother are affectionate, despite the stupendous misery of his childhood. He installed her in many stories, and in his pages she lives on. In his autobiography, he said that Matilda Carbury, the central figure in my favorite among his novels, *The Way We Live Now*, was based partly on Fanny. While she is a financially successful writer, Carbury emerges as a slightly dim figure of fun, seducing literary editors, writing absurd books and trying to force her children into good marriages. The victim of her wastrel son, Carbury works like a demon and rejects the role of the passive Victorian woman. Like Fanny Trollope, she was a successful transgressor. *The Way We Live Now* is a novel about a woman's escape from male uselessness and worse into a mostly sunlit land of redemption and emotional freedom. As Carbury herself notes, "How few women there are who can raise themselves above the quagmire of what we call love, and make themselves anything but playthings for men." Anthony deeply admired his mother. "She was an unselfish, affectionate, and most industrious woman," he wrote, "with great capacity for enjoyment and high physical gifts. She was endowed too, with much creative power, with considerable humour, and a genuine feeling for romance." In his novels, he creates people who rise from misfortune through ingenuity, hard work and even love, as she had. He saw her, as he saw his characters, with generous, forgiving eyes. But in his autobiography he said his mother was politically gullible, allowing chance acquaintance with "an Italian marquis who had escaped with only a second shirt" to shape her views. "With her politics were always an affair of the heart,—as indeed were all her convictions. Of reasoning from causes I think that she knew nothing." Tom said his brother had got their mother wrong in this regard. It was he, Tom, who lived with her for many of her later years. "We were inseparable companions and friends," he said, going on to defend the integrity and intellectual basis of his mother's political opinion. "She was the happiest natured person I ever knew," he wrote in his autobiography. "Happy in the intense power of enjoyment, happier still in the conscious exercise of the power of making others happy." What more could one want? "She was during all her life," Tom continued, "full of, and fond of, fun; had an exquisite sense of humour; and at all times valued her friends and acquaintances more exclusively, I think, than most people do, for their intrinsic qualities, mainly those of the heart."

Fanny never returned to America. She saw the USA and Britain moving together, culturally, as she had feared they would.* Through it all she found patterns in the messy, contradictory details of her own experience and salvaged redemption from the suitcase of shattered dreams. She died aged eighty-three at her

---

*The tiresome notion that America is responsible for the degradation of British culture is endlessly reiterated, like a Greek chorus. Philip Larkin told a friend in anguish that England was destined to become "one huge dismal wet imbecile Yanked-up slum."

handsome Florentine palazzo, the Villino Trollope. Like all writers, she went on talking after she was dead, and she speaks still. One obituary referred to her as "one of the most remarkable women of her period," which I would change to "of any period." Hers is a story of self-made success and of winning through by grit and hard work—an American story. She was more American than she imagined.

2

BRAVE NEW WORLD

Fanny Kemble Goes to Georgia

At thirty-one degrees of latitude, in a dimple of the South Atlantic
Bight, skeins of oat roots catch and hold the mushy Georgia Sea
Islands. High tides sloshing across the basin there nourish hundreds of thousands of acres of subtropical salt marsh. Each spring,
ruby-throated hummingbirds the size of a little finger fly across
the Gulf of Mexico and land in the cordgrass, and on the estuaries
terns gorge on the fat-filled eggs of horseshoe crabs. On the mainland, the Altamaha River, pouring down from the piedmont, in-
fuses fresh water into the salt marsh, which creates spongy islands
called "hammocks" in the inland delta. A thousand years ago,
Timucua peoples hunted right whale from the hammocks, living
off oysters, shrimp and crab. The conquistadores annihilated the
Timucua with European diseases and built garrisons on their
land. After the combined efforts of pirates, Yamacraw and Britons
in turn disposed of the Spaniards, Old World planters found that
the tidewater hammocks—places like Butler Island—made an ideal
environment for large-scale rice production, so they shipped in
West African slaves who spoke the Gullah language and knew
how to cultivate rice. The year after Fanny Trollope sailed home
in temporary defeat, another Fanny landed on the Sea Islands, a
tiny bird of paradise herself. The American press later called her
"the heiress of Mrs. Trollope," but she was a more neurotic species,

the most like me, internally, of all the women in this book. Externally, hers was a life of novelettish glamour; often tragic, often farcical, occasionally sublime. She was a Shakespearean leading lady, and, having conquered Europe, crossed the Atlantic to reprise the role. "We have never seen her equal on the American stage," announced one critic. Kemble adored America as much as Americans loved her. "This is a brave new world in more ways than one," she wrote home. The events that unfolded were more dramatic than a playwright could devise. When forces gathered momentum to break the nation's heart Kemble was a fat, middle-aged eccentric rather than a young woman who cast spells from the stage. So she did what she could—she wrote a book. As the Civil War approached, she distilled her experience on the Sea Islands into a powerful indictment of slavery. Southern historians say Fanny Kemble "influenced England against the Confederacy." She lived enough life for all seven of us.

Kemble's aunt was Sarah Siddons, queen of London's Drury Lane and the actress who dominated the English stage for three decades (Fanny Trollope had queued for six hours to see her play Lady Macbeth), and her father Charles was a leading man, an actor-manager at the Covent Garden Theatre. Fanny was born in 1809 to a nervy Swiss mother, also a thespian. The family favored the grand delivery style—a kind of hectoring declamation—and the phrase "like a Kemble" had entered the vocabulary in theatrical circles to indicate an especially florid acting style. Fanny grew up in the family home off what is now Oxford Street and mixed in the artistic circles of Regency London. She spent four years in France as a teenager and studied in the enlightened Edinburgh of the 1820s, reading widely in French, German and Italian. Like many young women, she was in thrall to the Romantics, and under the influence of Byron determined at an early age to become a writer herself. (Her youthful journal bears the imprint of the Romantics, "Rose at half-past four. The sky was black as death, but in the night winter had dropped his mantle on the earth, and there it lay, cold and purely white against the inky sky.") She was precocious, and when she was seventeen wrote a verse play. It was the first serious endeavor of a prodigious literary output through which Kemble wrote off her losses on the page, as Fanny Trollope had done. She had a passionate nature that needed an outlet, whether in a book, a love affair, or a cause, and all three got her into trouble. She was inconsistent and infuriating, but she refused to acknowledge defeat when crisis came in the middle of her life, and sailed into old age with enviable dignity.

In the mid 1820s the Covent Garden Theatre failed to flourish and Charles Kemble quarreled with the other shareholders. Eventually lawyers pinned bills of sale on the door of his playhouse. At the critical moment, he had his big idea. A flagging theater needs a new star, and he had one under his roof. He dragooned his nineteen-year-old daughter on to the boards to save the family exchequer. "My going on the stage," Kemble wrote, "was entirely an act of duty." After three weeks' rehearsal, on October 5, 1829, she went on as Juliet. Romeo was traditionally her father's part, but he correctly judged that it might look odd. Instead Charles took on Mercutio, and Kemble's mother played Lady Capulet. Sarah Siddons watched from a box.

This Juliet was not a classic beauty: she had large hands and feet and a face one critic described as "insignificant." Smallpox had coarsened her skin. "Well my dear, they cannot say we have brought you out to exhibit your beauty," her mother said before she went on. But she moved well and was sleek and graceful as a whippet (she was under five feet), and just as highly strung. It turned out that she had talent—lots of it. The verdict was unanimous ("A vision to the poet's heart!"), and on October 6, Fanny woke as Britain's leading lady.

As the run continued, London went Kemble crazy. Plates and mugs appeared stamped with her image, mobs of fans quickly dubbed "Kemblers" seethed round the stage door restrained by the unfamiliar figures of "bobbies"—Sir Robert Peel's Metropolitan policemen, making their first appearance in the capital that same week. Half of literary London wrote about her. "The divine Fanny!" mooned the young poet Arthur Henry Hallam. "I have seen her Juliet . . . I mean to live in her ideal." When Hallam and his friend Richard Monckton Milnes saw Kemble's Belividera, Milnes complained, "Hallam had an opera glass which whenever I asked for it he presented to me with a damn as deep as a paviour's [a pavement-layer's] and went raging home to write two sonnets about her." One could scarcely overdo the purple on the stage in those days. Critics often ominously described Kemble's style of acting as "poetic." But she had something. Hallam, a serious theatergoer, wrote, "Ellen Tree [a comic actress—she played Romeo to Fanny's Juliet in 1839!] lacks the touch of genius which Kemble put into her acting, which covered a multitude of faults." Success did not turn her head. Before appearing in the play she had written herself, she said, "I do not care a straw whether the piece dies and is damned the first night, or is cut up alive the next morning." Neither situation transpired. Critics loved her play, and the published version went through ten editions. The lionized actress (certainly not yet an "actor") was the trophy guest on that season's social circuit. The Duke of Rutland invited her to a house party at Belvoir Castle, where his band marched around the ramparts summoning guests to breakfast. "Such shoals of partners!" she wrote to a friend after a ball in her honor. "Danced until the day had one eye open, and then home to bed." When Covent Garden closed for the season, the company toured the provincial theaters. Everywhere Kemble went, star-struck young men gazed up from the front row, many for every night of the run. She sat to Sir Thomas Lawrence, president of the Royal Academy and the most fashionable portrait painter in Europe. (It was Lawrence who had got Fanny Trollope's protégé Hervieu into the Royal Academy.) He hardly missed a performance of her Juliet and was creepily obsessed—and had already seduced two of her cousins. "We were all of us in love with you," William Makepeace Thackeray told her years later, "and had your portrait by Lawrence in our rooms."

Fanny kept her distance from all her beaux, claiming in jest that she was "horribly in love" with George Stephenson, one of the great men of the 1830s, if not of the century. Twenty-eight years Kemble's senior, Stephenson was a civil and mechanical engineer widely revered as the "Father of Railways": he built the first public line to use steam locomotives, and invented the standard gauge. But although trains transformed everything in the half-century under consideration in this book—they are in many ways the emblem of the period—the railway was not yet the icon of Victorian progress it was to become. It was an unproven technological enigma, regarded by many with suspicion. When Kemble was reprising her Juliet in Liverpool, Stephenson took her to ride on the boilerplate in a trial run of his Manchester–Liverpool railway. The experience of standing aloft with her face to the wind and ribbons streaming from her bonnet was Kemble's ideal romantic fantasy. She wrote a long letter to a friend describing what a train looked like. "You cannot imagine," she continued, "how strange it seems to be journeying thus without any visible cause of progress other than the magical machine, with its flying white breath and rhythmical, unvarying pace . . . No fairy tale was half so wonderful as what I saw." On September 15, 1830, Stephenson invited Fanny to the opening ceremony of the same railway. It was a tremendous occasion, the unveiling of the fastest locomotives and longest piece of track in the world. Heavy rain failed to dampen the mood of the crowd. The twenty-one-year-old Alfred Tennyson, future Poet Laureate, was on board to witness the historic event and became sufficiently overheated to write a poem extolling the "ringing grooves of change," inadvertently revealing that he thought trains ran in slots like trams, rather than on raised rails. (Tennyson had a crush on Fanny, like everyone else, and addressed romantic poems to her.) The Prime Minister, the Duke of Wellington, also made the long trip to the north of England to ride on the inaugural journey, and attendant dignitaries included William Huskisson, Tory Member of Parliament for Liverpool and former Secretary of State for the Colonies. At Parkside Railway Station the train stopped to take on water. The rain had turned to drizzle. The duke got out, and Huskisson followed. At that moment one of Stephenson's glamorous locomotives thundered in from the opposite direction, striking Huskisson. He lay mangled on the track and died soon after, one of the world's first railway casualties. It was Hollywood before its time—an impossibly neat metaphor, adumbrating a darker side of industrial development.

The Covent Garden Theatre was again experiencing difficulties. It was the year Fanny Trollope arrived back from America, and supporters of the Reform Bill were busy rioting through London's theater district. "The streets," Fanny Kemble told her sister, "are thronged with people and choked up with carriages and the air is flashing and crashing with rockets and squibs and crackers to the great discomfort of the horses." Some feared revolution,

French style. "Society is becoming a sort of battlefield," Fanny wrote, "for every man (and woman too) is nothing if not political." She was playing Lady Macbeth, a role that ought to have suited the bloody public mood. But the public had again abandoned the theater, and Charles faced fresh financial crisis. He had to get his troupe out of England until trouble subsided.

Fanny's father organised one of the first American theater tours, a twenty-two-month enterprise that began in New York and continued up and down the East Coast, proceeding as far south as the Carolinas—or so Charles planned. Fanny would rather have stayed at home to burnish her literary reputation (besides the play, she had published translations and original poems). "I am weary and sad, and will try to go and sleep," she recorded in her journal at a tiny cabin table on the second day at sea. "It rains: I cannot see the moon." Later she wrote, "I have left my very soul behind me." But there was plenty of champagne and raspberry tart aboard, the captain gave her a sparrow in a cage, and she dazzled the other passengers when she sang at the pianola. After thirty days at sea with her father and her Aunt Dall, who was to act as chaperone, in September 1832 Fanny saw the low outlines of New York. Everyone had taken to the black steward who served them in the ship's dining room, and on the last night of the journey, Fanny poured him a glass of wine, and asked him to raise a toast with them. "Ah!" said the Yankee captain, who was dining alongside them, "One can tell that you are not American." The episode was a warning of horrors to come. She told the captain that perhaps it was just as well she was not American. The sparrow died.

Fanny's journal of the first weeks in New York records sticky rehearsals, hairdressers and three-hour sing-songs at the hotel piano ("I danced myself half dead," she scribbled one night). After rehearsing at the Park Theater she walked with her father across The Battery, then a small island attached to the rest of Manhattan by a wooden causeway and drawbridge. They paraded arm in

arm, he in a frock coat, she in a hooped skirt and bonnet, around
the dimpled sandstone of Castle Garden, a fort converted into an
open-air cultural emporium of the kind Fanny Trollope had tried
to create in Cincinnati.* Kemble was in raptures over the evanes-
cence of light where the Hudson and East rivers join. "In the early
evening," she wrote in her journal, "the moon shone full upon the
trees and the intersecting walks of the promenade, and threw a
bright belt of silver along the water's edge . . . The fort, now a cafe,
was brilliantly lighted with coloured lamps, shining among the
trees and reflected in the water." Later she called Castle Garden
"an aquatic Vauxhall." Fanny decided that she liked Americans
very much. They in turn revered her as a goddess, whereas they
had addressed Trollope as "Old Woman," a title which might well
put one in a bad mood at the age of fifty. *Domestic Manners of the
Americans* had just come out. "Mercy on me," Fanny wrote home,
"how sore all these people are about Mrs. Trollope's book and how
glad I am I did not read it. She must have spoken the truth now,

---

*The Battery's Castle Garden has reflected phases of a changing America. It
was built as an island fort after the War of Independence, and in 1850 landfill
joined it to the rest of Manhattan, creating Battery Park. Five years later, the
state of New York turned it into the Immigrant Landing Depot, the principal
U.S. landing port until 1892, when the facility moved to Ellis Island. Eight
million passed through the former Castle Garden on the way to some American dream, and one in six Americans descends from a hopeful man or woman
who purchased their first dollars and cents at the Battery immigration center.
After further incarnations, including an undignified stint as an aquarium, the
fort reverted to an earlier name, Castle Clinton (after governor DeWitt Clinton, not Bill), and entered peaceful retirement as a national monument. Its
distinctive sandstone now shoulders up to an outsize polished eagle and ranks
of twenty-foot concrete slabs carved with names of military personnel "who
sleep in the American coastal waters of the Atlantic Ocean"—the same Italian, Polish and German names inscribed a handful of decades earlier at the
immigration center. At dusk, the time when Fanny liked to walk at the Battery, a pane of light falls obliquely between the glassy office towers behind the
park, illuminating the lashed posts of the wharf, a row of slabs, and the names
that give the lie to the lofty promise of the Statue of Liberty rising from the
bay beyond.

for lies do not rankle so." There were some things in the book with which Fanny would already have concurred. She too had grown up in the stratified society of Regency London, and the lack of servility displayed by "ordinary people" shocked her. She could not grasp that the entire American project was founded on a measure of social leveling. After she had made her debut as Bianca in *Fazio* and appeared on the front pages, fame exacerbated the problem. Bizarrely reprising Trollope, Fanny had a shocking experience in a millinery shop. The salesgirl greeted her by name and told her how anxious they all were to make her stay agreeable. "Even though I had the grace to smile and say thank you," Fanny told a friend, "I longed to add, 'but be so good as to measure your ribbons and hold your tongue.'"

"As the day fell," Fanny wrote on the boat to Philadelphia, "the volumes of smoke from our steamboat chimneys became streams of fiery sparks, which glittered over the water with a strange unearthly effect. I sat on deck watching the world go dark, till my father, afraid of the night air, bade me go down." Her reputation had preceded her, and there had been fisticuffs over tickets at the Chestnut Street box office. Philadelphia had only just ceded ground to New York as the nation's literary capital, and theater was wildly popular. Fanny took to the place: she found it had "not so new and flaunting a look" as New York. She was sure she never "saw anything more lovely than the full moonlight on its marble buildings." The company opened with *Romeo and Juliet*, and this time the fifty-six-year-old Charles did play Romeo to his daughter's Juliet, scruples about incestuous connotations apparently abandoned in the liberal climate of the New World. "Kemblers" filled the front row at every performance and the actress's hotel overflowed with flowers and callers. "Came home: found a whole regiment of men," she wrote in her journal.

One man persevered until she noticed him. On Saturday October 12, Fanny recorded, "Came down and found a young gentleman sitting with my father—one Mr Butler. He was a pretty-spoken, *genteel* youth enough: he drank tea with us and offered to ride with me. He has, it seems, a great fortune, consequently I suppose (in spite of his lack of inches) a great man." Short but rich, as Fanny noted, twenty-two-year-old Pierce Butler belonged to one of the principal slave-owning families, based not in the South but in Philadelphia. Despite residing in the North, Butler was a politically active pro-South radical, mighty fond of girls and cards, and although nominally a lawyer, he never seemed to do much in the work department. Dandified and classically handsome, with a high forehead and a noble nose, his face was hard, like a face stamped on a coin. He wore sideburns. Butler was a beautiful rider, and every day he lifted his young actress on to one of his fine horses for a gallop along Wissahickon Creek. She wore a red velvet riding cap. One day he snapped a two-foot-long icicle off a rocky arch and presented it to her. "I never saw anything," she wrote that night, "so beautiful as these pendant adornments of the silver-fingered ice god." When this idyll came to an end, and she left on a steamboat, she declared, "I love Philadelphia for evermore."

Next stop D.C., where Fanny met the president, "a good specimen of a fine old battered soldier." Jackson was still fighting. Sensationally, the South Carolina Convention had just nullified federal tariffs on the grounds that they were unconstitutional. Protectionist taxes on imports had been agitating Southern landowners for some time: in the minds of those men, that kind of trading legislation existed to protect the manufacturing interests of the North and, in particular, to benefit New England mill owners. (The Butlers especially saw the hand of New England behind all their troubles.) Suspicious of a large federal government, they bitterly opposed Jackson. Tariffs were surely, they argued, a prelude to abolition, a word already stalking the imagination of Northerner and Southerner alike. As Fanny reprised her Juliet in the capital, troops gathered outside Charleston, and Butler, who had followed his heroine to Washington, talked of civil war. So did she. "So Old

Hickory means to lick the refractory Southerners," she had written in her journal on December 12, 1830, shortly after turning twenty-one. "Why aren't they coming to a civil war?" Charles Kemble canceled the Charleston appearances. Had Fanny had a taste of the South on her tour, she might have avoided the tragedies to come. But instead the company reached the safe ground of Boston, where Fanny spent a month headlining at the Greek Revival–style theatre on Tremont Street. Boston at that time was, according to Audubon, "the Athens of our western world." Fanny loved it. Bostonians loved her back, and soon every young woman in town was wearing "Kemble Curls." Butler had again followed her, and when she was not acting they walked on the Common close to the theatre, past the leaning gravestones of the Granary Burying Ground, or hired horses and galloped over Nahant beach, a panting Aunt Dall in the rear ("My spirits seemed like uncaged birds," Fanny wrote in her journal at the end of the Nahant day). They took a river trip up the Hudson, and followed the tourist trail to Niagara on an expedition for which Butler packed silver forks. The Falls inspired ecstasy. "Oh God!" Fanny wrote in her journal. "Who can describe that sight?!!!" Evidently she couldn't, as the entry ends there. Edward Trelawny had joined the party. The English writer, adventurer and professional ruffian was traveling aimlessly in the United States and had talked of setting up a commune, Nashoba style. Fanny had read his *Adventures* on the voyage over—it was a book in which Trelawny dilated on his friendship with Shelley and Byron. On the boat up the Hudson, Trelawny yelled Byron's "Isles of Greece" to her, and at the Falls he pirouetted her to the brink—a suitable backdrop for a young woman in thrall to the heroic sublime. "What a savage he is . . ." she gasped to her journal at the start of the expedition. "He wears two magical-looking rings: one of them he showed me is made of elephant hair." Trelawny, in a sub-Byronic gesture, threw himself into the rapids at the base of the falls and swam across— or so he claimed.

Fanny wrote home of "the universal kindness which has every-where met us since we first came to this country." Ominously, she liked New England best. "Of all the portions of the United States which I have visited," she said, it was "the most likely to afford gratification," largely because of its "tone," quiet dignity and, of course, its similarity to the Old Country ("a spirit yet most truly English in its origin"). She had made friends with Catharine Sedgwick, a New Englander twenty years her senior. Sedgwick was America's best-known female novelist and one of the first American women to write fiction that dealt with ideas. Like Fanny Trollope, though more sympathetically, she examined the nature of American democracy, and was much concerned with the inde-pendence of women in America. One of her later novels, *Married or Single*, even made the outlandish suggestion that it might be better for women not to marry (she herself had never taken a hus-band). Sedgwick lived in Lenox in the Berkshires, and her home became a refuge for Fanny. There the actress met William Chan-ning, presiding spirit of New England liberalism and the coun-try's most prominent Unitarian. Sedgwick was also a Unitarian, in revolt against the dogmatic Puritanism that still dominated re-ligious thought. As liberals, both held abolitionist views, and Channing had published a jeremiad on the subject. Fanny found them natural allies, as she instinctively hated slavery. When, in May 1833, she dined with former president John Quincy Adams at a private house in Boston, she listened to his views on the issue with horror. She was playing in *Othello* at the time. All Desde-mona's misfortunes, Adams informed her, were "a very just judge-ment upon her for having married a nigger." That night Fanny wrote to a friend suggesting that the play would have greater dramatic power, and better "realise Shakespeare's finest concep-tions," should Iago's opening line, "I hate the Moor," be changed to, " 'I hate the nigger,' given in a proper Charleston or Savannah fashion."

In October 1833 Butler and Fanny rode out from Boston to

Mount Auburn, according to Harriet Martineau "the most beautiful cemetery in the world." They walked among the sugar maples and smooth-skinned American yellowwoods, admiring the plain ashlar beauty of the brownstone monuments and the restraint of a landscape on the cusp of fall. It was, Fanny said, "a pleasure garden instead of a place of graves," and Eastern phoebes rustled the turning leaves. She was tired of touring and bored with acting. "I'm sick of the road," she had written recently in her journal, "and would be at my journey's end." Underneath the corkscrew branches of a star magnolia, Butler proposed marriage. She said yes.

The tour ended soon after the wedding, and Charles Kemble went home. He had mixed feelings about his daughter's defection.

Besides the fact that he loved her very much, she was a financial asset. But he was pleased that she had made a good marriage, or what looked like one. Once he had gone, the newly married couple moved to the 300-acre Butler Place on the Old York Road, close to the isolated village of Branchtown. It was separated from Philadelphia, Fanny wrote, by "between 5 and 6 miles of hideous and execrable turnpike road, without shade, and aridly detestable in the glare, heat and dust of summer, and almost dangerously impassible in winter . . ." Butler rode to his downtown office every day and the bleached landscape became a metaphor for the young bride's inner life. The Butlers had no close neighbors, and the largely Quaker residents of Branchtown disapproved of acting. When Fanny offered to teach their children, "I found that my benevolent proposal excited nothing but a sort of contemptuous amazement," and when she laid on a Fourth of July feast—pleased with herself for rising above any feelings of hurt English pride—the Quakers said it was a waste of a good working day. For something to do, she planted 200 trees, most of which died. Throughout that fall she listened to the felty beat of raindrops on the soft dust of her yard. Then Harriet Martineau came to tea. The English author had just published *Society in America*—she, Kemble and Trollope were the best known Englishwomen in the United States. Harriet's arrival in Philadelphia prompted a round of literary soirees and even a ball, the latter a highlight for Fanny ("I have had so long a fast from dissipation that I find myself quite excited at the thought of going to a dance again"). But Harriet was a rare exception in the social drought of Butler Place. Fanny was bored to tears. She missed her father, and Aunt Dall had died as a result of injuries sustained in a carriage accident on the Niagara expedition—Fanny had buried her at Mount Auburn, where Butler had proposed. When she did go into Philadelphia, she didn't like it. Unlike New England, the company in Philadelphian drawing rooms was dull, the conversation fatuous, opinions all alike. There was nothing strong-minded or fresh, and nobody did anything with panache. They, in turn, found Fanny pretentious—"too *pro-noncée*," one Philadelphian society figure said, apparently without irony. As for Butler: there was no chance of him declaiming "Isles of Greece." He had no interest in books and mixed with people of his own background—wealthy bullies who had grown rich on the slave states. His wife began to reflect on a topic that had preoccupied Fanny Trollope: the stifling conformity of this vaunted new democracy. "The fact is," Kemble wrote, "that being politically the most free people on earth, the Americans are socially the least so; and it seems as though, ever since that little affair of establishing their independence among nations, which they managed so successfully, every American mother's son of them has been doing his best to divest himself of his own private share of that great public blessing." It had been easy to give up the stage, as she had never liked it. But she was unwilling to give up stimulating company, or to abandon the life of the mind. Little Woman was a role she could not play.

To enliven the shattering dullness of married life she did a silly thing. It was typically flighty. She published *Journal of a Residence in America*, a diary of the thespian tour. It gave her something to do during the endless days of tedium at Butler Place. The book's value lies in its impressionistic spontaneity. Fanny records hours of rehearsals on creaky boards, ants on the hotel pillow and dinner of cold ham at three, as well as indulging in histrionic bouts of thespian self-pity.

> I acted like a wretch, of course; how could I do otherwise? Oh, Juliet! Vision of the south! Rose of the garden of the earth! Was this the glorious hymn that Shakespeare hallowed to your praise? Was this the mingled strain of Love's sweet going forth, and Death's dark vision, over which my heart and soul have been poured out in wonder and ecstasy? How I do loathe the stage, these tawdry, glittering rags, wretched, wretched mumming . . . What a mass of mimicry acting is!

America had taken time to grow on her, and the journal included negative remarks, both about the country, and about individual Americans. "30 Nov. 1832, sat by that ninny Mr—, who uttered inanity the whole of dinner time." Southerners came out badly. The Yankee, Fanny reckoned, is "as a race incomparably superior to the other inhabitants of this country." She did not stint on this topic. "I visited Boston several times," she wrote, "and mixed in society there, the tone of which appeared to me far higher than that of any I found elsewhere." She refused to hold back even though she must have been aware of what the consequences would be. "I saw more pictures, more sculptures, and more books in private houses in Boston than I have seen anywhere else . . . its charitable and literary institutions are upon a liberal scale, and enlightened principles. Among the New Englanders I have seen more honour and reverence of parents, and more witnesses of a high religious faith, than among any other Americans with whom I have lived and worked." She fulminated against the evils of slavery and looked to the day when it would cease: "Oh! What a breaking asunder of old manacles there will be, some of these fine days . . . what a sweeping away, as by a torrent of oppressions and tyrannies; what a fierce and horrible retaliation and revenge for wrong so long endured—so wickedly inflicted"—knowing of course that these words would drive her husband almost insane with fury. (Yet it could have been even worse. Fanny had shown proofs to Harriet Martineau, who advised her to suppress the most critical thirty pages.) Like Fanny Trollope three years earlier, when the book came out, its author felt the weight of American displeasure. Fifty members of Congress complained, the review in *Niles' Weekly Register* stated, "the authoress has unsexed herself," and lampoons appeared. One pamphlet was called *Fanny Thimble Cutler's Journal of a Residence in America Whilst Performing a Profitable Theatrical Engagement*. It mocked Fanny's pretension, as well as her frivolous self-obsession ("My conscience!" it begins. "Who'd have thought it; there, it is written, I am Fanny Thimble and no-one

else; this is my big toe and as I live, it has grown a crop of corns.")
Critics called Fanny "the heiress of Mrs Trollope," a remark not
intended as a compliment. The young Edgar Allan Poe reviewed
Journal of a Residence in America and said it was vulgar. Fanny's
friend Catharine Sedgwick loyally tried to gloss the debacle, and
in doing so, made an astute judgement. "It [the book] is like herself, and she is a complex being, made up of glorious facilities,
delightful accomplishments, immeasurable sensibility and half a
hundred little faults."

There was one person whose reaction mattered very much.
Pierce Butler. He was unaccustomed to being checked. His views
on the role of women were clear: stay at home, breed and look
decorous when wheeled on to the social circuit. Nobody can know
why Fanny had not seen her husband's heart clearly, unless love
really is blind. Butler made a scene about *Journal*, and Fanny
made one back. She left home, couldn't find a decent hotel, and
returned. But in May 1835, Butler and his wife produced baby
Sarah, known as Sally. Harriet Martineau had returned to Philadelphia and went to the christening, though one wonders why, as
since publication of *Journal* she had given up any pretense of lik-
ing Fanny and had little sympathy with her marital difficulties. An
ill-favored spinster, Harriet was industrious, progressive and
high-minded, intolerant of histrionic behavior or what she perceived to be feminine weakness. "By her way of entering up marriage," she wrote later of Fanny, "and her conduct in it afterwards
she deprived herself of all title to wonder at or complain of her
domestic miseries, terrible as they were. She was a finely gifted
creature wasted and tortured by want of discipline, principle and
self-knowledge." Wasted? Events were to prove Harriet wrong in
the long run. Fanny might have calmed the ongoing Wagnerian
tempests had she not been bored. She started writing letters to her
husband, a habit that got out of hand as her neuroses took hold. In
those moods, she talked to him as if she were on the stage. "My
heart still answers to your voice," she wrote to him, "my blood in

my veins to your footsteps." Then she would abruptly change register and tell him she regretted their marriage, and that she wanted
to go home to England. "I am weary of my useless existence," she
wrote to him; "my superintendence in your house is nominal, you
have never allowed it to be otherwise; you will suffer no inconvenience from its cessation." Her life was perpetual drama, and she
teetered on that perilous line between sanity and derangement.
She knew that if she left him he would never let her take Sally. In
a moment of desperation she even said she would leave the baby,
"as long as you procure a healthy nurse." He gave her a cage of
canaries; she was like an imprisoned bird herself. The great abolitionist push in the South began in 1835, and to provoke her husband, Fanny threatened to publish an anti-slavery tract she had
drafted. The word "abolition" invoked the same kind of reaction
in the parlours of Charleston, Savannah and New Orleans, or in
the Philadelphia drawing rooms of the slave plutocrats, as "socialism" in right-wing American circles in our own time. Pro-slavers
had burned a Philadelphia auditorium used for abolitionist rallies.
In the speechifying of New England liberals they saw their world
changing. Butler thought British abolitionists were fake democrats, loftily condemning slavery while pursuing imperial interests
around the world. Like her, he had a temper like a missile. The col-
lision between them was eruptive.

Periods of respite interrupted the fighting. "You cannot make
me cease to love you," he wrote in one of them. Another baby,
Frances, known as Fan, appeared in May 1838. But later that year
Fanny told her husband, "Since my marriage to you my life has
been one long incessant privation, which was all very well when
you were nice to me." Again she pleaded for company and mental
stimulation. "What need of intellectual converse, have you not an
affectionate husband and two sweet babies?" he retorted. "You
might as well say to a man who has no arms," she bit back, "Oh no,
but you have two legs." When they fought, her face twitched, like a
racing dog. Fanny packed to leave five or six times, and twice took

her jewels to Philadelphia to raise money for a ticket to England. Then doubts, like homing pigeons, returned to roost, and she never left him. She was torn between passion and self-criticism; one of those people who combine acute self-awareness with an inability to act on the knowledge.

Silky Sea Island cotton loves salt and moisture, and in the eighteenth century the colonies of coastal Georgia flourished. After the War of Independence Georgia joined the Union as the fourth state, and when Eli Whitney invented the cotton gin on a Savannah plantation, the population doubled in a decade. Whitney's gin separated cotton lint from seed, reducing labor to one fiftieth of what it had been. Fields bloomed white all the way to South Carolina. By 1800 a bridge over the salt marshes connected St. Simon's Island to the mainland and a stagecoach ran twice a week between Augusta and Savannah. Planters like Pierce Butler's grandfather came down from South Carolina to buy land, thousands emigrated from Britain to make their American fortune and in 1819 the *City of Savannah* made maritime history by steaming across the Atlantic. The friendly Yamacraw vanished, the Chickasaw followed the Creek and the Choctaw on the Trail of Tears across the Mississippi, and in 1832 Georgia's Sixth Land Lottery stole the Cherokee land in the north of the state. Jefferson had dreamed of turning the Cherokee into good Americans, which meant farmers, and those living among the strawberry fields of northwest Georgia had done everything asked of them: they had invented a written language, established a newspaper, adopted elections, courts, magistrates, a police force—they even had a constitution. But homesteaders wanted their land, and in 1838 the U.S. Army began the forced removal of Cherokee from the state of Georgia. Seven thousand troops hunted down Cherokee and sent them, like cattle, a thousand miles west to a new desert home. A visitor described a three-mile line of them in 1839: "even aged females apparently nearly ready to drop into the grave, were traveling with heavy burdens attached to the back—on the sometimes frozen ground with no covering for the feet." Jackson was doing to his southern tribes what previous administrations had done to the northern ones: pushing them west. "There," said Jackson, "your white brother will not trouble you."

Butler's Irish grandfather, the third son of a baronet, had served as a major in George III's 29th regiment. After being posted to the colonies he married the daughter of a wealthy South Carolina planter, and when his regiment transferred back to England, he sold his commission and stayed, devoting himself to agriculture and public service. His rise was spectacular, and contemporary historians recognize him as one of the Founding Fathers. Butler was one of the men who devised the language of the Constitution. "For census purposes," read a section Butler drafted, "a slave is one fifth of a person." In 1789 he accepted the role of South Carolina's first senator, and after re-election in 1793, the Democratic Republican Party considered him a possible vice-presidential candidate to run with Jefferson. As his political career advanced, the Major increased his holdings. He owned thousands of acres in South Carolina and Tennessee as well as property in Philadelphia and 1,500 acres on what became known as Butler Island, moving 600 slaves south to the Georgia coast. He also picked up a cotton estate close by on St. Simon's Island, where he shipped 400 more slaves. The Major never lived in either place—too hot, and too far away from the action—installing instead a resident manager. By 1809 he was the largest slave owner in Georgia and one of the wealthiest planters in America. "Few families," according to a Georgian historian, "can have played a role comparable to that of the Butlers in the southern slave economy." During the 1812 war with England, the Royal Navy seized 138 of his slaves and took them to Nova Scotia. There they gave them all freedom, and the surname Butler. The Major died in 1822, and when at the end of 1838 the resident manager departed to take over a plantation of his own, Pierce

Butler moved his family south for six months to look after the business himself. Sally was three, and baby Fan eight months. It took nine days to get to Georgia from Philadelphia. On the steamer across the Susquehanna they froze; and on a night boat they shared a fetid bathroom with fellow travelers. At Portsmouth, Virginia, they boarded an overcrowded train and, when the rails ran out, took a stagecoach to Stantonsburg, North Carolina, then another train to Waynesborough. This last experience was a good deal less heady than the occasion when the young Fanny stood on the boilerplate with Stephenson and felt the wind blowing through her hair. "We travelled all night on the railroad," she wrote to a friend from North Carolina. "One of my children slept in my lap, the other on the narrow seat opposite me, from which she was jolted off every quarter of an hour by the uneasy motion of the carriage, and the checks and stops of the engine, which was out of order. The carriage, though full of people, was heated with a stove, and every time this was replenished with coals we were almost suffocated with the clouds of bituminous smoke which filled it." The roads were made of logs, and at every moment the coaches threatened to propel their cargo into the pine swamps of North Carolina. From Wilmington the party proceeded by boat to Charleston. The food at the squalid port hotels was filthy, they never stopped anywhere long enough for a proper sleep, they had no privacy—and Fanny was still nursing the baby. Like Trollope she hated "that all but universal pest in this crowd-loving country, a public table." To take her mind off the horrors, she read the latest novel: *Oliver Twist*. She said it made her feel at home. Dickens was almost her exact contemporary, and she recognized the streets around Saffron Hill where the Dodger roamed. She liked Charleston, however, as she found taste and individuality in the architecture. But the visit was spoiled at nine o'clock when she heard "a most ominous tolling of bells and beating of drums" and learned that it was a curfew for blacks. It was more ominous for her than she knew.

In Savannah she admired the chaste squares and the towers of cotton bales on the cobbled wharves below Factors Row. For a generation, tidewater landowners had reaped bountiful profits from the cotton fields of the Sea Islands and the contiguous delta, and they formed a particular tidewater aristocracy. They kept townhouses in Savannah, then both the cultural and economic capital of Georgia, and pursued the archetypal antebellum life of horsewhips, flounced skirts and mint juleps on the porch. Their plantations were the most productive in the state, they were the largest slave owners, and they were politically influential. From her balcony Fanny watched slaves carrying tubs of water on their heads; small boys ferrying trays of sweetmeats; and black musicians attached to military bands marching through the streets drumming soldiers to the parade ground. She wanted to stay. But they had to get to Butler Island by rowing boat, traversing the sinuous channels of the Altamaha alongside reedy swamps "rattling their brittle canes in the morning breeze." The boatman sang in a lugubrious tenor, accompanied by the rhythmic shifting of the oarlocks. The forest beyond the swamp, Fanny noted, looked "savage," but from the dykes of the rice fields gangs of slaves put down their baskets and waved with shouts of "Welcome!" that reduced her to tears. They appeared, she wrote, "to hail us like descending deities." The steersman sounded a conch shell as the Butlers approached their new plantation home. "It seemed to me," wrote Fanny, "that we had touched the outer bound of civilised creation."

At the dilapidated house, situated close to the chimneys of a steam-powered rice mill, a battalion of household slaves gave the Butlers a rousing reception that including leaping and dancing, and from then on, representatives followed the new mistress everywhere. It was a long way from Belvoir Castle and the brass band that piped one to breakfast. The plastered walls of the house were without paint or paper and at dinner the carpenter cut up the salt-marsh mutton with a saw, so meat arrived at table in unidentifiable rhomboids. When Fanny asked the kitchen boy to wash the lettuce (it had been served accompanied by twice its weight in soil), he set about the task with zeal, deploying carbolic soap and a scrubbing brush. As for the landscape: in a letter she described Butler Island as "quite the most amphibious piece of creation that I have yet had the happiness of beholding . . .'Tis neither liquid nor solid but a kind of mud sponge floating on the bosom of the Altamaha." The same images appear elsewhere: Butler Island was "a hasty pudding of amphibian elements." Worse, it was too swampy to ride. Rice had overtaken cotton as the dominant crop on the Georgia coast, and Butler Island, with 900 acres under cultivation, was the engine of the family fortune. Most workers were still West African Gullah, and they knew how to work tidal creeks, as they had done so at home. The flat rice baskets, mortars and pestles used for decades on the southeast Georgia coast were all of African origin. Steam threshers dealt with a portion of the harvest, but mostly the slaves used hand flails. Their chief labor was clearing canals and drains and maintaining the banks of ditches that crosshatched the fields. Once she got used to its amphibious characteristics, Fanny found the landscape dazzling. She walked every day along the dykes between the marshy rice fields and the brimming river, reveling in the blue herons, the bearded oak and the great magnolia, and she loved the loggerhead shrike, the sharp citrus fragrance of the orange trees, and the milky blossoms of loblolly bay that rose higher than her house. "Every shade of green," she noted, "every variety of form, every degree of varnish, and all in full leaf and beauty in the very depth of winter." She learned to row, and relished the activity ("I do not weary of these most exquisite watery woods," she wrote in a letter) and watched mockingbirds swinging "from glittering graceful branch to branch." But a cry of "O missis!" greeted her wherever she went. Slaves importuned her constantly, touching her skirts and pulling her into reeking huts. In the first week she met a woman who had collapsed in the rice fields when pregnant, whereupon the overseer had summoned her husband to string her by her hands and thrash her with a hide whip, and when he had finished, she miscarried. Every single person lived in filth, most adults were crippled by rheumatism, and the older ones crawled to approach her, as their arthritic legs no longer functioned. Psyche, the slave who assisted the children's Scottish nanny, revealed that her husband was up for sale, and begged Fanny to intercede with Butler on her behalf. Individual slaves were frequently sold on throughout the South, irrespective of how many children they might have, and once they had gone down the river like Uncle Tom they would never return. (Between 1790 and 1860 more than a million slaves were shipped from the Upper South to the Lower in this domestic trade.) Fanny met a thirty-year-old woman who had given birth to ten children, five of whom had died. She was already a grandmother. Tara was the plantation to be on, if you were a slave. Margaret Mitchell's depiction of paternalism would not have been recognized by anyone at the Butler plantations.

Britain abolished slavery two years before Fanny was born, and had recently outlawed the practice in its colonies. The young actress had observed the industrialized wage labor which replaced it on her railway sorties with Stephenson, and had become a passionate participant in the abolitionist movement, one of the greatest social forces of her time. But she was also the wife of one of Georgia's largest slave owners. "It is too dreadful," she wrote, "to have those whom we love accomplices to this wickedness; it is too intolerable to find myself an involuntary accomplice to it." She said that when she married Butler she had not known about "these dreadful possessions of his," and that even if she had, she could never have imagined it would have been as bad as it was. She perceived slaves as human beings, he did not: this was the gulf that separated their interior worlds. Fanny's New England mentor Channing, the Unitarian sage, urged his followers to plead the cause of the individual slave with his or her owner. Fanny did, choosing the peaceful moment after supper when Butler was tugging on a cigar in front of the fire. He either walked out without a word or shouted at her, depending on his mood. Later, she would discover that the slave in question had been flogged for having appealed to her. "It seems to me," she wrote to a friend, "that I have come down here to be tortured." The slaves, meanwhile, were riveted by her. When Fanny was writing letters alone at night in the "great barnlike" drawing room, they would stealthily open the door, creep barefoot over the boards one after the other, and sit on their hams in the flickering light of the pinewood fire, silently watching her. When she finished her work she would look up suddenly and say, "Well, what do you want?" "Me come say ha do missus," they would murmur in unison, before trooping out as soundlessly as they had entered, like, as she said, "a procession of sable dreams."

Roswell King, the father and then the son, had occupied the post of resident manager at the Butler plantations for two decades. King Junior returned as a guest at Fanny's table, shortly after setting up as a slaveholding planter on his own account. Butler received his former manager warmly: the holdings had prospered under his stewardship. White managers were often more brutal slave-drivers than the plantation owners, and King had left a criminally neglected settlement. At the slave hospital, a four-room structure of whitewashed wood, Fanny found dying slaves huddled on the dirt in their own excrement, without sheets, medicines, beds or food. "And here," she wrote later, "in their hour of sickness and suffering, lay those whose health and strength are spent in unrequited labour for us." Some, including teenagers, had a disease that rotted their hands and feet. Babies suffered from a particular type of lockjaw. Rheumatism was "almost universal" in old and young, as were ulcerated legs, and prolapsed uterus was common among the women, as curvature of the spine was in both sexes. "Oh God," Fanny wrote, "Thou surely had'st not forsaken them?"

He had, but she didn't. She threw herself into cleaning the hospital, teaching basic standards of hygiene, and she sewed clothes. She learned a few words of the Gullah language and at home taught her houseboy his alphabet alongside Sally, despite the severe penalties for helping a slave learn to read. And she kept a detailed journal. Once again writing consoled her, however temporarily. She survived on Butler Island, she confided, only on account of "the childish excitability of my temperament," as the sight of the close embroidery of creeping green and red lichens "edged with an exquisite pattern of coral" lifted her spirits, and the gorgeous swarming of land crabs across the raised causeway over the salt marshes fired her imagination as she rode. In the solace she took from nature she was a true Romantic. "I sometimes despise myself," she wrote, "for what seems to me an inconceivable rapidity of emotion, that almost makes me doubt whether anyone who feels so many things can really be said to feel anything."

Every week, Fanny rowed over to Darien, the county seat. The town was founded on spongy ground by highland Scots and the people there were second-tier aristocrats. They were loutish, morose and isolated. Fanny saw none of "the restless spirit" Tocqueville had just identified as the great American peculiarity. Tidewater planters knew nothing of the westward pushes with which America was remaking itself, and as cotton culture had not yet spread inland, coastal society was quite different from that of the rest of the state. It was the opposite of the frontier: entrenched, sclerotic and backward-looking. Fanny's social visits were a failure. Darien women complained to her about the smell of their slaves. Fanny pointed out that this "smell" did not stop white men from impregnating slave women, or white women from attaching their babies to black breasts. She said, stating the obvious, that it was the state of slavery that made the slaves smell. French hovels smelled bad too, and so did Italian and Irish ones. "I pity them," she wrote of the women, "for the stupid sameness of their most vapid existence, which would deaden any amount of intelligence, obliterate any amount of instruction, and render torpid and stagnant any amount of natural energy and vivacity. I would rather die—rather a thousand times—than live the lives of these Georgia planters' wives and daughters." Philadelphia had not suited her but the rank magnolias of the Old South were worse. Visits to the Darien Baptist churches were disastrous. The most pious planters turned out to be the most inhuman slave owners. "Oh what a shocking mockery," Fanny wrote. They didn't like her, either, and gossiped about her low-necked dresses. Shopping too was a disaster. The goods were "three times as dear as in your northern villages" and worse quality. But she could not blame the planters for that. Yankee entrepreneurs ran the shops, foreshadowing the carpetbaggers who galloped into the ruins of the Old South after the Civil War.

By the middle of February 1839, when slaves were burning stubble and ivory blossom foamed from the narcissus, the Butlers moved to their cotton estate at the northern tip of St. Simon's Island, fifteen miles away from the Butler plantation by rowing boat. The family home jutted between a creek and the Hampton River, five miles from Frederica, the original fortified settlement. The house had a peach orchard, and a moat that filled and emptied with the tides. It was a poor period for Sea Island cotton. At one time, the crop was quoted separately on the Liverpool Stock

Exchange, and in the Major's era it fetched a half guinea a pound. Now it was barely worth a shilling. St. Simon's was higher and healthier than Butler Island, and consisted of swamp and sand, as opposed to just swamp. It had firm ground for riding, and as she galloped Fanny found solace in the wordless melody of the mockingbirds. But the sunlight hardened when a person walked into it. The tidewater plantations had already earned their place on the interminable list of settings in which the human need to inflict punishment on its own kind makes one long for the extinction of the species.

The devout slaves trooped up to Hampton Point on Sunday mornings to hear Fanny read prayers. Throughout the 1830s, Northerners had been pressuring slaveholders to allow religious teaching, and both Baptist and Methodist missionaries had been active in tidewater plantations. Southerners had turned the slaves' piety to their advantage, promoting a narrative in which slavery was ordained by God as a paternalistic system in which a superior race looked after its dependants in one big happy family. The Butler slaves attended church in Darien once a month to listen to white men tell them of the riches that awaited them in heaven. Fanny was a Christian, and she hated "these heaven-blinded negro enlighteners." The Darien preachers, "like most southern men, clergy or others," she fulminated, "jump the present life in their charities to the slaves, and go on to furnish them with all requisite conveniences for the next."

Next Fanny discovered that "the paragon" Roswell King Junior had fathered a tribe of mixed-race children. If a woman resisted, he had ordered her to be flogged, so she would not resist again. On one occasion, two slaves gave birth to his progeny in the same week. Mrs. King appeared a few days after the births, personally oversaw the flogging of the new mothers, and ordered the punishment to be repeated daily for a week. Fanny was disgusted. So was Butler—with her. He banned her from pleading with him on the slaves' behalf. "Why do you listen to such stuff?" he thundered. "Don't you know the niggers are all damned liars?"

The tension between marital duty and conscience was intolerable. "This is no place for me," she wrote to a New England friend, "since I was not born among slaves, and cannot bear to live among them." Again, she knew that if she left him, he would never let her take the girls. She was a slave herself. Her conscience moved and heaved like the ocean.

In the first week of March spring rushed over the islands like a tide. The air was light with wildwood fragrances, birds were singing, and delicate white blossom gleamed on the wild plum trees. But every day Fanny became more depressed, "surrounded by all this misery and degradation that I can neither help nor hinder." Eventually the rows were so bad and the imprisonment so unbearable that she packed her trunks and left without the girls. She rowed herself across the Altamaha to Darien. But there was no connecting boat to Savannah, so she went back, lay on her bed for two days and went on hunger strike. "I must, for their [the girls'] sakes," she wrote to a friend, "remain where they are, and learn this dreary lesson of human suffering to the end." The end was to come soon enough, in April, when the family returned to Philadelphia to escape the malarial ravages of a Southern summer. As for Butler, she knew him for what he was by now; he was a bully, a womanizer and a gambler—a man Georgians call a "no account."

Alone again in the cavernous Butler Place drawing room, she filled journal after journal with neat, looping sentences of regret and anguish. I had the dimmest insight into that, having written myself through the throes of a bitter parental divorce when I was fifteen, and that was just the start of it. The sanctuary of the page was always on my mind as I pursued Fanny to the Sea Islands in the winter of 2010–11. The creative impulse often shores up the border between neurosis and sanity, and Kemble's inky outpourings made her histrionics easier to understand. There was nothing American about her story. Although she lived through one of the defining episodes of U.S. history—slavery and its repercussions—I found

Fanny in many ways the least touched, among my girls, by her period. There was something so human, and so heroic, about her struggles that she rose above place and time. But perhaps it takes a neurotic to know one.

The plantations withered without slaves, and the population shifted inland, leaving St. Simon's to sink back to its miasma of refracted light and oyster middens. The air had a salty tang. The Sea Islands are a long way from the Atlanta metropolitan region, the Coca-Cola Company, and the busiest airport in the world. Like Venice, they were beached between land and sea. The yellow marsh grass is bleak from a distance, but close up it clicks and whirs with migratory birds and fishy nurseries. I rented a car in Savannah, and drove across a causeway on to the island at the long still moment of dusk. The grasses paled into the same watery hue as the sky, and the world quivered.

St. Simon's was a low-rise sprawl of boardwalks and simple summer houses where hummingbirds fed on sweet bay magnolia. The forest that spread over the north of the island had been cleared in places to make way for gated residential developments, and one of them, called the Hampton Plantation, had engulfed the ruins of the house where Fanny confronted her husband by candlelight. Besides a Pierce Butler Road, the municipality had called one street Roswell King Road. This was the man, Fanny said, who flogged pregnant women till they miscarried and raped a different slave each day. And now his name was installed on a handsome sign; evidence, as if it were required, that words can lie just as effectively as they tell the truth. At Fort Frederica, peaceful ruins spread out like a floor plan. Broken oyster shells jutted from walls and on the riverbank, the sun glanced off a pair of polished cannons. The Frederica ruins were the first Fanny had seen "in this land of contemptuous youth." She wrote, "In my country, ruins are like a minor chord in music; here they are like a discord; they are not like the relics of time, but the relics of violence." In 2011 they could not have seemed less violent: the scene was a study in tranquillity. But perhaps she was right. On the door to the Ladies' restroom a sign said, *No Firearms.*

The Civil War might have ended the era of plantation balls and crinolines, but a second age of prosperity rose over the Atlantic horizon with the appearance of an elite band of Vanderbilts, Astors and Carnegies. Bored with the overcrowded North, in 1886 the new millionaires—slave owners of the modern age—founded a hunting club on the island adjacent to St. Simon's. The Jekyll Island Club, built to look like a lighthouse, was to be simpler than Bar Harbor and more exclusive than Newport. The tycoons went skeet shooting, guzzled imported Scotch and competed for the biggest yachts. (J. P. Morgan's was so huge it couldn't dock.) For several decades at the intersection of the nineteenth and twentieth centuries the Sea Islands were the Southern playground of the new plutocrats—someone worked out that the members of the Jekyll Island Club owned one sixth of the world's wealth. A photograph still hanging on the ballroom wall shows the first transcontinental telephone call, made at the club on January 2, 1915.

The call was scheduled to take place in New York, but Theodore N. Vail, president of the American Telephone and Telegraph Company, sustained a leg injury shooting in the Jekyll marshes, and was unable to leave the island. Undaunted—he had been dreaming of a transcontinental link for years—he had a cable laid from Savannah to Brunswick. And it worked. The call marked a significant moment in American history. Forty-six years after the railroad joined the country together, the telephone line did the same thing in another way. Vail had a two-hour, four-way conversation with Alexander Graham Bell in New York, President Wilson in the White House, and Thomas Watson, Bell's former assistant, in San Francisco. One wonders what they talked about for so long. The photograph depicts the obese Vail talking in an armchair, Rockefeller sitting next to him with an earpiece clamped to his ear and J. P. Morgan standing gormlessly to one side. Vail, legs akimbo, has all his tackle on display, bulging down his left trouser leg. Such are the great historical moments. The club was still a hotel, but the Vanderbilt spirit had moved on. The tinkling piano and the languorous accent of the barman might have been redolent of 1915, but the pastel tracksuits of the middle-American clientele were not, and neither was the Christmas Shoppe.

Wealth was never enough wealth. Industrialist Thomas Carnegie, brother of Andrew, was dissatisfied with the shared accommodation of his *fin de siècle* country club. He built a winter retreat far from the Pittsburgh smog on the next island down—the seventeen-mile Cumberland, abutting the Florida state line. Dungeness was a retreat of the Gilded Age variety: a Scottish castle roofed with Vermont slate in a style later called Queen Anne Gothic. Thomas and his wife, Lucy, employed 200 staff to look after a heated pool in its own separate pool house, a barbershop, dairy, stables, poultry farm, multi-roomed Italianate guest "cottage" and an ice house stocked with blocks shipped from Maine (anyone could have hot food, the Carnegies argued; to have chilled food in the South, that was the thing). The couple gave each of their nine offspring 10,000 dollars with which to build their own island homes, and they had canvas wallpaper hand-stamped with Scottish gryphons and Tiffany lamps commissioned to look like Cumberland's loggerhead turtles. A century later there was still no paved road. On the long Atlantic beach, flocks of pelicans eyed the gannets bombing the ocean, and behind the pelicans, thousands of dunlins worked their beaks in and out of the sand like sewing machines. Horseshoe crabs—the ones Fanny called land crabs—had abandoned hinged shells over the beach. They looked prehistoric—and in evolutionary terms they are—but when I got three home and put them up on the wall, the children thought they were *Star Wars* masks. Behind the beach, ranks of dunes slipped towards the mainland, and behind them, green footballs of mistletoe hung in hickory trees. Swags of muscadine vine looped from cedars, and palmetto laced the feet of both.*

*Cumberland's almost untouched ecosystem includes a weird wild pig, one of which I glimpsed foraging on the banks of a tidewater creek. Conquistadores offloaded the original pigs on the island in the sixteenth century. Responding to an insufficient food supply, evolution stepped in with a process called *insular dwarfism*, meaning that natural selection favored smaller animals and the porcine metabolism was redesigned to maximize calorie storage. The one I saw had a hairy, mottled body so out of proportion to its stick-insect legs that the latter were barely visible.

Over on the mainland, where Fanny so often rowed, Darien was no longer at the heart of anything. It was a somnolent straggle of a town with a touch of the Wild West—until you learned that half of it was a retirement community. On Main Street, B & J's Steaks & Seafood sunned itself in wintry light next to a low-slung Baptist church. Everything was low slung, and seemed to be sinking. No wonder, because as Kemble wrote, "the whole town lies in a bed of sand." Darien burned during Reconstruction. But Georgia pine was considered the finest in the world, and in a decade Darien, phoenix-like, had risen from the forest and become the leading timber center on the Southern Atlantic coast. Overlogging brought that boom to an end, and in the thirties Darien reinvented itself as a seafood center. Overfishing duly finished that off too. Now, the retirement market was keeping Darien alive—decrepitude, unlike timber and shrimps, being infinite—and at Nautica Joe's Diner paper-skinned old ladies in wigs lunched under a slowly rotating fan. Nearby, on U.S. 17, one of the original New York–Miami routes, the Georgia Historical Society had erected a metal sign commemorating Fanny on the undeveloped land that was once the Butler plantation. The house was gone, but the thirty-foot chimney of the steam-powered rice mill still towered over the Altahama. The sky was aspirin white, blanched of blue, and the air still as a tomb. The blurb on the sign suggested that Kemble had influenced the outcome of the Civil War. How unlikely that must have seemed in 1839 when the distraught Fanny headed back to Philadelphia. Few would have bet that she would get her revenge on him, in death, on a signpost half hidden among the cordgrass.

On Factors Row the bricks of the cotton exchange were mottled with damp, and the Savannah River drifted in a ghostly pewter stripe. Older than Atlanta and more provincial than Charleston, Savannah is more sedate than New Orleans (and safer). The soil beneath the oaks and sycamore was red, with blue-black veins, and the air thick with stagnant humidity. One could see why Fanny

BUTLER ISLAND PLANTATION

Famous Rice Plantation of the 19th century, owned by Pierce Butler of Philadelphia. A system of dikes and canals for the cultivation of rice, installed by engineers from Holland, is still in evidence in the old fields, and has been used as a pattern for similar operations in recent years.

During a visit here with her husband in 1839-40, Pierce Butler's wife, the brilliant English actress, Fannie Kemble, wrote her "Journal of a Residence On A Georgia Plantation," which is said to have influenced England against the Confederacy.

liked it: the restrained architecture reminded her of home. The compact brick houses, grilled gateways and half-concealed gardens still today recall the Georgian England of the Founding Fathers. Fanny's admirer Thackeray visited in 1848, and he liked it too. He wrote of "a few happy negroes sauntering here and there," a description straight out of *Pravda*. In *Gone with the Wind*, Margaret Mitchell calls 1860s Savannah "that gently mannered city by the sea." It is an offstage presence in the story, aloof, dignified, refined, looking down its nose at Atlanta, just a teenage frontier town 300 miles inland. Since Mitchell published her bestseller in

1936, decades of economic decline and its associated problems have sharpened Savannah's edges: the modern city is more Tennessee Williams than Scarlett O'Hara. The fifties ushered in dire urban renewal projects and the seventies the dead hand of "historic preservation." It might be safe now but for a brief period the city was the murder capital not just of Georgia, but of America. When corporations started relocating to the South, they went to Atlanta, Jacksonville or Charleston, and the people of Savannah basked in their isolation. They colluded in it, discouraging Prudential from establishing its regional headquarters among them (the Pru went to Jacksonville). There was no longer a rail connection with Atlanta. The restored streets had a feel of arrested development and at the childhood home of Flannery O'Connor the windows were dark, like dead eyes. O'Connor's books are a useful foil to Fanny's—deeply sane portraits of an evolved, post-Butlerian Georgia. The modest house where she was born in 1925 was in the heart of Savannah's once-outlawed Catholic community; O'Connor's bedroom looked out on to the Gothic stucco of the Cathedral of St. John the Baptist, where she worshipped. As an adult, she attended Mass up in Milledgeville at seven every morning, hobbling on crutches when her lupus played up, which was most of the time. In her writing she was in permanent revolt against the moral standards of the North, in particular what she perceived as its mendacity, duplicity and penchant for shredding documents—so the thing had gone full circle, and Southern voices took the moral high ground. It's impossible to read O'Connor without reflecting on the sense of separation indigenous to Southern literature. She had her own vision of the divide between North and South. O'Connor thought the North had lost its moral compass. "When I'm asked," she wrote, "why Southern writers particularly have a penchant for writing about freaks, I say it's because we are still able to recognize one." In the reception room of her home, which is open to the public, a ponytailed curator was counting visitors in bundles of five, which he inscribed in pencil in an exercise book. He had not yet drawn a pencil bar across one bundle that day, and as I was the only visitor, he gave me a tour. We inspected the pots in the kitchen, the wallpaper and the back yard where the girl Flannery famously taught a chicken to walk backwards, a feat recorded by Pathé News, which sent a crew all the way from New York. The guide, Michigan-born, lived upstairs in a flat overlooking the square. I said he had a wonderful job. He smiled. "Everything bad that ever happened to me was erased when I got this position." A Northerner who had found redemption in the South—O'Connor would have loved that.

The Butler ménage staggered on. The only known photograph of the couple dates from this period: a water-damaged daguerreotype held in the University of Georgia archives. Butler looks as if he might have been cast out of concrete, his mouth and towering forehead stiff as his starched dress shirt. Kemble appears young, innocent and sad, her dark dress cut wide at the neck, creating a swanlike effect. Behind them, a slave stands in brocaded livery. But the livery was misleading. Butler's extravagance had reduced the family finances to ashes. Nonetheless, in 1841 they took off for London, where Queen Victoria received Fanny at court. Fresh skies did not dispel the storm clouds, and on one occasion Fanny called for a cab to leave him at two o'clock in the morning. She had discovered he was having an affair with their daughters' governess. Sexual humiliation is a punishing lesson. In a bid to establish financial independence, she translated and adapted a Dumas novel for the stage. But Butler said any money she earned was his by law (this was true). He was obsessed with her submission. "If you will govern your irritable temper," he wrote to her, "we may be reconciled and we may be happy." He might have been a pig as well as a moral invertebrate, but there was truth in his statement. Spawning good intentions like herrings, she promised to try to control her "nervous, excitable temperament." As for the rest: "I consider," she said, "that it is my duty *not* to submit my conduct to the government of any human being." Charles Greville was a leading public figure in England—he was a Clerk to the Privy Council—and a diarist of renown. He knew the Kembles, and had observed Butler at close hand. Greville left the following passage out of his published memoirs while Fanny was alive, but after her death, he reinstated it: "She has discovered that she has married a weak, dawdling, ignorant, violent-tempered man, who is utterly unsuited to her, and she to him . . . With all her prodigious talents, her fine feelings, her noble sentiments and lively imagination, she has no tact, no judgement, no discretion. She has acted like a fool, and now he has become a brute, the consequence is that she is supremely and hopelessly wretched." Before they returned to America, Butler threw such a lavish farewell party that six policemen were required to control the traffic.

Back in Philadelphia, Fanny found letters from another woman in her husband's writing desk. When she confronted him, anger at her snooping overcame any vestige of guilt. The couple moved into separate accommodations. It was as if he had turned the lights out one by one. But Fanny was still battling to save her marriage and keep her children. "For God's sake," she wrote to him at that time, consumed with remorse at her histrionic behavior, "and for your children's sake, Pierce, my husband, oh still my most tenderly beloved, let us be wise before it is too late . . . I implore you by that love which you once had for me, by that unalterable love which I still bear you, forgive me, forgive me . . ." She invoked her faith in God to help her stay sane, or to bolster her case. But nothing changed. In 1844, a "friend" caught Butler in bed with his wife and challenged him to a duel. The event took place in Bladensburg, Maryland, somehow ending up without injury on either side but with hectares of press attention. The starstruck rows of applauding Kemblers seemed to exist in some prehistoric region of the past, like the land crabs. Lying in her bed at night, Fanny had hallucinations and saw blood on the stairs. When the couple finally parted, she claimed he had made it impossible for her to remain in the marriage, and he claimed that she had deserted him. He controlled the children's movements and imposed conditions with Solomonic determination: if she wanted to see the girls, she had to break with her New England confidante Catharine Sedgwick. Fanny refused. Butler would not allow any concessions. The governess (presumably not the same one) had more authority over the girls than their mother. Fanny shuttled between friends' homes and boarding houses, fighting to wrest some kind of compromise from him. In September 1845 she retreated home to London, beaten. She was thirty-six.

She stayed at her father's lodgings in Fitzrovia's Mortimer Street and did what she did best: she went back on the stage, playing Desdemona to the tragedian William Macready's Othello. So she was not really beaten. I said at the start of this book that my working title was *No Surrender.** The phrase might have been coined for Fanny Kemble. She enjoyed a social life again ("I feel as if I had been growing idiotic out there") and planned to save enough money to return to America and the girls, and to buy a house in Lenox in the Berkshire highlands. In the meantime she published poetry in *Blackwood's Magazine*, visited her sister, now an acclaimed singer, in Italy, and wrote a book called *A Year of Consolation*. Then she went on tour. If the dressing rooms were damp and the house thin, she just kept going, always confident that something better lay over the hill, and she remained a keen observer of human foibles. Playing an antediluvian Juliet at the beginning of May at the Theatre Royal in Bristol's King Street (a venue haunted by the ghost of her aunt, Sarah Siddons), she noted the ways in which tradition persisted into the mechanical age. Stokers dressed their engines with hawthorn and laburnum on May Day "as formerly stagecoach horses used to be dressed with bunches of flowers at their ears." She wrote poems with titles like "Lines on Reading with Difficulty Some of Schiller's Early Poems." When her father retired from his famous program of solo Shakespeare performances, Fanny took over. It suited her, and she never appeared on stage with other actors again. The format remained unchanged for two decades: one play a night in a strict rotation of twenty-four, each cut to two hours, with a ten-minute interval. Fanny herself played all the parts.

In 1848 Butler began divorce proceedings, citing two years of wilful desertion. Fanny went back to face him in a Philadelphia

---

*My friend Nicky Shulman gave me that working title. One night while I was writing this book and thinking what it meant to these women to topple over into middle age, I met Nicky at a party. We talked about the purchase of several pairs of the elastic-waist trousers advertised in the back pages of the color supplements. Nicky is a writer of my own age, and at that point her mother breezed in. A perfectly judged couture dress, a fabulous haircut, a dazzling smile: still turning heads at the age of eighty-two. Nicky and I were lost in admiration, and lost for words, until Nicky finally said, "Look at that. No surrender."

court, as she still hoped to get custody of the girls, by then thirteen and ten. Her husband used her crazed letters in his statement. Fanny tried to make adultery charges stick, and to prove that he had driven her out. But his lawyers were lean and hungry. "She held," Butler stated incredulously in his submission to the court, "that marriage should be companionship on equal terms." The press gobbled it up, and everyone had an opinion. The misogynist genius Herman Melville knew Fanny from the Berkshires. He took a break from writing *Moby-Dick*, weighing into the saga with the comment, "The Lord help Butler. I marvel not he seeks being amputated off from his matrimonial half." Undaunted by spiteful public scrutiny, while the case continued Fanny raised funds to pay her own lawyers by giving play readings. She had not lost her touch. "Delicate women," wrote a theater-watcher, "grave gentlemen, belles, beaux, and critics, flock to the doors of entrance and rush into such places as they can find, two or three hours before the time of the lady's appearance." Another noted her versatility. "She has half a dozen voices in her . . . a deep sullen brute roar and snarl for Caliban that seemed an impossibility from any windpipe." One boy in the audience never forgot the experience. He went on to write himself, influenced, he said, by Fanny, and in her old age he sought her out, and worshipped her. He was Henry James.

The courts granted Butler his divorce in 1849, and awarded him custody. The case filled the newspapers until the end, most of them displaying little sympathy for either party. "Both are now free to marry again, if anyone will have them," wrote one Northern broadsheet, "and Mrs Fanny Kemble is entitled to wear the breeches in her own right." Fanny had severely limited access to the girls until they turned twenty-one. When she gave a reading in Savannah, Butler refused to let Fan visit her mother. He was supposed to pay alimony of 1,500 dollars a year and, while he still did, Fanny bought the house she had dreamed of, a gabled villa with eleven acres, in Lenox where she had spent so many happy days with Catharine Sedgwick. She called it The Perch as it stood halfway up a meadow,

overlooking Laurel Lake, and used it as an American second home after making London her permanent residence. The indomitable Fanny proceeded to settle into middle age with aplomb. She had a circle of intimates and was a loyal friend. The passing years had tempered the histrionics and reduced the flighty behaviour to eccentricities. She imposed rigid rules on herself, as she explained to her confidant Edward FitzGerald, the poet best known for his translation of *The Rubaiyat of Omar Khayyam*. These were laws, she said, "from which nothing short of a miracle causes me to depart; as, for instance, I never write till I am written to, I always write when I am written to, and I make a point of always returning the same amount of paper I receive, as you may convince yourself by observing that I send you two sheets of notepaper and Mary Anne only half one, though I have nothing more to say to you, and I *have* to her." It was a codification of what had been shapeless emotional energy. Wearing her dresses in color rotation, she would not change the order even if it meant appearing at a funeral in scarlet, which it did once, and she played the same number of games of patience each evening. Many found her formidable; an attention-seeking, wilful grande dame. But she inspired devotion. Her friend Anne, Lady Ritchie, wrote, "Mrs. Kemble possessed to a rare degree the gift of ennobling that to which she turned her mind. Kindness is comparatively commonplace, but that touch which makes others feel akin to qualities greater than any they are conscious of in themselves was, I think, the virtue by which she brought us all into subjection." She continued to cross the Atlantic each year, to see the girls, and to tour with her one-woman Shakespeare show. On the 1856 tour she gave the first readings of the Bard west of the Mississippi. Soon after that, Butler fell behind on her allowance. He had lost so much at cards that he had been obliged to sell 400 slaves at the Savannah racetrack. In 1859 Fanny turned fifty. Her weight had crept up to two hundred pounds and she described herself as old, fat and rheumatic. But she still had passion. When news reached her that her former husband had been arrested on charges of high treason after buying arms for the Confederate army, she threw herself into the brewing American drama. This was to be her most glorious moment yet: her second act.

When South Carolina split from the Union a month after Lincoln carried the presidential election in a wrinkled black suit, Butler adopted the motto of his cohorts, "Slavery is our king; slavery is our truth; slavery is our divine right." On February 18, 1861, he traveled to Montgomery for the inauguration of Jefferson Davis as President of the Confederacy. At home in London, his former wife looked on with alarm. "At that time," wrote one pundit, "it was the fashion among English critics to state that the whole secession question had no direct bearing on nor immediate connection with the issue of slavery. To the letter, there was some truth in this assertion; as to the spirit, there was none." Public opinion was divided. As a poem in *Punch* had it:

> *Though with the North we sympathise,*
> *It must not be forgotten,*
> *That with the South we've stronger ties,*
> *Which are composed of cotton*

INDIAN COTTON DEPÔT

OVER THE WAY.

MR. BULL. "OH! IF YOU TWO LIKE FIGHTING BETTER THAN BUSINESS, I SHALL DEAL AT THE OTHER SHOP."

Britain's economic stake in slave labor was plain to see, and Yankees attributed British acquiescence in Southern aggression to simple greed for cotton. "When the day of reckoning comes," snorted an American diplomat at the London legation, "I hope I shall be oblivious of mercy towards this [UK] government. As usually they will whine and sniffle for kind treatment and bring up the old Boston twaddle about the same Shakespeare, the same Milton, the same race and the same language." Public perception of the swanky Yankee poisoned the pro-North cause. "It is not necessary to admire the Yankees very much," the abolitionist Harriet Martineau wrote gamely, "to be on their side in the quarrel." Anglo-American relations in general were predicated on mutual suspicion and hostility, and maintenance of a polite but firm distance from the republic's problems formed a central plank of Palmerstonian foreign policy and the only point of agreement in that prime minister's quarrelsome Cabinet. Yet a great deal was at stake. Britons had well over 300 million dollars invested in stocks, bonds and securities in the United States, and 40 percent of export trade flowed to America. When Confederate troops fired on the Federal garrison at Fort Sumter in Charleston Harbor on April 12, 1861, Kemble spoke out against Britain's declaration of neutrality. Palmerston's determination to keep a distance splintered as factions mobilized behind both sides. Pro-secession arguments were political as well as economic, and the attraction of braking American power was obvious. A leader writer for *The Times*, on March 15, 1862, called for "two friendly Unions of moderate power and temper." In April, at Shiloh, the North won its first battle. The Welshman and future African explorer Henry Morton Stanley was serving with the Dixie Grays. "It was the first time that Glory sickened me with its repulsive aspect," he reported, "and made me suspect it was a glittering lie." The twenty-two-year-old Stanley was fighting with an obsolete muzzle-loaded flintlock, hamstrung, like most Confederates, by lack of ordnance and other supplies. The bodies, he wrote at Shiloh, "lay thick as the sleepers in a London park on a Bank Holiday." Both armies swelled monstrously after Shiloh, and so did casualty figures. At Antietam, the Irish Brigade lost half its men in twenty minutes. All told, 25,000 men fell in a single day. When the news reached Britain two weeks later, the public realized that a humanitarian crisis had developed on the stricken battlefields—the death toll was almost five times that of British losses in the Crimea, a memory still alive in the public imagination. And then there was Fredericksburg. Acres of dead piled up on the stony ground of Marye's Heights alongside tens of thousands of wounded and dying, and screams filled the cold December air through all the long nights. The living propped up frozen corpses to look like sentries. "It was not a fight," wrote an English volunteer. "It was a massacre."

Fanny found herself drawn into the unfolding drama. The blockade of Southern ports in America cut off the cotton supply, and by July 1862 the shortage was hurting hundreds of thousands of textile workers in Lancashire. Open-air public meetings pressurized the government to recognize the Confederacy, and for three years Britain supplied the Southern navy with ships and its army with ordnance. Twice in four years, Britain and the North teetered on the verge of war. Even among progressives and social liberals, many educated Britons supported the Confederacy. But on the other side, a phalanx of reformists rallied to the Union cause, as well as bankers heavily invested in the industrialized North and a faction of Liverpool dockers whose ideals were more powerful than their self-interest. Europeans might not have to deal with slavery, but the image of democracy fighting to protect the last best hope on earth gave succor to those campaigning for reform in the industrial north of England as it did to the enemies of Napoleon III. (It was to be a French abolitionist who in 1865 dreamed up the idea of a statue of liberty that would stand as a monument, slave shackles at her feet, to the shared ideals of two nations.) In the battle for public opinion, agents poured into England from the U.S. to stoke support on either side, along with equally divided returning Britons. The Revolutionary War in the previous century had made no emotional impact in Britain—the papers seldom even mentioned it. In the years between the two conflicts, America had moved from the periphery of British consciousness to the center. Now the country was obsessed, and crowds gathered outside municipal buildings to read newsprint pasted on the walls. Many papers favored secession, while others, such as the *Daily News*, in which Harriet Martineau hammered out triweekly editorials, supported the Union. For the first time, photography played a part in the propaganda of the conflict. Each side, both in Britain and America, deployed Mathew Brady's images of the dead—the ones Emily Dickinson

called "Piles of Solid Moan." Brady's picture of the corpse with
the buttoned jacket and open mouth at Gettysburg, with the
ghostly horse motionless in the background, makes one want to
die oneself.

Anthony Trollope joined in with *North America*, a two-volume
polemic supporting the North and reprising many of his mother's
themes. Rereading the history, America seems to be sleepwalk-
ing toward its doom. In 1863 the Confederates made gains at
Fredericksburg, Chancellorsville and Chickamauga, but the outcome at Vicksburg encouraged the Yankees, and Gettsyburg restored their morale. After that last bout of carnage, retreating
Confederate divisions loaded some of their injured on to wagons, but most remained, lying for days as worms feasted on
their wounds until they died. No wonder Fanny felt she had to do

something. Twenty-two thousand Confederate soldiers perished at Gettysburg. From then on, the South withered while the North grew strong. Lincoln spoke of "a new birth of freedom." The following year, in May, a horrified Fanny read in *The Times* that 11,000 grayjackets and 17,500 Union soldiers had fallen in the Wilderness of Spotsylvania. General Grant lost 55,000 men in a month. Seventy thousand perished in the Siege of Petersburg. "The men dropped here and there like bundles," Stephen Crane wrote in *The Red Badge of Courage*. "The captain of the youth's company had been killed in an early part of the action. His body lay stretched out in the position of a tired man resting, but upon his face there was an astonished and sorrowful look, as if he thought some friend had done him an ill turn." Based loosely on Chancellorsville, *The Red Badge* describes leaning towers of smoke stretching out to the sky in supplication, the mechanics of bleeding to death on a freezing battlefield, and windows glowing "murder red." The words on the page debunk the fallacy that war can be noble.*

When it really looked as if the South were going to win, Fanny Trollope, like many conservatives in Britain, had been quick to proclaim that the thousands of bleeding Americans on the fields of Shiloh and Spotsylvania and Chancellorsville provided a lesson in the failings of democracy. (She died halfway through the war, and never saw democracy triumph.) "We are now witnessing," an MP trumpeted in the House, "the bursting of the great republican bubble which had so often been held up to us as a model on which

---

*Hemingway called *The Red Badge of Courage* one of the best war stories of all time. "The good writers," he wrote in 1935, "are Henry James, Stephen Crane and Mark Twain. That's not the order they're good in. There is no order for good writers." Crane was like one of those fireworks that shoots up brighter and higher than the rest but dies soonest—he was only twenty-nine when he perished of drink and tuberculosis, but his collected works fill ten volumes. Here's the first line of *The Red Badge*: "The cold passed reluctantly from the earth, and the retiring fogs revealed an army stretched out on the hills, resting."

to recast our own English Constitution." Pundits in London and Edinburgh expressed the conviction that as American identity had been invented rather than inherited, the American people stood in an inferior position to Europeans, and were therefore unsuitable role models. The novelist Mrs. Gaskell was a fan of the country in principle, but, like many, confessed herself baffled by events. "I don't mind you thinking me dense or ignorant," she wrote to an American friend in June 1861, "but I should have thought . . . that separating yourselves from the south was like getting rid of a diseased member." Few Britons could foresee that America was to remain in a constant process of reinvention, which was the cause of its perennial optimism, at least until our own squalid era.

Fanny said publicly that blood would cease to flow only when the South was coerced back into the Union. She wanted to do something to make that happen; she felt compelled to act. There was a sense of a climax approaching in her life, as if she were at last making herself whole as America was splitting itself in two. Crucially, Fan, the younger Butler daughter, had turned twenty-one, so her father had lost his power. Few among us have a husband as rotten as he, thank God, but Butler's loss of authority symbolizes the shift that necessarily occurs in a woman's life when her children become adults. There is a sense of an ending, of sinking into the silt of coffee mornings and those elastic-waist trousers I mentioned earlier. But it doesn't have to be an ending. It can be a new beginning. For Fanny, it was. She was living proof that the post-fertile years do not have to be one long bleak descent into oblivion. It could be the best time of all—who knows? So many of the battles had been fought, and, won or lost, they were over. "You can wake on your fiftieth birthday," wrote Dorothy L. Sayers, "with the same forward-looking excitement and interest in life that you enjoyed when you were five."

Books were among the few arenas in which women could have influence. When Georgia followed South Carolina and seceded from the Union, Fanny published an account of the shameful scenes she had witnessed on the Sea Islands. She was fifty-two, no longer the neurotic young actress ricocheting between tantrum and crisis. The price of coming to rest, internally, had been appallingly high—but she had made peace with the inner America. The book would be a redemption of sorts, a beautiful creation fashioned from the festering garbage of the past. Nobody doubted the propaganda value of a good book. In the restless years before a shot was fired, the eruptive force of *Uncle Tom's Cabin* had inspired a renaissance in abolitionist clubs in Britain, selling a million copies in six months and spurring British Confederates into paroxysms of righteous indignation. Harriet Beecher Stowe's sentimental explosion of the myth of the paternalistic slave owner became one of the most successful feats of persuasion in world history, and in America it turned the tide of public opinion. When Stowe met Lincoln, he asked, famously, "Is this the little woman who made this big war?"* In Britain *Uncle Tom* had a similar effect, and Prime Minister Palmerston said he had read the book three times. In a counterblast of moral reprobation, Southerners retaliated with more than a dozen novels which allegedly revealed that Stowe had got it all wrong. Were not the New England factory workers wage slaves? And surely the average slave lived better than the average laborer in a Lancashire textile mill? Those Southerners appealed to a hallowed ideal of fine manners and gracious living remote from the materialism and vulgarity of mercantile Northern society. But as Fanny had discovered, there was nothing gracious about a young woman with ten children, dropsy and such appalling internal injuries from her many beatings that she could not crawl to Fanny in supplication from her corner of the slave "hospital" floor—she could only raise her hand. The image was on Fanny's mind all the time as she entered the trancelike

---

*By 1880, in excess of 500 Tom troupes were touring the States playing dramatized renditions of the novel.

state of the creative process. Her experiences in the tidewater were not anomalous. Few representatives of gracious living remained there, and little persisted of the stately planter's world even in Virginia. Southern nostalgia yearned for a paradise already lost—the world Confederates idealised was mostly an eighteenth-century memory, surviving only in knightly fantasies and what Mark Twain called "maudlin middle-age romanticism." Against that background, Fanny determined to pull off another *Uncle Tom*.

It is hard to think of a more vivid portrayal of slavery in the Southeastern United States than *Journal of a Residence on a Georgian Plantation*. By any standards, it is remarkable for the precision with which it skewers the vapid defences of slavery put about daily in both countries. Fanny still felt the shame she had experienced on the dykes when she saw a young woman die for her profit, and she found a way of translating it into prose. Was it that, like Lear, she had ever but slenderly known herself? Perhaps shame is the longest-lasting emotion—love and hate fade, but time fertilizes shame. Confected as a sequence of letters to a friend, *Journal* tells the story of the slave state before Hollywood cemented another version into the public imagination in *Gone with the Wind*. (The process began in 1915 with D. W. Griffith's silent film, *The Birth of a Nation*, a poisonous bit of drama deployed as a recruiting tool for the Ku Klux Klan.) In an adroit juxtaposition, Fanny makes the tidewater landscape function as a counterpoint to the horrors of the slaves' huts. "A sort of dreamy stillness seemed creeping over the world," she writes of one rowing-boat excursion, "and into my spirit as the canoe just tilted against the steps to the wharf . . . A melancholy, monotonous boat horn sounded from a distance up the stream, and presently, floating slowly down with the current, huge, shapeless, black, relieved against the sky, came one of those rough barges piled with cotton . . ." A third of the way through the book, she reports a conversation at the supper table during which Butler and his overseer refused to acknowledge the injustice of the flogging administered that day to a sick female solely because she had conversed with Fanny. "With this sauce I ate my dinner," Fanny writes after the grotesque denouement, "and truly it tasted bitter." She left out details of her personal life, referring simply to the pleasures of peace and quiet after the excitements of the stage ("twilight after glare"). Butler rarely speaks, featuring as a nameless, saturnine god brooding over the action. When it came to her appeals on a slave's behalf, Fanny restricts herself to the mention of "painful conversations." While she says little, the silent presence of a dissenting husband creates an inner drama linked to the outer drama enacted by the cast of slaves. Like Stowe, by giving her slaves names and personalities she makes the institution real. Who can forget the rheumatic Psyche, begging on her knees that the father of her young children might not be sold down the river? Also like Stowe, Fanny emphasizes the sexual mistreatment of slave women. When all is said and done, *Journal* is an anti-slavery tract. In case her readers failed to get the message, Fanny appended a closely argued abolitionist philippic, couched as a letter to *The Times* in London defending the veracity of *Uncle Tom's Cabin.**

Harper's New Monthly called it "the most powerful anti-slavery book yet written," and Henry James said it was "the most valuable account of impressions begotten of that old Southern life which we are apt to see today through a haze of Indian summer"—Twain's "maudlin middle-age romanticism." The Ladies' London Emancipation Society distributed 100,000 copies of excerpts culled from *Journal.* Confederate supporters dismissed the book as a work of malice. Other visitors after all had formed a favorable impression of the region. Sir Charles Lyell, Britain's top geologist, had visited both St. Simon's and Butler Island to inspect land formations.

*Lincoln once told a foreign correspondent, "The London *Times* is one of the greatest powers in the world—in fact, I don't know anything which has more power—except perhaps the Mississippi." *The Times* remained pro-South for most of the war.

The slaves, he reported, were "free from care"—another candidate for *Pravda*. Satirists again emerged from the shadows, as they had when *Domestic Manners* appeared. The pseudonymous Nil Admirari's verse epic *The Trollopiad* included the comment, "Mrs. Trollope and Mrs. Butler, the Alpha and Omega of travellers . . ." But scholars have since published weekly reports by plantation managers and other primary sources that vindicate Fanny's account. Like all the best books, *Journal* was inspired by a desire to tell the truth.

News of the Siege of Vicksburg broke as copies reached the binders. Major General Grant had crossed the Mississippi with buoyant Union troops and driven the Confederate army into Vicksburg. Yet the outcome of the war remained in doubt for a further year, until Sherman's March to the Sea ended in a broken Savannah when the visionary general telegraphed Lincoln, "I beg to present you as a Christmas gift the City of Savannah with 150 heavy guns and plenty of ammunition and also about 25,000 bales of cotton." Thousands of bales belonged to Butler—or did once. The Federal blockade had throttled the South and Davis' Confederacy was as good as bankrupt. When Richmond burned in April 1865, the pro-Southern correspondent of the mighty London *Times* resorted to Shakespeare. "Hell is empty," he wrote, "and all the devils are here." By the bitterest of bitter ends, the South had lost 30 percent of white males between the ages of twenty and forty-five. Fifty thousand civilians had perished and 600,000 all told—more than the American dead in the two future world wars combined. Civil War studies are an industry now, but as Whitman said, "The real war will never get into the books." For humanity at large there was neither victory nor defeat; there was only catastrophe.

Fanny had immersed herself in a phase of the American republican experiment criticized by Fanny Trollope for its leveling tendencies and had assisted the leveling. She said that she still felt deeply emotionally involved in the struggle. In April 1865, she was delivering a poem to the *Spectator* offices in London when she heard of Lincoln's assassination. She screamed so loudly that the editor came hurrying out of his office to find her in a heap on the floor.

Two decades later, Kemble's younger daughter Fan published, in London, *Ten Years on a Georgia Plantation Since the War.* Both girls had remained loyal to their mother and returned to her with joy once their father's jurisdiction came to its natural end. Sally had married and kept a house in Rome. (Her son, Owen Wister, grew up to write *The Virginian*, the first Western and a book that turned its author into the best-known writer in America—so Fanny's literary legacy lived on.) Sally was an abolitionist and close to her mother; her younger sister Fan was a Southerner to the marrow. The year after the war ended, Fan returned to the Georgia plantations with her father. "The white population was conquered, ruined and disheartened," she wrote, "unable for the moment to see anything but ruin before as well as behind, too wedded to the fancied prosperity of the old system to believe in any possible success under the new." It was a kind of Eden-gone-bad riff, like the opening credits of the famous film ("Gallantry took its last bow . . . a civilisation gone with the wind"). Hollywood was reluctant to let the South escape the Civil War, able to do so only by abandoning one stereotype for another. In literature, Erskine Caldwell's neglected *Tobacco Road* remains the superlative portrait of the Georgia sharecropper. Moreland-born Caldwell was a pulp fiction superstar guilty of selling too many copies for literary tastes: a quarter of a century after publication, *Tobacco Road* was more popular than any other book bar *Peyton Place* and the Bible, and the stage adaptation ran for seven and a half years. Caldwell, the six-foot-tall footballing son of an itinerant preacher, tells the story of Georgian tenant farmers dehumanized by poverty. A "tobacco road" is formed by rolling barrels of cured tobacco leaves across sand hills: I had seen many of them west of Savannah. Caldwell's prose has a visceral intensity, his characters possessed physically and emotionally by the poverty of the Georgian flatlands. Another novel, *God's Little Acre*, described the plight of mill hands ("lintheads") without Union protection in a newly industrialized Georgia. They were the next tribe of Georgia's dispossessed, after Fanny's slaves. So history marches on, mocking Kembles and Butlers alike. "There was a mean truth played on us somewhere," says Ty Ty Walden, Caldwell's protagonist. "God put us in the bodies of animals and tried to make us act like people." Margaret Mitchell denigrated Caldwell publicly, pointing out that *Gone with the Wind* didn't depict sadists or degenerates. After the New York Society for the Suppression of Vice tried to ban *God's Little Acre* (still one of the bestselling novels of all time) and arrested Caldwell at a book signing, a jury exonerated the author of obscenity charges. Sherwood Anderson, the bard of Ohio whom we last met in Cincinnati, spoke for him. The case was a landmark in First Amendment litigation, a pleasing example of the power of literature. Critics hailed Caldwell as America's first proletarian novelist, a soubriquet that won him a mighty following in the USSR and consequently, during the Cold War, the censure of American conservatives, who accused him, grossly unfairly, of being a tool of Moscow. Faulkner judged Caldwell one of the five greatest contemporary American novelists (he, Faulkner, was also on the list) and he was regularly tipped for the Nobel. What a tragedy he is not read today. Caldwell's time, I believe, will come again, and his idiosyncratic blend of empathy, truth, horrifying grotesque and macabre comedy might suit the zeitgeist to come. His influence was far-reaching in his own era. His depiction of Georgian sharecroppers cemented the image of the idiotic Southerner in the national imagination, spawning, among many other descendants, Al Capp's *Li'l Abner*, the thirties cartoon strip with a backwoods Southern hero and 60 million readers. In both the Second World War and the Korean War, GIs painted the noses of their bombers with Capp's bosomy girls, and when Abner married in 1952, newspapers carried the event on the front pages and *Life* ran it as a cover story. Cartoons invaded the world after that. None of my subjects foresaw, in their endless pontifications, that popular culture would turn out the great American triumph. Though in the long term it rang hollow.

In *Ten Years on a Georgia Plantation* Fan mentions neither her mother nor her mother's book, instead showing the former slaves' fondness for her father. While Fan was close to her mother, she instinctively took up her father's Confederate position. "The slaves received him very affectionately," she wrote of Butler's reappearance in the tidewater after the war. Father and daughter initially settled in Darien, their first act the installation of a picture of General Lee bedizened with gold lace. Four hundred former slaves came to apply for sharecropping work—the war had left them with nothing but freedom—and when Butler started planting rice again, he contracted to give them half the crop. In both Savannah and Darien, Fan found almost everyone in deep mourning. "The

South," she wrote, "was still treated as a conquered country . . . the local government in the hands of either military men or Northern adventurers." In the post-war devastation many thousands of former Confederate soldiers had gone west in pursuit of cheap land, while stump speakers from the North were touring the slave states and preparing blacks to vote (for them), setting people against their old masters and casting them, the freed slaves, as noble revolutionaries. "The baneful leaven of politics had begun working among them," wrote Fan. "Shall I not go back to Massachusetts," she heard a carpetbagger declaim, "and tell your brothers that you are going to ride in the streetcars with the young ladies if you please?" The bewildered Fan wrote to Sally, "Do you wonder we are all frightened? The one subject that southerners discuss whenever they meet is, What is to become of us?" Fan did not have her mother's gift for prose, but her story has a potent emotional backdrop.

Fan and her father moved from Darien to spend a year on St. Simon's, but not in Hampton Point, which had been destroyed when Northern troops had twice taken possession of the island. Instead they lived in the former overseer's house. There, looking out over the salt marsh, they lived on rice, fish and grits, supplemented with venison if Butler shot a deer. Many former slaves had left St. Simon's, the land had fallen into disuse, and labor was in such a chaotic state that Butler had to engage Irishmen to do the ditch clearing and banking. "*Sic transit Gloria (Si)mundi,*" Fan wrote as she looked out over the ruined cotton fields.

Butler died in 1867, two years after the end of the war. He was sixty-one. For his mourning former slaves, Fan reported, "Love for, and belief in, my father was beyond expression." But for the next two years, during Reconstruction, Fan slept with a loaded pistol by her bed. When field workers started speaking to her with their hats on, she accepted that there was no turning back. Then caterpillars ate the cotton. On July 15, 1870, Georgia rejoined the Union. That year Fan married James Leigh, a Hampshire parson on an extended visit to the United States, and together they made a success of the Butler Island rice plantation. The region settled down, but organized labor remained a challenge and the infrastructure was primitive. Leigh wrote an account of plantation life for his former parish magazine. "Savannah is our Leamington," he wrote. The comparison with the peaceful market town in the English heartlands revealed Leigh's positive attitude at its best. Shopping expeditions involved an eighteen-hour, hundred-mile journey to Savannah either in a train that broke down in a swamp, or in a steamboat, which ran aground on a sandbank.

Fanny returned to the United States after the war. "The country," she wrote, "is no longer English." In her lifetime the U.S. had become American. The year she arrived as a velvet-cheeked leading lady, approximately 50,000 Britons emigrated to North America, the majority selecting Canada. In just two decades that number had risen fivefold, and a quarter of a million Britons chose the USA over Canada. When the railroad joined the country geographically after a further two decades, the unification process came to its logical conclusion. The next century was the American one. In this new world Fanny withdrew to the shadows—now it really was "twilight after glare," as she had suggested in *Journal*. She spent long periods in Lenox, and in Philadelphia with the girls and their offspring, applying herself to grandmotherly tasks with devotion. When she was sixty-eight, she moved back to England permanently, setting herself up in Cavendish Square in London's West End and presiding over a coterie of admirers in a drawing room furnished in Russian leather which she dyed violet. A pair of American mockingbirds flew free, alarming guests when they alighted on a shoulder or knee. Fanny told her friend Lady Ritchie, "I do not care what anyone thinks of me, or chooses to say of me, nay, more than that, I do not care what anyone chooses to say of the people I love; it does not in any way affect the truth." She had no further romantic attachments. Bitterness had never taken hold in her, though it was there. When Fan, back in England, had a son, she christened him Pierce Butler Leigh, and granny Fanny told a friend privately that she could not go into church to hear "that evil name uttered." She inspired affection, even if neurosis still lurked in the background. Ritchie wrote that "what Mrs. Kemble did care for, scrupulously, with infinite solicitude, was the fear of having caused pain by anything she had said in the energy of the moment; she would remember it and think over it after days had passed. People did not always understand her, nor how her love of truth, as it happened to her, did not prevent her tenderness for the individual. Her stories of the past were endlessly interesting and various. She had known everybody interesting as well as uninteresting. She had most assiduous correspondents." She wrote religiously to this diligent band about whom she had seen and where she had been, how her eyesight was failing and how she forgot everything, and what was the best background and pose when the exciting day came to be photographed. Books, above all, preoccupied her; books, and her children and grandchildren. Despite the tumults, Fanny had always maintained a powerful sense of self, and her confidence as a mother neither wavered nor impinged on the other part of her life. I was beginning to think reunification might be possible.

Fanny continued to publish: she wrote notes on Shakespeare and articles on the stage, including a gossipy series for *Atlantic Monthly*, as well as a play about Pocahontas, which she tapped out on a typewriter she called a printing machine. In her eightieth year she brought out her first novel, *Far Away and Long Ago*, setting it in her beloved Lenox. But she never wrote anything half as good as *Journal of a Residence on a Georgian Plantation*. Her closest companion when it came to books and the theater was that New England Brahmin Henry James—she called him her "friend of many lonely hours." After hearing Fanny's Shakespearean declamations as a boy, James had met her at her daughter Sally's salon in Rome in

1873: "The terrific Kemble herself," he noted, "whose splendid handsomeness of eye, nostril and mouth was the best thing in the room." (Later he cast Sally's husband as the Vicar of Lockfield in *Portrait of a Lady*, the novel largely set in Rome.) They were both transatlantic types, and his creative life was engaged with the nuanced complexity of Anglo-American differences. They both too had ambivalent relationships with America: he was self-exiled, she, he observed, never heard the U.S. praised without expressing reservations, and never heard it abused without voicing admiration and faith in its future. The Jamesian rococo, periphrastic prose suited Kemble, as did the author's unwillingness to embrace any ideology. (James "had so fine a mind," according to T. S. Eliot, "that no idea could violate it.") Now James accompanied Kemble to the theater, where they both took fright at the increasing realism of British acting. "Good heavens, she's touched him!" Kemble whispered to James when Ellen Terry, as Portia, laid a hand on her Bassanio's arm, while James registered the strongest disapproval at the "hugging and kissing" disease that had infected the London stage. They both had liberal opinions and conservative taste. In front of The Terrific Kemble's fire in Cavendish Square, James provided the literary conversation she craved. She signed her letters to him "Your Old Gossip," or "Catherine the Great." He noted how her talk was so saturated with the language of Shakespeare that she made the Bard "the air she lived in," but even that didn't put him off. He had the writer's splinter of ice in his heart, that faithless shard of detachment that stores everything as material. As James recorded at length in his notebook on February 21, 1879, "Mrs. Kemble told me last evening the history of her brother H[enry]'s engagement to Miss T," going on to explain that Henry had jilted an heiress when he discovered her father was to disinherit the girl. This was the seed that grew into *Washington Square*, published in serial form in *Cornhill* the following year. When James wrote about Fanny, his images were fiery, featuring storms and volcanoes, and he summed up her life with the word "agitated." "There was no handy formula for Mrs Kemble's genius," he decided. "And one had to take her career, the juxtaposition of her interests, exactly as one took her disposition, for a remarkably fine cluster of inconsistencies." She was "always the tragedienne," and "the first woman in London" and "one of the consolations of my life." It was an *amitié amoureuse* of the Jamesian variety, despite or perhaps because of the thirty-four years between them. "A prouder nature than hers never confronted the long humiliation of life," he wrote, and he paid tribute to "the beauty of her deep and serious character." When Fanny died in 1893 at the age of eighty-four, James was among the mourners at her funeral, and many years later, in the long, cruel days of his own dying, he asked in delirium about The Terrific Kemble. The girls buried her at Kensal Green Cemetery in northwest London, close to Anthony Trollope, who had expired the previous month. The great thing was, James wrote in his journal that night, "she had abundantly lived."

3

❧

A GREAT EMBRYO POET

Harriet Martineau Goes to Massachusetts and Kentucky

Harriet Martineau, according to Dickens, was "grimly bent on the enlightenment of mankind." Bossy, sometimes silly, and almost always lovable, she was among the most famous women in England before she shipped out to America. Louis Philippe read her pamphlets on social improvement to his family, as did Nicholas I. In the end both banned her books, but Harriet remained a revered social commentator: prime ministers competed for her attention and she became what we would call a celebrity, though it was a more dignified business then, and she adapted to it with dignity of her own. When an envelope arrived at the post office addressed to "The Queen of Modern Philanthropists," a clerk scribbled on it, "Try Miss Martineau." She was governess to the nation, an early social-theorist and self-help guru. Men considered sociology an unfeminine subject, and found it hard not to snigger, especially when Harriet's sales figures rocketed beyond their own. "How very fortunate it is, she is so very plain," Darwin noted in a letter to his nan, "otherwise I should be frightened." The radical Harriet picked apart every argument ever made against female suffrage—and that was just one of her causes. Alone of my subjects, she set out, as a girl, to be a professional writer, and in the end earned more from her pen than any female author before her. She is rarely read these days outside the universities, which is an irony, as she considered herself a popularizer. At first, when I set out on my travels with Ms. Martineau, I found it hard not to laugh at her myself. But as I got to know her I admired the way in which she sacrificed the private self to the public good. "The best happiness in this world," she wrote, "is found in strenuous exertion on a right principle."

America had convinced Fanny Trollope that democracy would fail. Harriet, twenty-three years her junior, returned from her own tour publicizing its virtues. "I am more democratic than ever," she declared, "since I have seen what democracy is." Dickens, ten years younger again, may have disapproved—Harriet was too much like a man for his taste—but the pair had a lot in common. Both were republicans and social reformers. Both were passionately interested in prisons and asylums, viewing them as touchstones of progress. Equally hyperactive, they rearranged furniture in hotel rooms to create a more practical set-up, the better to get on with the business of *achieving good things*. Dickens had praised Fanny Trollope's *Domestic Manners*, but he judged that Harriet had written the superior book. *Society in America*, he declared, was the best thing ever written on that country.

Before the railway, the marshy Norfolk fens nestled alongside the bulbous east coast of England retained a provincial identity separate from the rest of the country, attracting dissenters and nonconformists in search of a bracingly unrestricted social climate. The Martineaus arrived at the end of the seventeenth century, one of many Huguenot families in flight from persecution in Catholic Europe. When Harriet was born in 1802, the 105-mile coach journey from Norwich to London took fourteen hours, unless highway robbers pounced. She was the sixth of eight, and grew up in a bow-fronted house in Magdalen Street, Norwich. Her father was a textile manufacturer and Unitarian—a dissenting Christian who believed in practical morality and rational enquiry. Unitarians were sane and intellectual, promoting education for girls and other heresies, and unlike Calvinists they thought it was fine to have a good time. Parties, dancing and card games were regular events in Magdalen Street. Harriet read everything, learned French, Latin, German and Italian, and as a young adult contributed to Unitarian publications under the pseudonym Discipulus. She was a tireless worker, which was just as well, as when her father died she and her mother had to earn a living by taking in darning. Like many nineteenth-century women who dismantled barriers, she was delicate and highly strung. Her hearing began to fail when she was twelve, and she was almost deaf by twenty, losing at the same time her sense of taste and smell. She was medium height, and her eyes were hazel; her lower jaw was prominent, and her mouth small. Her fingers were unusually long. "I was astonished to find how ugly she is," noted Darwin. An elaborate ear trumpet involving a long rubber tube did little to mitigate the vaguely comic appearance. Harriet had a fiancé for a short period, an unstable Manchester priest. He went mad and died in an asylum when Harriet was twenty-five, and forty years of romantic silence followed.

As a young woman she absorbed Nonconformist concern for social problems and embarked on a crusade to enlighten the masses with fictional morality tales. Instructive literature for children was popular, and Harriet reckoned the use of dialogue, fable and plot to illustrate complex laws could be applied to adults. The idea of the tales obsessed her, even when publishers rejected the proposal on the grounds that the Reform Bill and cholera were depressing the market (most authors are familiar with the rejection letter, but few have one citing cholera). In 1832 *Illustrations of Political Economy* came out in monthly installments: effectively Harriet self-published. The 132-page stories covered universal education (good), colonial monopolies (bad), slavery, free trade, demands for freedom of the money market, the evils of privileged trading corporations, the Poor Laws, the disestablishment of the church, and much more. Harriet had judged the national mood correctly. *Illustrations of Political Economy* sold in the hundreds of thousands and their author, aged thirty, became a public figure. She never darned socks again.

She was aggressively didactic, but not arrogant. "I believe myself possessed of no uncommon talents," she said, "and of not an atom of genius; but as various circumstances have led me to think more accurately and read more extensively than some women, I believe that I may so write on subjects of universal concern as to inform some minds and stir up others . . . of posthumous fame I have not the slightest expectation or desire. To be useful in my day and generation is enough for me." Her publishers—she could take her pick now—called her "a national instructor." She lost no time in leaving Norwich, moving to the capital in November 1832 and settling in modest lodgings at 17 Fludyer Street, behind the prime minister's residence in Whitehall. Her mother and aunt moved with her. For two years Harriet worked to a cycle of monthly deadlines. She was a quick researcher and a natural journalist, writing rapidly and never rereading copy. The *Illustrations* are not literary. The characters are ciphers, the dialogue stilted, and even the moralizing is simplistic. But the reading public devoured every one. When the Lord Chancellor, Lord Brougham, paid court at Fludyer Street, he said Harriet was doing more good than any man in the country. Brougham was so keen to prepare the masses for his forthcoming Budget that he commissioned Harriet to continue her series with a sequence of stories called *Poor Laws and Paupers Illustrated,* based on material collected by government commissioners.* In between long sessions at the writing desk she went to three parties a day and sat to sculptors who made casts of her. She spoke as she wrote, and talked everyone into the ground. After Hans Christian Andersen was introduced to her at a garden party, he said he had to lie down for the rest of the afternoon. Harriet was a tremendous gossip. Hearing the news that George Eliot's common-law husband was ill, she wrote to a friend, "Do you know that Lewes is about to die? All but hopelessly ill, Matt. [sic] Arnold told me the other day. What will she do? Take a successor, I shd expect." She issued peremptory orders, telling Florence Nightingale which way the hospital beds should face, and she could be oracular, which annoyed people. She was always quick to take up an extreme position. In later years she quarrelled in print with Dickens over factory legislation and wished *Adam Bede* had never been written. George Eliot obviously just got on her wick. Carlyle wrote to Ralph Waldo Emerson about Harriet. "She is one of the strangest phenomena to me. A genuine little Poetess, buckrammed, swathed like a mummy into Socinian and Political-Economy formulas; and yet verily alive inside of that!"†

She produced thirty-four volumes in thirty months and in

---

*The radical Whig Brougham was an abolitionist, an educational reformer and a thoroughly unpleasant man. He holds the House of Commons record for non-stop speaking, having droned continuously for six hours. "If I was not a Christian," wrote Fanny Kemble, "I think every now and then I should like to shoot Brougham." He looked, she said, "as if he had been gnawed by rats."
†Socinianism was an unorthodox brand of dissenting Christianity founded in medieval Poland. It was allied to Unitarianism.

1834 she went to America. Her friend Lord Henley had suggested it (he was a member of parliament in his own right, and married to the prime minister's sister). Harriet was planning to follow the established tourist route to Italy and Switzerland. "Oh, do not go over that beaten track," said Henley. "Why should you? Will you not go to America?" She asked for one good reason why she should. He replied, "Whatever else may or may not be true about the Americans, it is certain that they have got at principles of justice and mercy in their treatment of the least happy classes of society which we should do well to understand. Will you not go, and tell us what they are?" *Domestic Manners of the Americans* had been out for two years, and the merits and pitfalls of New World democracy remained a contentious topic in Britain. Fanny Kemble, entombed outside Philadelphia, was discovering its shortcomings for herself. Harriet needed little encouragement—she was longing to take off. The 10,000-mile, two-year tour, she said, was conceived "chiefly because I felt a strong curiosity to witness the actual working of republican institutions," and "partly" because a shared language is all the more important when one is deaf. One could argue the opposite.

For the voyage on the sailing packet *United States* she packed a stone hot water bottle and a horsehair glove for rubbing herself down as a substitute for exercise. The captain gave permission for her to tie herself to the post of the binnacle to watch hurricanes. There was no letting up: she knocked off a short book during the six-week crossing—*How to Observe Manners and Morals*. She was like a ferret, constantly worrying away at the next task. The *United States* reached the East Coast just as early fall breezes were cooling off the summer heat. "All that I had heard of the Pilgrim Fathers, of the old colonial days," Harriet said after the first sight of America, "of the great men of the Revolution, and of the busy, prosperous succeeding days, stirred up my mind, while I looked upon the sunny reach of land on the horizon." When the hills of New Jersey, Long Island and Staten Island grew purple in the cloudy sunset, a steam packet emerged from the Narrows jammed with people coming to greet the incoming ship. Harriet had made friends on board, many among them waiting to be reunited with loved ones. "O the speculations and breathless suspense as to whether the boat was coming to us!" she wrote. "In a few minutes, there remained no further doubt, then there was a rush to the side, and one of the young ladies saw through her tears her two brothers . . . I never liked introductions better than those which followed. With broad smiles my passenger friends came up, saying, 'I have the great pleasure of introducing to you my brother.'"

From the outset, Harriet liked both America and Americans. Being in the U.S., she said, "was like stepping into a warm bath." Within weeks, she had adopted American habits, drinking raw egg and holding her fork in her right hand. At first she based herself in New England where Unitarianism was fashionable. Followers who had been reading her books and pamphlets for years competed to host a star author, flying up like snipe when she entered a room. People liked her as much as she liked them: she had an open manner that made her easy to know, and new acquaintances appreciated her fresh, frank opinions. "We had wintry hearts," said a disciple, "and she melted them." She went gallivanting—Dr. Channing, the unofficial leader of Massachusetts Unitarians and Kemble's friend, invited Harriet to stay in his holiday home in Rhode Island, and Ralph Waldo Emerson took her in at Concord. "She made us all love her," said one acolyte. The English accent helped—as I have often found myself—as did Harriet's determination to step out of Fanny Trollope's shadow. "No nation can pretend to judge another nation's manners," she said publicly. Kemble's other friend, the forward-thinking novelist Catharine Sedgwick, called Harriet an "extraordinary woman who found us all strangers and left us friends." But a chill descended during a walk along the banks of the Housatonic after an altercation over the quickest way to abolish slavery.

Guided by a cast of well-wishers, Harriet explored Massachu-setts Bay from Gloucester to Yarmouth, lying on the rocks in autumn sunshine watching smacks returning loaded with mackerel, or Quakers fertilizing fields with fish heads. Among the Cape Cod dunes—"of so dazzling a whiteness as to distress the eyes"—she found "a private race of fishermen and saltmen, dwelling in ground-floor houses, which are set down among the sand ridges without plan or order. Some communication is kept up between them and a yet more secluded race of citizens, the inhabitants of Nantucket and Martha's Vineyard . . ." She and her companion walked across Nahant sands where Kemble had galloped with her beau. A man called Dexter, someone informed her, had bought the land there from the Indian Black Willy for a suit of clothes. Nahant had since grown into a gentrified resort, and in the season a steamboat ran daily to Boston. "The gay birds of summer have flown," Harriet wrote in Nahant in October. "We were alone with our own voices and the dashing of the sea, which seemed likely to take us off our feet." There was little greenery, but the distant views and intricate rocks made up for it. "Here and there," she said, "was a quiet strip of beach, where we sat watching the rich crop of weed swayed to and fro by the spreading and repeating of the translucent waters; and then at intervals we came to where the waves boil among the caverns, making a busy roar in the stillest hour of the stillest day. Here all was so chill and shadowy that the open sea, with its sunny sail and canopy of pearly clouds, looked as if it were quite another region, brought into view by some magic, but really lying on the other side of the world." The sun vanished behind the Lynn brickworks and the sands darkened. "Never," she said, "was the world bathed in a lovelier atmosphere than this evening."

I envied my girls when they led me to places that had been beauti-ful to them. At those times, when I stood on a bluff or turned a bend in a river and saw something made of concrete, more often than not eructating emissions, I felt as if I were following them into the shadows and groping for the America that had captivated them. But Nahant allowed glimpses of the country they had swooned over. The fairy dust of the East Coast elite had vanished, and so had the mackerel, and the sun had long ago sunk for the last time behind the Lynn brickworks. But the light on the pearly sand was just as she had described. I was there at the beginning of November, on my way to Boston to take a flight to Provincetown. The air had a seaweed tang, and gulls swooped over the empty beach. Softening pumpkins grinned from the stoops of the clapboard houses. In a hair salon on the coast road, women with foil on their heads sat under dryers, their isolation reprising the insularity of the quiet streets. I felt so lonely that I went in and had a trim I didn't need. Despite the numinous light, there was something standing between me and the landscape, and between me and Harriet and the others. Journeys tend to go in fits and starts, like life. Sometimes, like that day at Nahant, too much clogged up the interstices between them and me. Too much of the crap of contemporary America, and too much metaphorical concrete inside my head.

Later I walked up to Greenlawn Cemetery. Slats of watery light fell through maple branches onto the mini Stars and Stripes flapping over military graves. The whole of Nahant was like a cemetery. A lone bar was open on the beach, its lights on at two in the afternoon. I saw the winks of a flat-screen television and the backs of three or four heads looking up at it. Was it possible that televisions were even more ubiquitous in the U.S. than they are in the UK? I believe it was. A pair of pickups occupied either end of the gravel car park. The Boston smart set had evacuated to Osterville, Chatham and Martha's Vineyard. I saw them later in the day, at the Cape Air desks at Logan, patrician Democrats in sport jackets.

Harriet traveled up and down the East Coast, quizzing everyone. The trumpet, Harriet thought, "seems to exert some winning powers by which I gain more in *tête à têtes*." Not everyone found that the device facilitated intimacy. "Her deafness is a serious bar to her enjoyment of society," wrote one American observer, "and some drawback to the pleasure of conversing with her, for, as a man observed to me last night, 'One feels so like a fool, saying, "How do you do?"' through a speaking-trumpet in the middle of a drawing-room'; and unshoutable commonplaces form the staple of all drawing-room conversation." Whatever the difficulties, Harriet's interlocutors met the challenge. Whenever she made an inquiry, "the person questioned seemed to feel himself put upon his conscience to give a full, true and particular reply; and so he went back as near to the Deluge as the subject would admit, and forward to the millennium, taking care to omit nothing of consequence in the interval." It was rich, coming from her. She found regional rivalries amusing. "I was even told in New York," she wrote, "that the Rhode Island people were all heathens and the New Jersey folks no better. Some Baltimore ladies told me that the Philadelphia ladies say that no Baltimore lady knows how to put on a bonnet." In Michigan and Ohio people were arguing so bitterly over territory that the legislature in the new town of Columbus had just voted 300,000 dollars to raise troops.

Her reputation and its press coverage preceded her, and Philadelphian hostesses competed to throw parties and balls in Harriet's honor. Fanny Kemble had misgivings, despite longing for the parties. "I am afraid she is not likely to like me much," she wrote to a friend before meeting Harriet. "I admire her genius greatly, but have an inveterate tendency to worship at all the crumbling shrines, which she and her employers seem intent upon pulling down; and I think I should be an object of much superior contempt to that enlightened and clever female Radical and Unitarian." Fanny worried about the "great disparity of intellect" between them. When Harriet eventually appeared, her new friend presented her with a hummingbird's nest from the garden. The pair went on to see a good deal of one another, and Fanny said she liked Harriet "very much indeed, in spite of her radicalism," a sentiment that was not reciprocated. The words "chalk" and "cheese" come to mind. "I really strove hard to like and approve of her," Harriet wrote in the posthumously published *Autobiography*, "and I imposed upon myself for a time, as on others in conversation, the belief that I did so: but I could not carry it on long. There was so radical an unreality about her and her sayings." Conforming to English prejudice, Harriet disdained the acting profession. Referring to "a green-room cast of mind," she took against Kembles in general. "There seemed to be an incurable vulgarity clinging to them . . ." In theory Harriet believed in the right of women of all classes to obtain a divorce—a deeply unconventional view at the time—but in practice, when events unraveled, she had little sympathy with Kemble's loss of her children at the hands of a patriarchal legal system. Like others who strive to improve humanity, she didn't care much for its individual representatives.*

Consumed by the conviction that she must examine every aspect of American society, Harriet visited jails, interviewing inmates and pontificating on how to "regenerate some self respect." The embattled prisoners had only just been interrogated by Tocqueville. Harriet also appointed herself inspector of lunatic asylums. "The insane in Pennsylvania Hospital should be removed to some more light and cheerful abode," she announced. Asylums for the blind were especially vexing. "The fault in general," she pronounced, "is that mirth is not sufficiently cultivated." But overall in the north of the USA she found "society basking in one bright sunshine of good will," and all Americans in possession of "a sweet

---

*Bertrand Russell was another of that ilk, as was H. G. Wells, and so are certain campaigning individuals hacking at the coalface of social and political improvement today. It is a peculiarly British condition. Mark Twain was the opposite: he had a low opinion of the human race, but admired individuals. The message of all Twain's work concerns human equality. Which is why he is still the great American writer on the condition of whites and blacks in the nation they share.

temper and kindly manners." Just as Trollope and Kemble had recoiled at the equal status of servants, Harriet rejoiced in it. "I had rather," she said, "suffer any inconvenience from having to work occasionally in chambers and kitchen . . . than witness the subservience in which the menial class is held in Europe." As the journey proceeded, Harriet flourished. She found fresh energy in America; a sense of renewal that eluded her in the Old World. Contact with the U.S. ushered in a second act for Harriet. But clouds were gathering over the American tour. Everyone knew Harriet's views on slavery, as she had published an *Illustration* in support of abolition. Her New England friends warned her not to visit the Southern states, suspecting that they might prove a colder bath. But she did. Naturally, the abolitionist Fanny Kemble thought it was a good idea. "She is gone to the South," Fanny wrote, "where I think she cannot fail to do some good, if only in giving another impulse to the stone that already topples on the brink—I mean in that miserable matter of slavery." Harriet travelled widely in the South, and the more primitive the conditions, the better. In Virginia her coach got stuck ten times in a day and the coachman was obliged to cut down trees to lever them out. The stages stopped at roughhouses where passengers bedded down for three or four hours before setting out again at two in the morning. Harriet describes candles flickering on log walls and the cold grope for reticules in the darkness. Early one morning she saw a slave coffle, a line of chained men and women slipping through the mist, and she could not see the beginning or the end of the line. It took nine days to travel 350 miles from Richmond to Charleston. She went to the Carolina slave markets and saw a boy of eight being sold. He was standing on the auctioneer's table. "There was no bearing the child's look of helplessness and shame," she wrote. "It seemed like an outrage to be among the starers from whom he shrunk." She was staying in a fine house in Charleston at the time, the guest of a Unitarian clergyman. But after that, "every laugh had lost its gaiety." All her friends supported the burgeoning abolition movement, and despite the intractability of Southerners, Harriet sensed hope. "The crescent streak is brightening towards the full," she wrote with determined bombast, "to wane no more. Already is the world beyond the sea beginning to think of America less as the country of the double-faced pretender to the name of liberty, than as the home of the single-hearted, clear-eyed Presence majestically passing through the land which is soon to be her throne." It was not going to be all that soon, and there was not going to be anything majestic about it.

In Georgia and Alabama she visited cotton gins and learned how pods were drawn through the cylinders to extract seed. In New Orleans she watched Quadroons take an airing on the levee while men smoked and veiled ladies stole through the streets. "It is an absorbing thing," she said, "to watch the process of world-making." She felt, as a traveler, that being a woman conferred advantage. "The nursery, the boudoir, the kitchen are all excellent schools in which to learn the morals and manners of a people." She even tried to adopt a little slave girl who had been sold on down the river and parted from her parents, but the girl's owner refused. Finally, Harriet witnessed a duel. There were more duels than days of the year in New Orleans and fifteen on a single Sunday morning.

From New Orleans Harriet followed Trollope's route up the Mississippi. At the embarkation wharf, she had noticed a man sneak up the gangplank "with his bundle" some time after the captain had declared the ship full. He lay down on the second deck, "without attracting particular notice from any one." The first night passed. When Harriet left her cabin before six the next morning to observe dawn on the river, "I was privately told by a companion that the man who had forced his way on board had died of cholera in the night and had been laid under a tree at the wooding place a few minutes before . . . We sped away from that lonely grave as if we were in a hurry to forget it; and when we met at breakfast, there was mirth and conversation and conventional observance . . . This was no more than a quickening of the process by which man drops out of life, and all seems to go on as if he had never been: only seems, however. Even in this case, where the departed had been a stranger to us all, and had sunk from amid us in eight hours, I believe there were few or no hearts untouched, either by sorrow for him or fear for themselves."

For three glorious weeks in Kentucky, Harriet was a guest of a wealthy political family in Lexington. She had rifle lessons, and saw buffalo roam the bluegrass. The country there revealed itself to her as a world of opportunity and promise. The wilderness set her free, and she responded with a delight normally beaten down by her remorseless pursuit of theories and categories. An excursion to the Mammoth Caves of Kentucky turned out to be the highlight of the two-year tour. The caves were the apotheosis of wilderness. "If any of us should ever happen to be banished," she wrote later, "and to have a home to seek, I fancy we should look out for a plot of green sward, among flowering kalmias, near the mouth of an enormous cave, with hummingbirds flitting about it by day, and fireflies and summer lightning by night." The longest known cave system in the world, Mammoth has close to 400 miles of limestone passageways and chambers under a sandstone ridge irrigated by the springs of the Green River, and although surveyors had been mining portions of it for saltpeter since the War of 1812, a new breed of American tourist had recently begun to make the trek to visit the untouched segments.* As the land around was hardscrabble, too poor to farm, that part of Kentucky was thinly populated and even the bison had abandoned it (as a result,

---

*Over the years the enterprising people of Kentucky have found numerous purposes for their caves. The temperature inside remains stable at fifty-four degrees, and as the medical profession once believed in the health-giving properties of cold, damp air, a specially appointed commission set up a TB hospital inside the Mammoth complex, a project that reached a natural conclusion when all the patients died. The limestone chambers were later used as a wine warehouse.

so had the Shawnee). As guides, Harriet and her four companions hired a pair of dashing brothers who lived with their mother in the only house at the site. The family used the passage into the caves to refrigerate joints of ham. Harriet left her ear trumpet in her valise, tucked up her gown, tied a hanky over her head ("like the witches in Macbeth") and spent the day scrambling over loose limestone. The guides' candle cast monstrous shadows. "Everything appears alive," she wrote: "the slowly growing stalactites, the water ever-dropping into the plashing pool, the whispering airs—all seem conscious." She swooned at "that Rembrandt light on the drip of water" and decided she had found the most romantic place in the world.

The party lodged in the guides' house and washed in a milk pan. The next morning they crawled through an opening eighteen inches high to get to the grotto. "Whether the singularity of our mode of access magnified to our eyes the beauties we had thereby come into the midst of," she wrote, "or whether Nature does work most *con amore* in retired places, this grotto seemed to us all by far the most beautiful part of the cave." In the deeper recesses Harriet found bits of charred cane scattered on the limestone floor, remnants of a hearth. It had been, she concluded, "perhaps the most remarkable walk we had taken in our lives." She compared the last cave with "a magnificent sepulchre," and it later turned out that it was one: in 1935 someone spotted a pre-Columbian mummy under a boulder.

The year before I began to research Harriet, I swapped my house in London for an antebellum stud farm in Lexington, Kentucky (for a month, not for good). The house was, it turned out, much like the one where Harriet stayed, and close by. My two feral sons, then aged eight and thirteen, came along, and so did their Canadian father. He and therefore our children are descended from Ogilvies who emigrated from Scotland before the War of Independence. They were plantation people in Virginia, and later made claims against the Crown for slaves lost in that conflict. When the game was up, in 1865 they shifted to Nova Scotia. So the American experience was in my infants' DNA. At any rate the children took to Kentucky: we all did. The humidity clubbed us to a stupor, so we stayed close to water, cruising Laurel Lake in a flat-bottomed skiff hired for forty dollars a day. The marina was crowded with gin palaces and boaters ferried gear from cars to vessels in shopping trolleys, a fleet of which were stabled in the parking lot. The lake was so large we could spend whole days alone, a feat inconceivable in the crabbed confines of Europe, skinny dipping in thirty-degree water and leaping off limestone outcrops. One afternoon a hailstorm struck. We had a long journey back to the marina. Surrounded by bluffs as the hail beat down, we glimpsed the untamed America Harriet and my other girls had seen. Then as the moon rose over the forests of Kentucky we ate with the good old boys at the Gator Grill clubhouse. The food was prison fodder: hot dogs, chicken nuggets and unidentifiable fried vegetables ladled out of steel drums. Later we canoed down the Green River, a tributary of the Ohio that rises in Lincoln County, and stayed the night in Wigwam Village on the North Dixie Highway. The concrete wigwams, built in the fifties and still furnished with the original Formica, were owned by a charming family of Indians (Bengali as opposed to Cherokee). The thirty-five-year-old receptionist, a nephew of the owner, had recently arrived from Calcutta. He yearned for New York or Chicago. "This," he said, gesturing toward the straggly highway and a dog engaged with an upturned trash can, "was not the America I had in mind."

The Kentucky River drains the bluegrass wold that makes up the northern part of the state. Between Madison County and Frankfort, the water cuts a canyon through the Palisades, a hundred-mile series of striated gorges dotted with yellowwood, blue ash and sugar maple. Among white fences, Adirondack chairs and blue spruce, country stores and worn-out truck stops revealed

a vanishing backwoods America infinitely charming to sentimental Europeans, if not to a Bengali seeking a better world. I found
the Kentucky plots of green sward as liberating as Harriet did,
even if the buffalo had vanished. The only failure was Mammoth
Caves. When the federal government conferred National Park
status on the attraction in 1941 it might as well have consigned it
to one of the less important circles of hell. The year before the
house swap, driving north in a hurry through Kentucky on a
magazine assignment, I arrived late at night at the hotel near
the entrance to the main cave system—on the site, presumably, of
the house in which Harriet had washed in a milk pan. I could see the
silhouettes of tour buses dozing like dinosaurs in the parking lot, but
the rest was silence. In the forest, draughts of cold air wafted from
invisible caves. The ubiquitous Kentucky fireflies danced and a
long-legged deer cantered out of the gloom. I had to leave early
the next morning, and when I returned with my children the
next year we took the road in from Cave City, skeining through

miles of amusements built to service the mammoth Mammoth-bound tourist trade. Consulting my notebook, I see that these included:

Dinosaur World
Yogi's Water Slide
Mini-Golf
Hillbilly Hound Fun Park
Debbie's Minerals and Fossils
Big Mike's Rock Shop
Golgotha Fun Park

At the Caves, tens of thousands of people were eddying around a Visitors' Center. There was to be none of Harriet's happy scrambling: we had been obliged to book a tour weeks in advance. Halfway through it, the ranger shone a powerful electric beam into a pool of black water. In the depths, he said, were troglodytic shrimp that had been in the caves for so many generations they had lost both sight and pigment. One was tempted to draw an analogy with the biped electorate outside, busily sanctioning Creationism on the statewide school syllabus.

She was crazy about Cincinnati. No town compared with it "in beauty of setting." It was "a glorious place," with only one blemish. "This Bazaar is the great deformity of the city," Harriet wrote after a concert at Fanny Trollope's emporium. "It is built of brick, and has gothic windows, Grecian pillars, and a Turkish dome, and it was originally ornamented with Egyptian devices, which have, however, all disappeared under the brush of the whitewasher." She instinctively disapproved of Fanny, judging her vulgar and insufficiently serious, just as the actress Fanny had been. But Harriet liked Cincinnatians. As in Philadelphia, press coverage noting Harriet's fame in her homeland had enflamed people's imagination. One adoring magazine editor wrote a sonnet to the ear trumpet, perhaps the first ever penned ("Thrice-precious tube!"). At the Western Museum, where *The Infernal Regions* was still pulling in crowds, the owner showed Harriet views of the basin and the river of blood flowing from the pig slaughterhouses at Deer Creek, explaining enthusiastically why "Buckeyes [Ohioans] were superior to all others of God's creatures." This was the West, a region without a past. The frontier was an ideal place for someone obsessed with human perfectibility. "We should foster Western genius, encourage Western writers, patronize Western publishers, augment the number of Western leaders and create a Western heart," proclaimed the museum owner, and Harriet agreed. The bold, open complacency of Cincinnati—the very characteristic Fanny Trollope disliked—made the East Coast seem dim and old-fashioned to a radical. But publicly expressed enmity between North and South shocked Harriet. "Many a time in America," she wrote, "I have been conscious of that pang and shudder which are felt only in the presence of hatred." Back in New England after five months in the South, she expressed dismay at the extent to which Northerners outside New England had no interest in the abolition struggle. "I suppose, while Luther was toiling and thundering, German ladies and gentlemen were supping and dancing as usual; and while the Lollards were burning, perhaps little was known or cared about it in warehouses and upon farms." She was right, and still is right. People supped and danced and farmed in 2010 while the Gulf of Mexico burned and shrimp fishermen starved.

In November 1835 Harriet appeared on a platform at the Boston Female Anti-Slavery Society, speaking plainly in support of immediate abolition. "Mrs. Trollope herself could not have done worse," thundered the *Charleston Mercury*. Many who had hosted her in their homes now froze her out. She was "an ugly, deaf, sour old crabapple," said one New York commentator, and the *American Quarterly Review* called her "a poor flimsy tool of a nest of poisonous radicals." She liked that.

A New York publisher offered to produce any book she might like to write. She said she had not planned such a volume. "Why, surely madam," replied the publisher, "you need not be at a loss about that. You must have got incident plenty by this time, and then you can Trollopize a bit, and so make a readable book." In fact, Harriet had been assiduous in her investigations. During her tour she had been to four weddings and a congressional funeral, and at a spa in the Virginia Alleghenies she had participated in a public weigh-in. She had stayed at a Rappite colony near Pittsburgh and visited the Shakers, finding both rich and miserable. She had visited cemeteries in mosquito-ridden swamps in New Orleans and among the sugar maples of Mount Auburn, the "museum without walls" where Kemble had said the fatal yes to Pierce Butler. Former presidents competed to host her and she had been present when an assassin fired two shots at President Jackson (both missed). Food was the only subject she left alone, because she could not taste anything. She had gathered material for one purpose. Yet she said, "I am sure no traveller seeing things through author [sic] spectacles can see them as they really are," a statement which at first glance seems clever, but on closer inspection turns out to be wrong. Many of Harriet's aphorisms are meaningless. She just couldn't stop herself coming out with them, like a sausage machine jammed to ON. "If there is any country on earth where the course of true love may be expected to run smooth," she wrote, "it is America." One wonders what Fanny K. would have said about that.

Her chaperone went home, and Harriet made her last trip unaccompanied. It was to the Great Lakes. On Lake Huron she shared a cabin with a fat man, their bunks separated by a white counterpane fastened by four forks. Chicago she found to be crawling with land speculators—a plot worth $750 in the morning sold for $5,000 in the afternoon. The female population of Milwaukee totalled seven.

As my two maps flapped in the breezes of Lexington and Philadelphia, I glimpsed what Harriet's emotional reckoning had been. It was a sublimation of the self—by which I mean the feminine self and its sexual dimension. I admired her greatly for sticking to her choice, even though it's not one I could ever make. Harriet's work no longer has much significance; she is worth remembering for her achievements in a man's world and for her personal commitment to winning through.

"I regard the American people," she wrote to a friend at the end of her tour, "as a great embryo poet, now moody, now wild, but bringing out results of absolute good sense: restless and wayward in action, but with deep peace at his heart, exulting that he has caught the true aspect of things past, and the depth of futurity which lies before him, wherein to create something so magnificent as the world has scarcely begun to dream of. There is the strongest hope of a nation that is capable of being possessed with an idea." "Futurity" notwithstanding, this is not all tosh. Frederick Jackson Turner quoted it admiringly in his influential book *The Frontier in American History*. The frontier, according to the Yankee Turner, forged the American character. Writing at the end of the nineteenth century, he argued that the existence of an area of free land, its continuous recession, and the advance of American settlement westward explained American development. The frontier formed the crest of the wave, the meeting point between savagery and civilization, and it was the line of most rapid and effective Americanization. Turner argued that decade after decade, West after West, the rebirth of American society had gone on, leaving its traces behind it like a glacier. The frontier was a metaphor for social progress for both Harriet and Turner. "In the crucible of the frontier," Turner wrote, "the immigrants were Americanized, liberated, and fused into a mixed race." In the atomic conditions of backwoods society, the individual had the upper hand. Turner was reprising Tocqueville's themes: the Frenchman had noted the elevated role of the individual in the elastic social conditions of the frontier. Both men said that America became more democratic as the frontier moved west because free lands promoted equality among settlers and acted as a check on the aristocratic influences of the East. Two generations before Turner, Fanny Trollope had made the point that expansion westward stimulated equality. She thought that was a bad thing, whereas both Turner and Harriet approved.

A year after returning to Fludyer Street, Harriet brought out her two-volume *Society in America*. Kicking off with two paragraphs on the impossibility of summing up a country, the author used up 500 pages defining the U.S. before concluding "it is too soon yet to theorise." Talk about cake and eating. She tried to establish whether the nation had achieved the goals of its Constitution. The resulting chunks of theory would send all but academic sociologists into a coma, and by the time she wrote her autobiography, even she agreed that *Society in America* is tedious. Her strength was in purveying common sense, not original thought: she did not have a truly speculative mind. In *Society*, she made what she saw confirm her pre-existing opinion, blinded by idealism and dogmatic to the point of absurdity. America ceased to be a real place once she sat at her desk and shut down that part of herself that had responded so profoundly to the Kentucky palisades. The country became a blueprint and the curtains came down before the second act got started. "Every factory child," she gushed, "carries its umbrella, and pig-drivers wear spectacles." She said she found in America less crime, poverty and "mutual injury of every kind that has ever been known in any society." She could not possibly have proved that nor can it have been true. Fanny Kemble knew America, and admired *Society*, but not uncritically—she wondered if a malfunction of the ear trumpet might be responsible for the misinformation. She considered Harriet gullible. "The details of her book are sometimes mistaken," she said, "but that was to be expected, especially as she was often subjected to the abominable impositions of persons who deceived her purposely."

The young Disraeli recognized Harriet's intellectual method when he reviewed her volumes in *The Times*. "There is something infinitely ludicrous in the vanity and presumption with which this lady squares the circle of American morals and discovers the longitude of impending civilisation of a new world," Dizzy barked. He was right. Harriet was more interested in proving her principles than learning about America. She believed in the potential of the individual and was convinced that the application of theory could achieve its fulfilment. America was a stage on this sunlit path from barbarism to enlightenment. "They have realised many things for which the rest of the civilised world is still struggling . . . they are, to all intents and purposes, self-governed," she wrote. "They have risen above all liability to a hereditary aristocracy, a connection between religion and state, a vicious or excessive taxation, and the irresponsibility of any class." But *Society in America* was not uncritical. Fanny Trollope had noticed with irritation that Americans, allowed to say whatever they liked, ended up all saying the same thing, and there was Harriet making the identical observation. The great American fault, she wrote, "is deficiency of moral independence." Nobody had a mind of his own, or, if he did, he was frightened to reveal it. "When Spurzheim was in

America," she said, "the great mass of society became phrenologists in a day." New Englanders were especially unwilling to break ranks, and "detestably so—the restraint imposed by the servitude to opinion makes for a misery and dullness without parallel." In addition, people drank too much. Intoxication was "as remarkable as licentiousness of other kinds ever was in Paris, or at [sic] Vienna." These were sins to which she could only aspire. She wrote at length about the moral bankruptcy of the South, suggesting that cricket might bring the national character up to British standard.

Her bitterest vituperation she reserved for men of the cloth, reprising Fanny Trollope's observations in Cincinnati and those of Fanny Kemble in Darien. "Seeing what I have seen," Harriet thundered, "I can come to no other conclusion than that the most guilty class of the community in regard to the slavery question at present is not the slaveholding, or even the mercantile, but the clerical: the most guilty, because not only are they not blinded by lifelong custom and prejudice, nor by any pecuniary interest, but they profess to spend their lives in the study of moral relations, and have pledged themselves to declare the whole counsel of God." She is a heroine in those passages.

After slavery, the position of women mattered most. "Is it to be understood that the principles of the Declaration of Independence bear no relation to half the human race?" she asked. "If not so, how is the restricted and dependent state of women to be reconciled with the proclamation that 'all are endowed by their Creator with certain inalienable rights; that among these are life, liberty and the pursuit of happiness'?" The lack of women in politics distressed her. At least Britain had Queen Victoria at the helm. "The principle of the equal rights of both halves of the human race is all we have to do with here," she wrote. "It is the true democratic principle which can never be seriously controverted, and only for a short time evaded." *Society in America* was a feminist call to arms. Harriet alone of my subjects supported a woman's right to vote. None of the others joined the nascent suffrage campaign, no matter how many Women's Studies departments try to shoehorn them in retrospectively. The transatlantic women's movement didn't take off until the second half of the century. But by the time Harriet was in her stride, demands for feminine education, marital and property rights and the franchise were voiced with increasing regularity, as were opinions expressing the opposite view. Harriet might in these pages be an exception in her commitment to the feminist cause. But all six women in *O My America!* expressed themselves in a man's world. The journey goes on. At the time of writing, women hold 16 percent of seats in Congress, the Senate and the House of Representatives, 12 percent of mayoral positions in large cities and the same 12 percent of governorships. A disappointing advance in 175 years.*

Harriet emerges from her book as a likeable and deeply impressive figure. Disraeli notwithstanding, Britons thought so

---

*Britain does a little better with 22 percent of MPs in the House of Commons. In 1979 it was 3 percent.

highly of *Society* that they installed its author as chief national expert on transatlantic affairs. Kemble said most Englishmen who read Harriet's book at least respected the author's character, integrity and courage. Americans, on the other hand, were furious. From Louisiana to Michigan, the national cry went up, *Not Again.* People sent Harriet letters weighted with stones so she had to pay postage. New England Unitarians regarded *Society in America* as a breach of hospitality. "They would," her erstwhile friend Mrs. Jameson reported, "have willingly roasted the author before a slow fire and eaten her up afterwards." The Unitarian saint of New England William Channing observed that *Society in America* was "in as bad odor as Mrs. T.'s book, perhaps worse." Five years after the book appeared, the young Dickens toured the U.S., reporting that people competed to hurl abuse on Harriet in his presence. "But what has she done?" he asked them. "Surely she praised America enough?" "Yes," they replied, "but she told us some of our faults, and Americans can't bear to be told of their faults, don't split on that rock, Mr. Dickens, don't write about America; we are so very suspicious." He did. According to one of his biographers, "It is Martineau with whom he seems to be most in dialogue in *American Notes.*" But he didn't like her—he talked of her "vomit of conceit"—and there is more than a touch of her in Mrs. Jellyby, the vaudevillian quasi-philanthropist in *Bleak House.**

It was impossible to stop writing. In 1838 she brought out *A Retrospect of Western Travel*, a conventional travelogue more digestible than *Society in America* despite extending to three volumes. So she got an impressive thousand pages out of her trip—a page for

---

* Dickens was so famous in America that when he had his hair cut in New York the barber sold strands of his discarded locks. But when Dickens raised the issue of royalties (transatlantic copyright legislation was not yet in place), press and public turned against him. U.S. readers perceived *American Notes* as hostile; the temperature rose; Dickens sharpened the point in *Martin Chuzzlewit*, a book which reveals America to be a land of savages and con men. On his second tour, in 1866, both sides stepped down and mutual admiration broke out all around.

every ten miles. Harriet's pen portraits of American political satraps in *Retrospect* are among the most entertaining pieces she ever wrote. Vice President John C. Calhoun appears as "the cast-iron man, who looks as if he had never been born and never could be extinguished." She raced on to produce another triple-decker, a domestic novel called *Deerbrook*. The protagonist, an unmarried governess, had something of Harriet in her. "There are glimpses of heaven for me in solitude," she says to a confidante, "as for you in love." Meanwhile, the author was still at the heart of things in London. The actor William Macready, who played opposite Fanny Kemble, got a box for her at Covent Garden whenever she wanted and practically everyone came to dinner. Sir Charles Lyell, the revolutionary geologist who had started a craze for rocks, was a frequent caller between his own visits to America examining carboniferous swamps. But many had reservations about Harriet, or at least enjoyed mocking her. Someone called her "a sour apple crushed with a hobnail shoe." In the letter to his grandmother mentioned earlier, Darwin recalled an encounter with Harriet after an agreeable visit to the zoo. "So much for Monkey, & now for Miss Martineau, who has been as frisky lately [as] the Rhinoceros . . . She is a wonderful woman: when Lyell called he found Rogers [Samuel, the poet], Ld Jeffrys [Lord Francis Jeffrey, judge, literary critic and fan of America] & Empson calling on her;—what a person she is thus to collect together all the geniuses." Rogers said that Miss Martineau had a charming laugh, and that it was like listening to a child being tickled in a cradle. Darwin's brother was close to her. "Erasmus has been with her noon, morning & night," gossiped Charles. "If her character was not as secure as a mountain in the polar regions she would certainly lose it." Other men courted her, but she viewed the whole business as "an occasional annoyance, presently disposed of. Every literary woman, no doubt, has plenty of importunity of that sort to deal with." Well, yes; but some of us like it, in small doses, and from the right quarters. For the majority of men, however, the logorrhea grew tiring. A friend called on the writer Sydney Smith and asked what sort of night he had had. "Oh, horrid, horrid, my dear fellow!" said Smith. "I dreamt I was chained to a rock and being talked to death by Harriet Martineau and Macaulay."*

In her journal, Harriet rebuked herself for not doing enough thinking. You can see her trying to obliterate herself in work. But that usually reliable sanctuary from fear failed her in 1839, when she collapsed at the age of thirty-seven. She had a mysterious variety of symptoms from backache to depression, fatigue and a prolapsed uterus. For five years she could work only intermittently, and when she was too frail to write she knitted blankets and sent them to the Boston anti-slavery bazaars. Her health remained an obsession for the rest of her life, and she did not spare her many correspondents, issuing daily bulletins on the state of her bowels and "the quality of the excretions." She carried on thinking, even if the publications slowed up. God, it turned out, was no longer important. Her higher power was the perfection of society. When she went public on the subject of her atheism, the writer Douglas Jerrold quipped, "There is no God, and Harriet Martineau is His prophet."

In 1844 an acquaintance suggested that mesmerism might help with her portfolio of illnesses. Mesmeric mania had taken hold in England just as phrenology had gripped America, and Harriet, despite her barbs about American gullibility, was as susceptible as everyone else. Animal magnetism was a supposed magnetic fluid present in human beings, and mesmerists reckoned they could manipulate it by what was, essentially, an early form of hypnosis. When Anthony Trollope was ill, his mother had engaged a mesmerist to treat him. Dickens himself learned to "mesmerize,"

---

*Smith's legacy lives on in the United States, as he composed a rhyming recipe for salad dressing that appeared in a popular cookbook. Millions of housewives knew the poem by heart. The rhymes are suspect—though an American accent helps: 'And lastly in the flavored compound toss / A magic spoonful of anchovy sauce.'

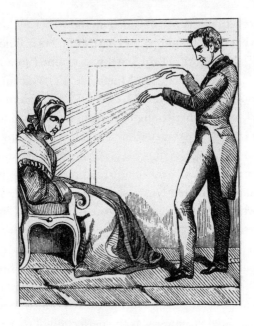

practicing enthusiastically on family and friends, and once he mesmerized his wife by accident, just by thinking about mesmerizing someone else while he was sitting next to her.

Mesmeric theory had a profound effect on Dickens' attitudes to scientific phenomena, as it convinced him of the powerful effects of the human mind—he grew increasingly convinced that all seemingly supernatural experiences could be accounted for by rational, scientific explanations. Victorians were keen on the supernatural (hence the crowds of ghosts in Dickens' novels) and mesmerism allowed them to square rational beliefs with apparently supernatural events, which is why one finds a rationalist like Harriet falling for hocus-pocus. (The respected medical journal *The Lancet* deduced at the time that her love affair with mesmerism had sexual implications.) But her health improved! When there was no professional available, she taught her maid to mesmerize her. As her recovery quickened, Harriet took up this new cause. It suited her wider agenda, as the medical establishment represented vested interests—the enemy. She set about attacking the conservative opinions of the profession and insisted that the miracles of the mesmerists were as great as those of Christ and the Apostles.

In renewed health, Harriet moved to Ambleside in the Lake District. Between the Grasmere and Windermere lakes Harriet built a gabled house of dark-grey Westmoreland stone. She called it The Knoll, and from the eglantine hedge at the bottom of her sloping garden she could look up at Wansfell, a mountain forming part of the long southern ridge of a wide moor.

It was a remote part of the country for a Norfolk lass to pick—but possibly the most heart-stopping when it came to scenery, so she did have an aesthetic sense after all. She soon became a familiar figure on the village scene, preaching at the tall Methodist chapel directly behind The Knoll and pouring her formidable energies into the civic problems of the tenant farmers and laborers she lived among. Other neighbours included the Wordsworths at Rydal Mount and the Arnolds at Fox How. (Harriet managed to get The Knoll built so quickly that Mary Wordsworth, the poet's wife, said she must have mesmerized the workmen.) William Wordsworth often came to call in the evening, tramping over rocky fells under moonlight, though when he took his false teeth out in Harriet's drawing room, as he liked to do, the ear trumpet couldn't cope with his mangled consonants, and the dialogue that ensued was that of the deaf. When posterity yielded up the various Wordsworth and Arnold journals, it turned out that neither family liked her, despite the frequent exchange of visits. Mary said she was "a pest," and on hearing of Harriet's death Matthew Arnold wrote, "What an unpleasant life and unpleasant nature." Charlotte Brontë visited The Knoll many times from her home in Yorkshire, often staying for a week, and the pair walked around Grasmere, looking down at the shining lake. *Jane Eyre* was so popular in America at the time that Southerners were naming their plantations "Rochester." "Miss Martineau I relish inexpressibly," wrote Brontë. "I believe she almost rules Ambleside. Some of the gentry dislike her, but the lower orders have a great regard for her." She didn't mind being mesmerized by her hostess, but Brontë found Harriet's secular moral stance hard to swallow. After reading a volume she had co-authored in support of secularism, Brontë wrote, "It is the first exposition of avowed Atheism and Materialism I have ever read. The strangest thing is that we are called on to rejoice over this hopeless blank." She had recently lost three siblings in under a year and badly needed to believe in an afterlife. Then Harriet wrote a cool review of *Villette* in the *Daily News* (there was, she said, apparently without irony, "not a touch of lightheartedness in it"), and the friendship ended. Harriet was slightly autistic in her inability to engage with the emotions of individuals. I wonder if she ever had any real friends, or wanted any. She found it easier to connect with strangers, like the passengers she met on the ship to America, than to sustain lasting friendships. When it came to intimacy, Harriet did have a series of close but not long-term relationships with younger women. Her best biographer, an academic historian, thought she was a lesbian. She once described herself as "the happiest single woman in England," perhaps an admission that something was missing. Elizabeth Barrett Browning said she was "the most manlike woman in the three kingdoms." But at the end of her life she said she was glad she had not married, claiming she had not been tempted since her fiancé died in the lunatic asylum. In all the decades since that broken engagement, she claimed, "My mind has been wholly free from all idea of love affairs." Harriet brought feminist perspectives for the first time on big topics—marriage, children, work—yet in her personal life she seemed to want to be sexless. There were no passions, small kindnesses or tears. One of her contemporaries, a well known but now forgotten novelist, said that "as a born lecturer and politician Martineau was less distinctively affected by her sex than perhaps any other, male or female, of her generation." There had to be more to it—some inner conflict. Perhaps it emerged in the maniacal work rate. Edith Wharton, another friend of the ubiquitous Henry James and a resident, like Kemble, of Lenox in the Berkshires, was as sexually frustrated as Harriet. In her case it seemed to come out in gender inversions in the work. She gave the heroine of *The House of Mirth*—her best-known book—a beard. (Wharton might be the first novelist to portray a recognizably modern America. She even wrote a book about celebrity.) There was something of the mineral about Harriet, as if ferocious activity enabled her to transcend her womanhood and even her humanity. What did childlessness mean to her? The reproductive wasteland that follows the menopause looks like a gloomy place as one approaches the frontier. How much more poignant that journey must seem to a childless woman.

At the menopause, childless or not, women face their own mortality, perhaps for the first time. Death was part of life in the nineteenth century, and my girls saw a good deal of it, whereas for us, today, if we are lucky, death is an alien thing. Many of my girlfriends are going through the change while burying their parents—not me, thank God—and they find themselves on the generational front line. I was beginning to see, on these American interludes, that perhaps my unnamed anxieties were not about motherhood at all. They were about moving forward, crossing that Rubicon. Friends talked about the changes they observed in their own lives all the time. Many noted attitudes shifting as they went about their business. "Invisible" was a word that cropped up a lot. My friend Miranda lived in her twenties in the area of South London called Battersea, close to the Thames. Renovation was always in progress in the handsome Victorian terraces there, and Miranda rarely reached her bus stop without a symphony of wolf whistles from the scaffolding. She was an ardent feminist like the rest of us then and fired off letters to the head offices of the construction companies complaining about this egregiously sexist behavior. Thirty years later, Miranda found herself again living in Battersea, this time in a whole house in a street parallel to the one in which she rented an apartment in her youth. To my eyes she was a wonderfully handsome woman with all the experience of a life well lived visible on her face. The next generation of construction workers, however, showed no interest, no matter how many times Miranda passed. "I'm going to write to the head office," she moaned to me, "complaining that the builders don't take any notice of me." I was waiting for this kind of invisibility to happen to me—waiting with a little too much trepidation.

———

Harriet's posthumous reputation emits the fumes of high Victorian self-mortification, and in this she resembles Florence Nightingale. The Lady of the Lamp was eighteen years younger than Harriet, and from a different social class. The two women shared the most extraordinary strength of spirit, a powerful sense of duty and a lifelong psychological restlessness, and both remained determined to avoid that menace of feminine achievement, a husband. They channeled intense passion into duty, rather than romance. It's quite a trick to pull off, and not altogether to be pitied. They did something noble, and were a bit ridiculous at the same time. Both exercised tremendous influence over the men officially in charge of England and the world: Nightingale issued orders on the administration of India just as Harriet advised on the deleterious effects of colonial monopolies. Both women maintained indefatigable vigilance and a superhuman work rate. After a fifteen-hour day addressing audiences, producing pamphlets and drawing up architectural plans for her house or somebody else's, Harriet would sit at her desk in a pool of smoky light and write a dozen tightly spaced letters, just as Nightingale had done at Scutari when darkness swallowed the long miles of beds. Sometimes, they wrote to one another. They shared a lively interest in sanitation and drains and could dilate endlessly on those topics as on many others. Work was everything, and in both cases internal strain emerged in neurasthenic illnesses: for months they never got out of bed (not the same bed), and for decades both expected death hourly.

Harriet turned fifty on June 12, 1852, though in spirit she had always been fifty. The age that was looming with such glowering intensity for me had not the slightest significance for her. Infertility, invisibility, that tiresome thickening of the waist—these were anxieties Harriet had banished. Instead of indulging in menopausal fretting, she wrote a guidebook to the lakes and fells around

The Knoll, and the volume quickly became a bestseller. Next, a glimpse of a man with a scythe in his hand stimulated several hundred pages on the necessity of improving the education of labourers. In her spare time she knocked off a volume on Norway. Harriet had never been to Scandinavia and saw no need to visit just because she had to fill 300 pages. She wrote for the shop-keeper, not the critic. "I am not afraid of censure from individuals or from the world," she said in a letter. "I must and will bear everything." And she did, laughing off a piece in the *Quarterly Review* calling her false, foul and unfeminine. She just got on with it, taking a cold bath at five every morning, drinking carrot tea for a neuralgic tic and smoking cigars for her general health. "From week to week," she wrote to Jane Carlyle, "I sit under the still lamp-light every evening alone; and my brain seems to grow young and strong in the peace and quiet." Evidently the cigars did not work, because in 1855 Harriet fell ill again. This time, nothing was said of mesmerism. She sat down and wrote her autobiography. For the next twenty-one years, she sensed death round the corner.* Her output during this period was prolific even by her standards. Swathed in bombazine and surrounded by pot plants, she wrote pamphlets entitled *Cow Keeping* and contributed articles on sanitation to Dickens' periodical *Household Words* and a series of papers on army hygiene to *Atlantic Monthly*. The *Daily News* engaged her as chief leader writer, and if the newsroom was short-staffed, Harriet wrote six pieces a week. The paper was the Liberal equivalent of the Establishment *Times* and the ideal forum for Harriet, who

---

*Having written the autobiography in a week in 1855, she had it typeset, proofread and printed on to sheets, which she instructed London publisher Smith, Elder to bind and issue on her death. The sheets lay in storage for twenty-two years before appearing between hard covers. In the book she talks of childhood fears of inadequacy, and of a rage against injustice. Victoria Glendinning once called it "one of the best autobiographies of all time," though she didn't say why. I can't say I agree. The book is a useful historical document, but to glean anything from Harriet's story one has to read between the lines.

sat at her defenseless Underwood typewriter to give the royal family a talking to, hammer away at Napoleon III or go full tilt on Ireland. She never missed an opportunity to reveal that Canadians sent her to sleep: "So *very* mediocre,—neither heroic, nor clever, nor gay, nor accomplished,—nor any thing but intensely commonplace." On the other hand she warmly supported the Association for the Prevention of Steam Boiler Explosions. She covered unsettled conditions in the Isthmus of Panama and at least once a week told people how to improve themselves (this included learning to swim). Naturally she fell on deteriorating relations between Confederates and Unionists with gusto, and rejoiced when the Civil War finally broke out, as she felt it was the beginning of the "renewal of the soul of the genuine nation." When The Ladies' London Emancipation Society distributed excerpts from *Journal* Harriet fought shoulder to shoulder with Fanny Kemble after all those years—and what a delicious irony that it was the "intellectually lightweight" Kemble who had more influence on public opinion. In addition to all of the above, Harriet wrote voluminous letters gossiping about the collapse of the Dickenses' marriage ("He is *awful* at home now—restless, despotic and miserable"). She carried on campaigning till the end, petitioning against a bill proposing the extension of flogging and, when she was in too much pain to leave the house, sending postal orders to an Edinburgh society providing medical education to women. When in the warm spring days of 1876 she knew the end really was near, she wrote her own obituary, staggered to the pillar box and sent it to the *Daily News*. She had never lost hope. A new dawn would come; though it might take a bit longer than she once thought.

4

IS THIS AMERICA?

Rebecca Burlend Goes to Illinois

A little boat was lowered into the water and we were invited to collect our luggage and descend into it, as we were at Phillip's Ferry; we were utterly confounded: there was no appearance of a landing place, no luggage yard, nor even a building of any kind within sight; we, however, attended to our directions, and in a few minutes saw ourselves standing by the brink of the river, bordered by a dark wood, with no one near to notice us or tell us where we might procure accommodation or find harbour . . . It was in the middle of November, and already very frosty. My husband and I looked at each other till we burst into tears, and our children observing our disquietude began to cry bitterly. Is this America, thought I?

This sounds more like an American nightmare than a dream. But most Englishwomen in nineteenth-century America were homesteaders, and many of them cried on some lonely riverbank. Their voices are rarely heard, as they were too busy cutting corn with blunt sickles and delivering their own babies. The God-fearing Rebecca Burlend had never strayed more than ten miles from her Yorkshire village when she left England with a husband, five children and one hundred pounds in cash, bound for a lonely bit of sod in western Illinois. The family were desperate tenant farmers, undone by the falling price of corn. It was the winter of 1831 and the Burlends were among the first to break the soil of the Old Northwest. Although the yeoman farmer was central to the Jeffersonian ideal, the Homestead Acts were still a long way off when Rebecca brought in the harvest while breast milk leaked through her calico dress. There was nothing but land on the plains: not a country at all, but the material out of which countries are made. The myths of the West had yet to be forged, and in Illinois, Chicago was not incorporated. Rebecca was not quite a writer—she was a storyteller, and in middle age dictated a memoir to her eldest son, a gripping account of the hardship, grind and disappointments of literally breaking new ground. The book is a masterpiece of oral literature, a Homeric Black Earth saga, and Rebecca's story reveals a very different America from those glittering East Coast citadels already described. Before I found her memoir—quite by chance, while I was researching something else in the British Library Rare Books Room—I had been looking for a homesteader to include in this volume as I knew what a significant role that disparate tribe played in the formation of the nation. But I never dreamed I would find a character as memorable as Rebecca Burlend. She inspired me more than any of the other women, mainly because she proved what I already knew: that hard work is 90 percent of the battle.

Rebecca was born into a poor family near the Yorkshire town of Wakefield in 1793, six years before Fanny Trollope and sixteen years before Fanny Kemble. Unlike those two, she received little education, although she did learn to read, write and sew. She was strong, and had nimble long fingers. As a young woman she married a good, hard-working man and in 1817, when the price of corn was high, the Burlends took a fourteen-year tenancy on a farm in Barwick-in-Elmet, near Leeds. They were thrifty and trusted in God: they were members of the Wesleyan Methodist Society. By the time the lease ran out on the farm, John and Rebecca had seven children. The rent went up, the price of corn went down, and even with grind and stringent economies, it was impossible to make ends meet. "The gradual diminution of our little property," she said, "and the entire absence of any prospects of being able to supply the wants of a large family, had tended effectually to fix my husband's purpose of trying what could be done in the western world." John heard talk of the Barwick man George Bickerdike, who had emigrated to what was then known as the American Northwest. Propelled by a powerful sense of destiny, John walked to the house of the man's brother to read letters extolling the lush and fertile Illinois River Valley. England was in chaos on account of the Reform Bill, a piece of legislation that many feared would shatter the social order, and as a result parliament had recently been dissolved. In addition, agriculture was in the doldrums. John wrote to Bickerdike at his cabin in Illinois. The mail took many weeks. It was possible, came the eventual reply from the pioneer, for a diligent farmer to make the land pay; Illinois soil was "flowing with milk and honey." Bickerdike offered to host the Burlends until they acquired a cabin of their own. He sent travel instructions. John made up his mind. The eldest of the children, Edward, was already an under-teacher at a boarding school, so he was to remain in England, as was the next oldest, Mary, who was in service. The other five, ranging in age from nine months to nine years, were to accompany their parents to the New World. As for Rebecca: "I gave up the idea of ending my days in my own country with the utmost reluctance," she said, "and should never have become an emigrant, if obedience to my husband's wishes had left me any alternative." That was a hard thing for me to read. It made her seem as if she were dwelling in a foreign land even before she emigrated.

Having sold their sticks of furniture to raise cash for their passage on the sailing ship *Home*, in the last week of August 1831 the Burlends arrived at Liverpool docks. Many years later, Rebecca still remembered the loneliness that descended as she walked up the gangplank and looked out over the brick warehouses gleaming in the summer sun. Liverpool had grown fat from the slave trade, and as the *Home* weighed anchor, Rebecca noted "the immense forests of ships, which on every hand strike the eye of the beholder as he sails out of the harbour. Whatever might have been my ideas of the greatness and wealth of England before, I am sure they were enlarged when I beheld for the first time in my life those unwieldy instruments of commerce . . . I felt as if I was leaving all I had been wont to prize; and when I could no longer see the shore, I shall never forget how enviously I looked upon the vessels that were approaching the shores I was leaving." The U.S. was still a closed book even to educated Britons. The week Rebecca left, *The Times* reported the news that "in North America pauperism is almost unknown."

For more than two months Rebecca cooked for seven over a shared fire in the unventilated steerage, rationing a supply of oatmeal, flour, bacon, biscuits, tea and coffee. The company was rough, but, during one apocalyptic storm, Rebecca recalled, "You might have seen those, who yesterday could not conclude a sentence without the usual flourish of an oath, now on their knees serious enough." More than fifteen years later, she said, "I shall never forget the horrors of that night." Robert Louis Stevenson joined the poor of Europe in the search for a new life in a promised land. "At breakfast," he wrote of the sea voyage in his best book, *The Amateur Emigrant*, "we had a choice between tea and coffee for beverage, a choice not easy to make, as the two were so surprisingly alike." And he traveled in second class, not steerage. His companions were not young, strong, hopeful men straining at the leash. "We were a company of the rejected; the drunken, the incompetent, the weak, the prodigal, all who had been unable to prevail against circumstances in the one land, were now fleeing pitifully to another; and although one or two might still succeed, all had already failed." Stevenson delivers not the myth, but the reality. But he writes fondly of the voyage, and of his companions, "all now belonging to one small iron country on the deep." He generally slept on deck, finding it preferable to the stuffy cabin. Listening to the clear note of the clapper on brass and the seaman's cry, "All's well!," he wrote, "I know nothing, whether for poetry or music, that can surpass the effect of these two syllables in the darkness of a night at sea."

The Burlends sailed to New Orleans rather than an East Coast port, in order to facilitate travel up the Mississippi to Illinois. When the *Home* approached the misty shore after breasting the Gulf of Mexico, a sailor suspended a lantern on the mast, as a signal for a pilot to come on board. "The captain and cabin passengers had been very kind to us during the voyage," Rebecca said, "and on going away my children were severally presented with small tokens of approbation, of which they were not a little proud." As for New Orleans: "Its appearance was really brilliant, and gave me more exalted ideas of the country to which we were hastening." They landed on a Sunday, but shops and stalls were open, "and streets thronged with lookers-on more in the manner of a fair than a Christian Sabbath country . . . I could scarcely believe it was the Lord's day. I remembered that frequently on our passage I had heard it remarked that the time varied with the time in England a few hours, and for a moment I supposed that the Sabbath varied also."

Now for the 680-mile, twelve-day voyage from New Orleans to St. Louis. On the steamer, John and Rebecca quizzed passengers about Illinois as the Mississippi sugarlands floated past. "Our unsettled condition was ever the uppermost in our thoughts," Rebecca recalled, "and shed a settled gravity over our conduct." This vessel turned out to be less friendly than the last one, and rather than offering the children gifts, a crewman tried to rob John as he slept, foreshadowing acts of random cruelty to follow in Illinois. At St. Louis the seven boarded another steamer for the final 120-

mile leg to Pike County, where Bickerdike had instructed them to disembark at Phillip's Ferry, a landing two miles from his cabin. "Our enquiries of the sailors, 'How much further to go?' almost exhausted their patience," Rebecca said. Twenty-four hours out of St. Louis, as night fell, the packet stopped. They climbed down on to the cold black earth, and that was when they burst into tears.

While Rebecca knelt and prayed, John set off to find Bickerdike, or to find someone. On the edge of the forest, he spotted a curl of smoke above the ash trees, and followed it to a log cabin that turned out to belong to a Mrs. Phillips, a pipe-smoking homesteader after whose husband the landing had been named.* She agreed to take the family as paying guests until they found Bickerdike. During the three days Rebecca spent in the windowless home, Mrs. Phillips taught her the etiquette of the Illinois backwoods. Language, apparently, was the only link between England and America, and even that link was fragile. "No person, however slender his pretensions to knighthood," Rebecca reported with surprise, "or how long so ever the time since his small-clothes were new, is addressed without the courteous epithet of 'Sir'; and this practice is observed by the members of the same family in their intercourse." This was an agreeable revelation—the only agreeable one that would appear on Rebecca's horizon for some time.

After three days, the Burlends followed the swell of the prairie over two miles of frozen country and moved in with Bickerdike. The homesteads of western Illinois were far apart, and the Yorkshireman's cabin stood gaunt against an Arctic blue dome. Winter comes down savagely on the prairies in any year but the region was experiencing a period of exceptional cold: snow that deadened. Rivers seized up and wind hurtled across hundreds of miles of open country. On the first night at Bickerdike's, Rebecca got so

*The landing was originally the site of a canoe operation known as Van Deusen's Ferry. The owner rowed passengers across the river, and swam horses. The site lies at the present location of Valley City, Illinois, once a prosperous settlement, now flooded and as empty as it was when the Burlends arrived.

chilled that John had to iron the soles of her feet (he heated a flat iron, wrapped it in flannel, and applied it to the afflicted zones). The thirty-seven-year-old Bickerdike was a bachelor who had been obliged to leave England in a hurry—a proper remittance man. As for the milk and honey he had described, Rebecca noted, "his appearance would have led any one to suppose that he gathered his honey rather from thorns than flowers. He was verily as ragged as a sheep, and his house like the cell of a hermit." Still, the Burlends were to remain friends with Bickerdike until his early death. He rescued them from several scrapes and in the end was the architect of the whole project: hundreds of Burlends prospering in twenty-first-century Illinois are his legacy.

The first settlers to west-central Illinois found heavily forested land with prairie running like fingers between the creeks, its surface lush with waist-high grasses. In 1831, only tiny patches had been cleared. Illinois had been a state for thirteen years and in the capital, Vandalia in Fayette County, the state treasurer still worked from home. (It was in Vandalia three years after the Burlends landed that an aspiring politician made his first stump speech in a suit bought with borrowed money. He was Abraham Lincoln.) Although it was not a slave state like the contiguous Missouri, slaves worked the southern part of Illinois, a zone known as a result as "Egypt." But the indigenous peoples had gone. During the Burlends' first twelve months, following the Black Hawk War, government militia drove the Sauk and Foxes from Illinois and the Winnebago ceded all their territory southeast of the Wisconsin and Fox rivers. In 1833, at a grand council of chiefs in Chicago, the Potawatomi, Ottawa and Chippewa also relinquished their holdings and, in the month they called "the time of the moon when the deer paw the ground," prepared to cross the Mississippi and put up skin tents on the reservations. That secular saint Lincoln hanged thirty-nine Sioux who had led a violent revolt against federal regulations that starved their nation.

Pike County was originally enormous, stretching up from its present position on the Missouri border as far northeast as Chicago. An 1822 gazetteer mentions Chicago as "a village of Pike county, containing twelve or fifteen houses and about sixty or seventy inhabitants." A decade on, the county had shrunk to a slice of unconquered prairie and forest between the Illinois River and the Mississippi. On the western side it abutted Missouri inches from the township of Florida, where Mark Twain was born while the Burlends were clearing their land. Pike had not yet fully entered the cash economy. Its remote and scattered stores accepted produce in exchange for seed, clothing, agricultural tools, coffee and medicines. On December 1, 1831, the Burlends took mortgaged possession of an eighty-acre farm that included a spring, a log cabin and 400 maple trees. The boundaries were marked out by stones set at each corner. The family had no furniture except two large boxes, two beds, and a few pots and cooking utensils, and their food had run out. On the second day, John walked several miles across the frozen sod to the nearest store and purchased a bushel of ground Indian corn, and on the return journey he procured milk lumpy with ice from a neighbour half a mile away. The first meal Rebecca cooked in the cabin consisted of paste baked in a frying pan on hot ashes. John spent most of his time cutting wood for fuel. Eking out their remaining dollars as winter deepened, they bought a cow and calf, a young mare, two pigs, and an iron pan. With five dollars remaining in the coffer, all seven members of the family broke out in livid, itchy spots. It was an affliction, common to newly arrived settlers, called the Illinois mange. The Burlends had to spend their reserves on medicinal sulphur. John came back from the store carrying it under his coat, white as a snowman.

Rebecca made candles from lard and rags, and soap, as Mrs. Phillips had taught her, from ash and pigs' entrails. She doctored the children with plants and herbs. However hard it was, she could still appreciate the beauty of the land. "The nights in winter are at once inexpressibly cold," she said, "and poetically fine. The sky is almost invariably clear, and the stars shine with a brilliancy entirely unknown in the humid atmosphere of England. Cold as it was, often did I, during the first winter, stand at the door of our cabin, admiring their lustre and listening to the wolves, whose howlings, among the leafless woods at this season, are almost unceasing." The natural world was a healing presence, even without its medicinal herbs. Meanwhile, every two weeks, John returned to the store. Blue smoke puffed from a stovepipe that stuck up out of the snow on the roof and blanketed horses looked out through frozen lashes. The store was the only meeting place for miles around, and during the winter its fug of pipe smoke, damp woollens and kerosene gave homesteaders the opportunity to talk over their unequal fight with the land. While women checked groceries and pinned shawls about their heads, men drank raw alcohol tinctured with oil of cinnamon and discussed the weed called "cheat" that spoiled the corn. The days faded before four, and the streaks of watery light glimmering in the leaden sky vanished before John reached the cabin. He sometimes caught quails and rabbits for the pot. Once he even got a turkey, and according to his wife, "brought home his game with as much apparent consciousness of triumph, as if he had slain some champion hydra of the forest." The following day, they invited Bickerdike to lunch.

We accordingly dressed our bird, and congratulated ourselves with the idea of having our countryman to dine with us on a fine boiled turkey. Sunday morning arrived, and in due time our turkey was in the pot boiling for dinner. Mr. B came; we told him how happy we were on account of the treat we were going to give him. He was surprised at our story, as those birds are difficult to obtain with a common fowling-piece, and desired to see the feet and head. But the moment he saw them, he exclaimed, 'It's a buzzard,' a bird which, we subsequently learnt, gourmandizes any kind of filth or carrion; and consequently is not fit to be eaten.

They were shackled to the seasons. In mid-March, they had to sow corn. As they didn't have a plough, the Burlends and their nine-year-old son, the eldest one, set to work with hoes. They toiled solidly for three weeks, until the spring showers. At least there was rain. If Rebecca had got off the steamer on one of the rivers in eastern Colorado like many settlers, her first two years would have been much worse, and they were bad enough as it was. When the Illinois torrents died to a soft, dripping rain, sky and land turned a dark smoke color and came together like two waves. The next week, the prairies shone with bloodroot and ginger. With the corn sown, John worked ten hours a day with his grubbing hoe and axe, tearing up underwood roots and chopping down some of the largest trees. Rebecca and the boy helped, and by the end of May they had cleared three or four acres and made a zigzag fence halfway round a new field. In June, they had to purchase meal on credit, a practice they had tried to avoid. The previous owner of the land, a squatter, had broken up twelve acres and sown three with wheat, which was now ripe, so, at the end of the month the Burlends walked to Bickerdike's to borrow sickles to harvest the crop. On the journey home, John stumbled and fell on to a sickle blade. The wound went septic. As the leg swelled, John grew delirious. Days and nights passed. "I could not but perceive," Rebecca remembered, "I was likely to lose my dearest earthly friend, and with him all visible means of supporting myself, or maintaining my family . . . Despair began to lay hold of me with his iron sinews; I longed to exchange situations with my husband; there was no one near to assist or encourage me. My eldest child alone manifested any signs of sympathy: the poor boy went up to his father's bed, and with affectionate and child-like simplicity said, 'Don't die, father, don't die.'"

If it were not cut soon, the crop would be lost. So she had to do it, leaving the younger children to attend to their father and the unweaned baby. The fields smelled of wheat and clover and the temperature rose above 95 degrees. The chaff went down her neck and stuck to her skin. She tried working at night, but even then it was close and hot, and heat lightning played softly on the horizon, the distant booms metallic like the rattle of sheet iron. Thunderheads checkered half the sky and the lightning made the west look like deep blue water with the sheen of moonlight on it. But she had to do it—she had to be the ox. In little more than a week, she had the wheat cut. Then she had to gather it in, otherwise it would dry out and be spoiled. Having neither horses nor wagon, she arranged two thin ash trunks on which she piled the wheat at one end, prevailing upon her son to carry the lighter end. Thus she stacked the wheat crop. As they had no winnowing machine, she had to winnow with the wind. They got fifty bushels in the end, and John, restored to health, borrowed a wagon and a yoke of oxen to transport it to the store. There he settled the meal account and paid ten bushels of wheat for two pairs of adult shoes. With the rest he bought a plough, two tin milk bowls, a few pounds of coffee and a little meal, reserving the rest for seed. Meanwhile Rebecca bartered a china teacup for hens. Asked if after six months she thought emigrating had been the right thing to do, she said no. She regretted it very much. "We had indeed some good land, but it was nearly all uncultivated, and we had nothing to sell except our cattle, which we wanted. The only ground of hope we had was in our industry and perseverance. My husband worked very hard; the little time we had to spare, after feeding the cattle and procuring fuel, was spent in splitting trees to make rails."

The Plains cast spells, and I think of all American novelists, Midwesterners remain most faithful to the landscape that raised them. Willa Cather conjures the scent of Rebecca's black earth: in her books, the landscape itself is the leading character. "The great fact was the land itself," Cather writes in *O Pioneers!*, "which seemed to overwhelm the little beginnings of human society that struggled in its somber wastes." Cather makes a vanished Nebraska live again. In *My Ántonia*, her most accomplished book, the narrator, having moved east from the plains, talks to a childhood friend of "burning summers when the world lies green and billowy beneath a brilliant sky when one is fairly stifled in vegetation, in the color and smell of strong weeds and heavy harvests; blustery winters with little snow, when the whole country is stripped bare and grey as sheet-iron. We agreed that no one who had not grown up in a little prairie town could know anything about it. It was a kind of freemasonry." It's a novel that slips the shackles of its period and enters the immortal zone. At the time, critics accused Cather of nostalgia and a refusal to engage in the present. But nostalgia is fond recognition of the past, and history has been kinder to Cather, respecting her role in the charting of the American journey, at least in a small part of the Plains states. "We come and go," she wrote in *O Pioneers!*, "but the land is always here. And the people who love it and understand it are the people who own it for a little while." She was a romantic who wore masculine clothes and periodically called herself William. "It does not matter much whom we live with in this world," she wrote, "but it matters a great deal whom we dream of."

In October the pioneers sowed wheat. Although the Burlends now owned a plow, they had no team. The matter caused considerable anxiety, and was turned over endlessly in the candlelit evenings. The problem was solved at the store, when another farmer, spotting John's wristwatch, offered to plough and harrow the whole eight acres in exchange for the item. Soon afterwards, the Burlends were able to buy three young pigs. In addition, the potato seeds they had planted under the interlacing shadows of a honeysuckle produced more than they could eat and the sugar orchard delivered a lucrative crop. The maples were Rebecca's responsibility. When the trees were ready for tapping, she pierced holes in the trunks and inserted tubes made from what was called in Illinois the shoemaker's tree. Sap drained through the tubes into wooden troughs, then was ladled into borrowed copper kettles and boiled down to a liquor the consistency of thin treacle. After straining the liquor through a coarse woolen cloth, she boiled it again until it hardened. In this way she obtained three hundredweight of sugar and a barrel of maple syrup. But they badly needed two steers and a milk cow. Cash had begun to work its way into the local economy and farmers increasingly asked for money rather than goods. When a moneylender appeared at the cabin door offering thirty dollars at 25 percent, the unworldly couple agreed to the deal without a repayment schedule. Before fall was out, the lender returned, demanding his money: the Burlends had been counting on the spring harvest to generate income to pay off the debt. The next day a legal representative, a wizened, sinister figure officially called an Esquire, rode out from Quincy and served the Burlends with a writ. As Frederick Jackson Turner had written in his Frontier Thesis, "in the atomic conditions of backwoods society, the individual had the upper hand." After all they had gone through, they faced the seizure of their property. "Remorse the most pungent preyed on our heart-strings," Rebecca said later. "The emaciated appearance of our cattle condemned our cupidity." It was almost the end. At the eleventh hour, Bickerdike paid the debt, and so another crisis was averted.

November 1832 marked the first anniversary of their arrival. The year had unspooled in a series of small battles to grow corn for the animals, harvest wheat for the bipeds and fight off a lively cast of rogues roaming the backwoods. One interloper had insisted on keeping his horses in the Burlends' cornfield, and when John asked him to remove the beasts, he got a punch in the face. Had John not immediately withdrawn, the man later boasted that he would have stabbed him with a dirk he kept in his pocket. Now the family again faced winter, with even less warm clothing than they had in the previous one, as most of their garments had worn out over the course of that hard first year. The day fell on a Sunday, but they could not walk to a worship meeting to give thanks as they were in rags. "This was one of the gloomy days in our history," Rebecca recalled, though she acknowledged that, "in all respects except clothing, however, we were better situated than we had been the foregoing season. We had four acres more of wheat sown this year than the year before; we were now in possession of a plough; our cattle had likewise increased in value; the cow had calved again, and the former calf had grown a fine-looking heifer. We therefore saw, after all, we were gaining ground."

As the second year wore on, the Burlends continued to gain ground, but it was slow progress, and the weather was often unkind to their plans. ("On the farm," wrote Cather, "the weather was the great fact, and men's affairs went on underneath it.") When the second corn crop was ripe, John had to work elsewhere to pay a debt, so Rebecca again was obliged to haul herself up and down like an ox. This time, she was seven months pregnant. The heat was stupendous. Once, when she took a break, "a large full-grown rattlesnake crawled idly out of the sheaf on which I was sitting; I seized my rake and struck it on the head several times, whereby it soon died . . . The sudden start made me so feeble for a while that I could not proceed with my labour. I however took care not to rest on a sheaf: shortly after, as we expected, we saw another snake, apparently in search of its mate, which I destroyed in like manner; when they were dead, my children took them home as trophies of triumph . . ." In September she gave birth to twins. She did not know she was having two until the crown of a second head appeared. She was forty, and had delivered nine children.

By the time two years were up, the Burlends could enjoy what they called "a moderately comfortable existence." The cattle had done well and they had wheat and heifers to spare. They had established themselves within a fragmented community of uprooted people. Almost everyone had come to Illinois with little knowledge of the land, and almost all had borrowed money against their meager claim. Pike County remained isolated, and the settlers relied on one another. Knowledge of Rebecca's skill with medicinal herbs had spread, and she was summoned by wagon whenever a settler fell sick. The election of Martin Van Buren to the White House in 1836 barely registered on the prairie, and nor did the financial panic that swept the East Coast the following year after the banks funded rampant speculation—though elsewhere Illinois was establishing a firmer foothold. In 1839 State Representative Abraham Lincoln succeeded in his fight to get the capital moved to Springfield. For the Burlends, although the very worst was over, the next shyster was waiting in the wings. When land contiguous to their own came on to the market, after much hesitation they decided to buy it. Disaster intervened when a villain illegally claimed possession of the cabin on the new land and forcibly moved his family in while Rebecca and the twins were in residence. "It was most uncomfortable," she recalled with characteristic understatement, "for me to be thus left with only two little children under the same roof with a family whose sentiments towards me were the most unfriendly imaginable, and whose character stood assuredly not very high for probity." A prolonged legal battle ensued before the problem was resolved in the Burlends' favor at the Quincy courthouse.

Rebecca remained devout, despite the absence of formal worship, and she read the Bible every Sunday. She once visited a Methodist group that met in a cabin two miles away. After a circuit rider had opened proceedings, she reported, "A sort of circle or ring was then immediately formed, by the whole assembly taking hold of hands, and capering about the house surprisingly . . . This done, worship commenced with extempore prayer . . . All the persons present being again seated, an individual started from his seat, exclaiming in a loud and frantic shriek 'I feel it,' meaning what is commonly termed among them the power of God. His motions, which appeared half convulsive, were observed with animated joy by the rest till he fell apparently stiff upon the floor." The performance frightened her off, but like a good Christian she did not judge. "I have no right to question the sincerity of the individual," she said, "and if his taste differed from mine it was no proof that his was wrong." She subsequently discovered—like my other subjects—that "some of the most rapturous members were far from being exemplary in their conduct." In 1843, more orthodox Methodist pioneers built a church, Bethel: a shingled chapel with wooden slab benches. On Sundays she walked there across the Illinois River Valley carrying her shoes and stockings.

Unlike all the other women in this book, including me, Rebecca hadn't the slightest wanderlust. Nor was she a reader. I wondered what it would be like to satisfy one's inner needs without recourse to those two reliable sanctuaries.

After fifteen years, the Burlends had accumulated 360 acres, more than half of it cultivated. When July came round with its breathless heat Rebecca said she could hear the corn growing in the night, and there was so much motion in the prairie that the whole country seemed to be running. They had become landlords, renting out two small farms on their land for a dollar an acre. The children grew strong, with fresh faces, sandy hair and blue eyes. Twenty head of horned cattle, seven horses and large numbers of pigs, sheep and poultry lived in pastures and enclosures, and in the cabin pots of geraniums stood in deep sills behind a stove with nickel trimmings. "There are after all few cottagers in England that would not be on an equality with us," Rebecca said, "with this exception, theirs are generally rented, while ours is our own freehold." Many more homesteaders had arrived to turn the black earth. "We have seen a neighbourhood rise around us," Rebecca said, "and in some situations, where at our first coming, everything appeared in its native wildness, small villages have now begun to rise." As Frederick Jackson Turner wrote, "In the crucible of the frontier, the immigrants were Americanized, liberated, and fused into a mixed race."

Despite the rogues, Rebecca had continued to find most Americans uncommonly courteous, just as Mrs. Phillips had explained on the bleak day of the Burlends' arrival. Her experience was close to my own. On the whole Americans are a friendly, polite lot, lacking that northern European reserve that edges so easily into *froideur*. I remember, on my first ever visit, fetching up as a nineteen-year-old at the University of Alabama when the students were engaged in the frenzied ritual of Rush Week. Everyone raced wildly between sororities and fraternities named after Greek letters as if a great deal depended on the outcome. The whole performance was as exotic as the moon, but I was endlessly touched by the students' warm hospitality and their determination to include me in what was apparently such an important rite of passage.

In the spring of 1846, Rebecca went home to England for the summer, arriving just in time to see the reforming Whig Lord John Russell enter Downing Street as prime minister. Her daughter Mary had married, and introduced the fifty-three-year-old Rebecca to two grandchildren. Edward was prospering as a schoolmaster, and while they sat in front of his fire she told him the story of the first years in Pike County. Edward went on to transform his mother's words into a sixty-two-page pamphlet published anonymously under the title *A True Picture of Emigration: or Fourteen Years in the Interior of North America; Being a Full and Impartial Account of the Various Difficulties and Ultimate Success of an English Family Who Emigrated from Barwick-in-Elmet, Near Leeds, in the Year 1831.* Rebecca's clear, plain-speaking voice sings out of the pages, even though Edward, a part-time poet, spiced up the text with extracts from Milton and other writers unknown to Rebecca. The pamphlet was designed to be a guide for settlers, though I don't know who would contemplate emigration having read it.

Rebecca returned to Pike County accompanied by Mary and her family and spent the next twenty-five years sitting in a rocking chair tugging on a pipe. God knows she deserved the rest. John died aged eighty-eight in 1871. They both lived long enough to see their likenesses in a photograph. She buried him in the Bethel cemetery, and joined him there a year later.*

*I found many Burlends prospering close to the site of the first cabin—the picture depicts Butch Burlend in the grounds of Bethel chapel, showing me the graves of Rebecca and John: his great-great-great-grandparents. Pike remains an agricultural county, and the corn Rebecca harvested by hand covers many thousands of acres.

5

ABOVE LOVE AND HATE

Isabella Bird Goes to Colorado

Isabella Bird was a Victorian lady traveler, one of that tribe of battleaxes who sailed through malarial swamps, parasol aloft, or scaled unnamed Pamirs trailed by a retinue of exhausted factotums. History has written them off as mad eccentrics. (The titles of their books don't help: one thinks of Kate Marsden's *On Sledge and Horseback to Outcast Siberian Lepers*.) At the time, the Establishment declined to take them seriously. When the Royal Geographical Society honoured Isabella as its first female Fellow, *Punch* magazine spoke up for the nation:

> *A lady an explorer? A traveller in skirts?*
> *The notion's just a trifle too seraphic:*
> *Let them stay and mind the babies, or hem our ragged shirts;*
> *But they mustn't, can't and shan't be geographic.*

Tongue-in-cheek? More head up arse.

At home in Scotland, Isabella was an invalid, often too frail to hold her head up without a steel support. Yet in Colorado, already middle-aged, she talked about the "up-to-anything free-legged air," signed letters to her sister "your frugiferous bat," and fell in love with Rocky Mountain Jim, a one-eyed desperado with a whiskey habit. Dossing down with dudes, tenderfeet and cowboys at 7,500 feet, "where the boar frost crisps the grass every night of the year," Isabella wrote, "I have found far more than I ever dared to hope for." It was the freedom to be truly herself. Jan Morris once referred to Isabella as "that indomitable original" (it took one to know one). Like me, and unlike my other girls, she was a professional traveler, boarding a ship to escape her demons, or at least to escape the curtain department. When she was alone she was safe in the travel writer's natural habitat; nobody would ever recognize her. Anonymity can be a powerful aphrodisiac. It was to Isabella. She was a transgressor, an outsider everywhere, standing two inches short of five feet. Toward the end of her life she said the Front Range of the Rocky Mountains was the place she loved best in the world, especially a blue hollow below Longs Peak, a serrated 14,250-footer that dominates what is now the Rocky Mountain National Park. She lived in a log cabin in the shadow of the peak, listening to coyote scream in the forest. Six years after her Colorado adventure, Isabella published *A Lady's Life in the Rocky Mountains*, a classic combination of fresh personal narrative with observations on the perils of riding through ten feet of snow without a map. "I have found," it begins, "a dream of beauty at which one might look all one's life and sigh." The book made her name. Framing the volume as a sequence of letters to her sister, Isabella said it was "written without the remotest idea of publication." That may or may not be true. Within her portrait of the settlers she composed a hymn to the parsed mountain landscape they were struggling to tame. On page after page, Isabella expressed the wonder that communion with nature can bring. Conjuring the setting sun over Donner Lake, she wrote of peaks glowing in amber light and the sensation of "a hardly bearable joy, a tender anguish, an indescribable yearning, an unearthly music, rich in love and worship." Isabella was a Romantic, and the force of emotional expression overcomes her creaky prose style. "You can form no idea," she wrote home, "of what the glory on the Plains is just before sunrise."

———

Isabella's father was a cousin of the abolitionist William Wilberforce, a kinship that was moral as well as biological. A devout man of the cloth, Reverend Bird was a fanatical dispatcher of missionaries to heathen lands and a Sabbatarian, which meant he campaigned against Sunday trading. His churches were generally empty, and his sulphurously puritanical views led to an abrupt departure from more than one living: the worshipers at St. Thomas' in Birmingham stoned him out of the parish. Bird home-schooled his two daughters. Isabella, born in Yorkshire in 1831, was a sickly child who grew into a sickly adult. When she was twenty-three, her father gave her a hundred pounds to visit relatives in America, believing that a change of climate would restore her health (either that, or he wanted to get the stench of sickness out of the rectory). In Boston she stayed, for two dollars a night, in an immense granite hotel on the corner of Portland and Hanover. Chandeliers sparkled in mirrored walls and a fountain threw up iced water scented with eau de cologne. Isabella discovered how prudish Americans could be when she took out her goose-quill pen in the drawing room and started writing a letter. A porter appeared to tell her sharply that writing was not permitted in public. She felt out of place, she said, among the gilded pedestals and brocade couches, and could not find anything to say to the sleek women purring over schooners of French champagne. Back in Britain she wrote up the journey in a spiritless book she called *The Englishwoman in America*. Then she took to her bed once more. A pattern was established: ill at home, Isabella set off on her travels and recovered, only to collapse again when domesticity loomed. Some inner fire burned, one that never found fuel in a conventional setting. Between trips, she wrote. Besides contributing to theological journals she published *The Aspects of Religion in the United States of America*, having returned for another, year-long tour. *Aspects* looked at "the great revival" of the Protestant religion in the U.S., its varied manifestations, and the attitude of the church and its branches to slavery. Isabella was infinitely more temperate than

Fanny Trollope had been three decades earlier. "It is a matter of regret," she wrote in *Aspects*, "that so much prejudice still exists against America. It is full time that old jealousies should be buried, and that in a larger faith and a more comprehensive charity the children should forget the separation of their sires."

In the 1860s the Birds migrated to Scotland, and Isabella and her sister Henrietta flitted between Edinburgh and Tobermory on the Isle of Mull in the Inner Hebrides. Isabella was almost always ill during this period, suffering fevers, lesions, rashes, nausea, tumors, chest pains, muscle spasm, hair loss, neuralgia, jaw ache, insomnia and constipation. Her medical record reads like a list of possible side effects on the back of a pill packet. According to a modern specialist, she probably had carbunculosis, a deep staphylococcal skin infection, in her case on the spine. In a fruitless attempt to cure a generalized infection, she had all her teeth out. As a proper Victorian neurasthenic and something of a depressive, Isabella drank alcohol for health purposes. "I have wine at 11," she reported, "lunch and beer at one, wine at 4 taken out if we are driving, dinner and beer at 6, tea wine and bed at 9." Her doctor had actually prescribed wine: along with a change of air, it was thought that alcohol could boost the aging woman's spirits. So medical advice was not all against hapless crones. But booze failed to solve any problems (does it ever?), and in 1872 Isabella's despairing doctors recommended a world tour. She was forty-one.

Setting off in July, Isabella sailed to Australia, and after three months in the Antipodes proceeded to Hawaii, still known to Europeans as the Sandwich Islands. Sunshine and the absence of Caledonian drear raised her back to life, Lazarus style, and during her seven-month sojourn she received a marriage proposal (she refused it) and became the first woman to climb Mauna Loa, the largest volcano in the world. As for marriage: the proposer said the sight of her knitting needles had made him think of his mother. Isabella was like a duck, toothless and sedate on the sur-

face, and furiously energetic below the waterline. On one sea voyage she wrote to a friend, "No bills . . . no conventionalities . . . no dressing [presumably not literally] . . . I feel like a Viking wild." From the Sandwich Islands she sailed to California, landing in San Francisco in the dog days of the summer of 1873. She planned to make her way to the Rocky Mountains and the seasonal hunting grounds of Estes Park, chiefly because someone told her it was hard to get to. After having had her photograph taken in a studio on San Francisco's Montgomery Street (it was a craze), she boarded a ferry across the bay to Oakland and the sierra beyond where the dipping valleys were crimson-sided with poison oak. Isabella then took the Central Pacific Railroad. Throughout the American tour, she found lodgings in settlers' homesteads. She had to: there was nowhere else to stay. She was oblivious to hardship. At Truckee in northern California, her landlord served, for supper, "a small slice of bread which looked as though it had been much handled," and drunken fellow guests discussed chopped-up human bodies in sacks. At the sight of this filth and disorder, Isabella's spirits rose. She hired her first horse, and when a grizzly frightened it and it threw her, she simply remounted—it was water off her back. "I dreamt of bears so vividly," she wrote the next morning, "that I woke with a furry death-hug at my throat, but feeling quite refreshed. When I mounted my horse after breakfast, the sun was high and the air so keen and intoxicating that, giving the animal his head, I galloped up and down hill, feeling completely tireless. Truly, that air is the elixir of life." She rode with legs astride, like a man, though for the sake of propriety, when she entered a town she adopted the feminine position, which she greatly resented. In a note to the second edition of *A Lady's Life*, she added advice, "for the benefit of other lady travellers," explaining that her riding habit included "a skirt reaching to the ankles, and full Turkish trousers gathered into frills falling over the boots, a thoroughly serviceable and feminine costume for mountaineering and other rough travelling."

"As night came on the cold intensified, and the stove in the parlour attracted everyone," she wrote from Cheyenne, which she reached on the mail train. Unlike the Fannys, Isabella took Americans as she found them. She had an egalitarian spirit, and less investment in the British status quo than the others, and as a result she appreciated the fluidity of Colorado society. "True democratic equality prevails," she wrote of the West, "not its counterfeit." The reader will search *A Lady's Life* in vain for the trope about cocky servants not knowing their place. "Womanly dignity and manly respect for women are the salt of society in this wild West," Isabella wrote. Her first impressions endured. "I have met nothing but civility," she reported at journey's end.

After leaving Wyoming Territory Isabella saw the Rockies. "Five distinct ranges of mountains," she wrote, "one above another, a lurid blue against a lurid sky, upheaved themselves against a prairie sea." It was the Front Range, a southern spur of the Rockies and the first barrier homesteaders faced when they trundled west across the Great Plains to fulfil their Manifest Destiny— though its eastern flanks had formed a human migration route when Paleo-Indians were hunting the American lion. The Continental Divide bisects the Range from northwest to southeast, at one point looping, with the result that the Pacific drainage basin is momentarily east of its Atlantic counterpart. For Isabella, it was love at first sight. "They are gradually gaining possession of me," she revealed to Henrietta when describing the mountains. "I can look at and *feel* nothing else." At Fort Collins she walked among beehive-shaped cacti before riding nine hours in a buggy across plains teeming with buffalo, wild horses and antelope. "Plains, plains everywhere," she wrote, returning to the same oceanic imagery, ". . . like waves of a sea which had fallen asleep." At the next boarding house, the embattled family ignored her. "I sat down and knitted for some time," she wrote, "—my usual resource under discouraging circumstances." Her landlord had uprooted to Colorado on account of its salutary climate, and having staked a squatter's claim, set up a primitive sawmill and began planting. But grasshoppers ate the crops and he could not get his wood to market. However rhapsodic Isabella might be on the subject of the Western landscape, she never romanticized the homestead experience. She recognized the grind involved in wresting any kind of living from the land. "Except for love, which here as everywhere raises life into the ideal, this is a wretched existence," she wrote in one miserable shack where two exhausted parents labored day and night to ensure their children did not die of starvation and had already failed once.

She joined a group of trappers for a ten-hour ride to the tiny settlement at Estes Park (park in this context meaning a broad high basin, as opposed to a defined zone managed by human hand). There was only one pass in and out. "This is another world," she wrote. At Muggins Gulch, a prairie-like dale on the pass, the party stopped at a "rude, black log cabin" on the edge of a copse of willows. The mud roof was covered with lynx fur, and antlers and offal lay on the muddy ground outside. It looked, said Isabella, like the den of a wild beast. Out stalked the beast then, a grizzled figure with one eye, blue as a gas jet. "A broad, thickset man," breathed Isabella, stars already shining in her eyes, about the middle height, with an old cap on his head, and wearing a grey hunting-suit much the worse for wear (almost falling to pieces, in fact), a digger's scarf knotted round his waist, a knife in his belt, and "a bosom friend," a revolver, sticking out of the breast-pocket of his coat; his feet, which were very small, were bare; except for some dilapidated moccasins made of horse hide. The marvel was how his clothes hung together, and on him. The scarf round his waist must have had something to do with it. His face was remarkable. He is a man about forty-five, and must have been strikingly handsome . . . He has a handsome aquiline nose, and a very handsome mouth. His face was smooth-shaven except for a dense moustache and imperial. Tawny hair, in thin uncared-for curls, fell from under his hunter's cap and over his collar. One eye was entirely gone, and the loss made one side of the face repulsive, while the other might have been modelled in marble.

His first impulse was to swear at the mastiff at his heels, but, seeing a lady, he kicked it instead. He offered Isabella water in a battered tin, "apologising gracefully for not having anything more respectable." When she admired a set of beaver paws hanging on the wall of the cabin, he presented her with them. This was the America Isabella sought: rude, romantic and wild, many mountains from the tinkling pianos of Boston. Riding on, her companions regaled her with stories of the beast in the den. "Rocky Mountain Jim" Nugent was a scout, a trapper and a fisherman who galloped into Boulder with 300 pounds of trout in his panniers. Most of his activities were disreputable, even by the standards of the frontier, and the seditious effects of whiskey were plain on his face, which was pink as a ham. The men riding with Isabella disapproved. She didn't.

Estes Park consisted of a low valley and meadowlands threaded with the silver coils of the Big Thompson. "There," she wrote, "no lumberer's axe has ever rung." It had been recently named for Joel

Estes, a Kentucky-born rancher with thirteen children who for three years made a living hunting, fishing and raising stock. Hay did well in the valley, fish bit as fast as Estes could pull them out and one of his sons shot a hundred elk in a single year and sold the dressed skins and hindquarters in Denver. But the winters were long and the isolation severe, and maintenance of a cart road that followed the Little Thompson through the foothills an ongoing saga. Estes left for pastures new in 1866 and when Isabella arrived the valley had no permanent settlers. A handful of ranchers struggled to make a go of squatters' claims and the occasional city man came to rough it for a season. Isabella was thrilled with the set-up. The very words "Estes Park," she decided, "mean everything that is rapturous and delightful—grandeur, cheerfulness, health, enjoyment, novelty, freedom, etc. etc. I have just dropped into the very place I have been seeking, but in everything it exceeds all my dreams." She expressed revulsion at the way settlers were replicating the urban development of the East Coast in their rush to develop the West. Deciding to make Estes Park her base until winter set in, she took board and lodging in a cabin on a ranch run by the Evans and Edwards families. Sam Edwards was a teetotal veteran who had assisted General Sherman in the razing of Georgia during the March to the Sea at the conclusion of the Civil War. His partner in the Estes ranch, the curly-headed Welsh-born Griff Evans, was an irascible drunk and fine cook who had arrived in the park with wife, children, a gun and a single dollar. Thirty miles from the nearest settlement and accessible only by a steep track, the ranch nestled at the foot of Longs Peak. "Somewhat dazed by the rarefied air," Isabella wrote at the end of the first day,

> entranced by the glorious beauty, slightly puzzled by the motley company, whose faces loomed not always quite distinctly through the cloud of smoke produced by eleven pipes, I went to my solitary cabin at nine, attended by Evans. It was very dark,

and it seemed a long way off. Something howled—Evans said it was a wolf—and owls apparently innumerable hooted incessantly. The pole-star, exactly opposite my cabin door, burned like a lamp. The frost was sharp. Evans opened the door, lighted a candle, and left me, and I was soon in my hay bed. I was frightened—that is, afraid of being frightened, it was so eerie; but sleep soon got the better of my fears. I was awoken by a heavy breathing, a noise something like sawing under the floor, and a pushing and upheaving, all very loud. My candle was all burned, and, in truth, I dared not stir. The noise went on for an hour fully, when, just as I thought the floor had been made sufficiently thin for all purposes of ingress, the sounds abruptly ceased, and I fell asleep again. My hair was not, as it ought to have been, white in the morning!

It turned out that the cabin, which she named Queen Anne Mansion, rested on six legs above a skunk's lair. From her hay-bale bed, she watched the sun rise over Mirror Lake. Rent included the use of a horse. "There is health," she wrote, "in every breath of air." She waddled to the river to wash her skirts, ecstatic with the sheer joy of existence. In the wilderness she found a better understanding of God than she did in a church, and better reasons for loving God. She remained devout—a faithful daughter of the Manse—till the end. But she followed the rich tradition of Christians who find the divine in nature. In the confused religious climate of our own age, hers is a tempting position—though some of us have a weakness for the consoling poetry of the King James Bible.

Throughout September 1873, the sky was a deep, brilliant blue. Besides helping in the kitchen, and in the dairy where a waterwheel powered a butter-churner, Isabella drove cattle with the cowboys and rode for five hours a day. Evans and the other ranchers hosted a variety of boarders and in the evenings Edwards lay on the kitchen floor and told stories about marching through Georgia with Sherman, and a French-Canadian played Yankee Doodle on a harmonium.

Longs Peak obsessed her. "In one's imagination it grows to be more than a mountain," she wrote. "It becomes invested with a personality." Rocky Mountain Jim offered to guide the diminutive Isabella to the summit. Any fourteener is tough to climb and although Longs is not among the most challenging, in mid-October snow had already fallen and the faces were occluded with ice. Accompanied by two young boarders eager to bag a peak, Isabella packed steaks sliced from a steer suspended in the ranch kitchen and hung a pair of Evans' hunting boots over the horn of her saddle. Nugent, wearing deerskin trousers belted with a scarf, kept his rifle across his horse's neck. The frost was twenty-five degrees below when they camped on the lower slopes of Longs, but they huddled round the fire singing "The Star-Spangled Banner." When the young men turned in, Jim recited poetry. What woman would not have fallen in love? That night she used her saddle as a pillow and young pine shoots as a mattress, and Nugent's mastiff tucked into the small of her back. The final ascent was hell: Evans' boots were so big she walked like a clown, tripped and dangled by the hem of her frock, which Nugent had to cut with his hunting knife, whereupon she tumbled into a crevasse. The thin air made one of the young men bleed from the mouth. But they did it. Then they wrote their names and the date of their ascent on a bit of paper and left it in a tin at the summit. When Isabella described the climb, she did not stint on the purple. "It was something," she wrote, "at last to stand on the storm-rent crown of this lonely sentinel of the rocky range, on one of the mightiest of the vertebrae of the backbone of the North American continent, and to see the waters start for both oceans. Uplifted above love and hate and storms of passion, calm amidst the eternal silences . . ."

The feat brought Nugent and Isabella close. "He has pathos," she gabbled to Henrietta, who was taking Ladies' Greek lessons at Edinburgh University, "he has poetry, and humour, an intense love of nature [they had that in common] . . . a considerable acquaintance with literature, a chivalrous respect for women in his manner . . . His conversation is brilliant, and full of the light and fitfulness of genius." He was known across the free Territory— so she wrote—for bravado and brawling, and she said you could barely open a newspaper without finding a paragraph detailing his misdeeds. She fell for his "breezy mountain recklessness," and in flickering campfire light he revealed that he had a heart. "You're the first man or woman who's treated me like a human being for many a year," he told her as they sat under the stars. When they rode to the beaver dams of Black Canyon, he revealed that his father, from a good Irish family, had served as a British officer in Montreal; and that he, Nugent, had worked for years as an Indian scout in the service of the government, galloping into camps with golden curls eighteen inches long and a red scarf round his waist. He had recently lost his left eye to a grizzly. "The handsome, even superbly handsome, side of his face was towards me as he spoke," Isabella wrote. The animal, "after giving him a bear hug, tearing him all over, breaking his arm and scratching out his eye, had left him for dead." On another occasion she rode to Nugent's cabin to nurse him when an old arrow wound in the lung was troubling him. She begged him to forswear whiskey, but he said he could not give up the only pleasure he had.

Everything Nugent revealed about himself was a lie. Others were less gullible than Isabella. An English doctor who attended Nugent after a shooting said he was called The Mountainous One "because of the altitude of his lies." He sometimes claimed to be a defrocked Catholic priest, and at other times a Canadian school-teacher. As a correspondent of the *Greeley Tribune* wrote at the end of 1873, "The mountains overflow with Rocky Mountain Jims, Sams, Bills and Jakes." But who has not wilfully selected facts when emotions are engaged? To do otherwise would be to deny life itself. It is always the moment that counts, not the hours or the days or the years. Isabella was Boswell to Nugent's Johnson. Per-haps she was not as simple-minded as her academic pursuers maintain. I like to think she built up her Rocky Mountain beau to further the popular commercial appeal of her book.

I rented a log cabin under Longs Peak. I had heard enough lovers' lies for one lifetime, but I wondered if I could find the "hardly bearable joy" Isabella had experienced in the Front Range. My cabin was on the grounds of Aspen Lodge, a motel which, like the cabin, was more 1973 than either 1873 or 2011. The television had a humped back, the cups were made of Styrofoam and the sheets nylon. There were no guests at the motel, and the screen in the cavernous reception displayed an advertisement for catheters. Like Isabella, at the sight of tat and discomfort, my spirits rose. Over the next days I pursued Isabella up and down the backcoun-try trails she described, though they weren't trails then. It was she who broke them. Elk grazed in wetlands and meadows where In-dian paintbrush were blooming in a persimmon haze. Higher up, montane forest of ponderosa pine and aspen merged into a denser subalpine landscape tufted with bighorn sheep. The sun shone hard, and the thin tang of high air sharpened the outlines of the trees, which stopped abruptly around 11,500 feet, like a lifted curtain. The eye of a frozen lake shone in the distance. I did not pass five thousand head of Texas cattle traveling 700 miles on their way to Iowa, like Isabella did. But it was still possible to be alone in a wilderness that, once the railroad had joined up the country, wove itself into the American imagination. Clippering altocumulus created a dappled interplay of light and shade on the rock faces. It was bleak country, after the vulgar luxuriance of tidewater magnolia: one had to get one's eye acclimatized. Isabella repeatedly used the words "exhilarated," "intoxicating" and "sublime" in her descriptions of the Front Range, and she referred to an "elasticity" in the air that made her feel more alive than she had ever felt before. It brought her close. Out there on the road, so often one ceases looking inward at last. That's the attraction: like writing, the anonymity of travel encourages a welcome escape from personality.

The year before Isabella discovered the blue hollow, the Earl of Dunraven made an appearance in the Park. The Limerick-born lord already had 40,000 acres in Ireland and Wales, but he fancied he might augment his portfolio with private hunting grounds in America. Like other European sportsmen, Dunraven viewed the Western United States as one great playground in which to kill things. Having crossed the Atlantic, he rode the Union Pacific to North Platte and hired Buffalo Bill Cody, legendary hunting guide and one of the ultimate showmen of the Old West. Bill galloped for the Pony Express, scalped Cheyenne braves in the Plains wars, panned for gold and supplied the Kansas Pacific Railroad with buffalo meat for its workers. In this latter role he shot 4,280 American bison in eighteen months. He was literally a showman, as when he could no longer ride fast or shoot straight, he toured the country with a Wild West show. "It is often said on the other side of the water," commented Mark Twain, ". . . that none of the exhibitions which we send to England are purely and distinctly

American. If you will take the Wild West show over there you can remove that reproach." And Bill did, staging 300 sell-out performances in London alone including a private one for Queen Victoria. Cody and Dunraven hunted buffalo and elk for a month, and the teeming plains of Colorado enraptured the Irishman. At the end, boasting of his bag in Denver's Corkscrew Club, Dunraven heard talk of the limitless hunting in Estes Park. He ended up buying the whole park, chiefly as an investment, though he built a lodge on the North Fork of the Big Thompson where he repeatedly returned to hunt, allegedly burying emergency cases of whiskey that have yet to be found. Wealthy Britons had begun to invest in stockraising in Colorado, and in Estes Dunraven combined his love of shooting with commercial acumen. "The Earl of Dunraven and party," reported the *Rocky Mountain News* on July 22, 1874,

. . . have been cutting up high jinks in Estes Park and enjoying all sort of hair's breadth escapes. They have killed any number of "beasties" of various sorts, and the Earl had a pitch battle with a female mountain lion not long ago that came very near to causing much weeping and wailing at Dunraven Castle . . . The Earl arose much flustered at his narrow escape, but otherwise none the worse for it, although he privately told our correspondent that, "those mountain lions were blasted nasty things to meet when alive, you know."

Reaction to the Irish interloper was amiable enough at first, but as Dunraven increased his holdings, and more Europeans came to sample the good life in Colorado, the phrases "land grabbing" and "land sharks" began to appear in newspapers. Dunraven eventually lost interest, and in time the federal government acquired most of his land, out of which, later, it carved the Rocky Mountain National Park.

I drove east through Big Thompson gulch, ending up in the fractal backcountry around Masonville, a granite landscape thrust from eroded volcanic rock 10 million years ago. The buttes of chaparral blazed red and the air hung heavy with heat and burned light. There was nobody anywhere. Masonville had two shops, both selling Harley Davidson leathers and moccasins. I looked out at the Front Range from the ridge of the Dakota Hogback. It was a view that moved Isabella. In those mountains she saw the aspirations of mankind, our hopes, fears and dreams, rendered absolute. It made her feel she was not alone. She believed that natural beauty could knock down the wall between past and present, compressing all of life into one timeless moment. It was a kind of transfiguration, and she understood that a journey was more than the sum of its parts. I was beginning to understand it too. I saw the leaves of the overhanging cottonwoods precisely defined, each holding its droplet of rain or fleck of granite dust.

As one slows down, time speeds up. Martin Amis (born 1949)

remarked recently that a year used to last a year but now it lasts an afternoon. Perhaps that was why the world had become such an unspeakably beautiful place, with all its fragility and human horrors. I had spent so very many long months in the polar regions, in my youth down south, and more recently in the north, feeling myself deeply in love with those pristine landscapes. But the piercing joy I found now in a high wood or a bluebell dell was richer and deeper. It was I who had changed, not the world. I had feared, at the outset of these American journeys, that motherhood meant a loss of freedom and that the rest would follow a downhill trajectory (and not whizzing downhill in an exhilarated way, either). Perhaps that fear, and the concomitant anxiety about the future, were necessary stages in the process of letting go. Now and again, as I strode across prairies and thought about the women who were here before me, I glimpsed a truer freedom that lay ahead. There is no rite of passage for women entering the barren years. I realized that this journey—all these actual journeys in the America I loved, and the metaphorical journey of writing this book—was a private way of marking that shift. Perhaps that had been my subconscious intention all along, but the passage of time, a dose of America and, of course, my girls had allowed it to float to the surface. I did not want to sail through this period of my life without thinking about the profound changes it brought. It was time to confront the "problem" of aging, and let it go.

In October Isabella left Evans' ranch to tour Platte Canyon, intending to return to Queen Anne Mansion before winter. She borrowed a bay pony called Birdie with legs of iron. There were no maps. Isabella knew only that she must "steer south, and keep to the best beaten track." Heading initially for Denver, on the second day out she met a migrating family in a covered wagon. They had been three months on their journey from Illinois, and had buried a child on the way. But when Isabella rode into Denver she saw banks, two-story grocers and silver barons conferring outside

195

the Corkscrew Club. Loafers drank after months in the country and Yankees chose saddles before setting out on the great hunting adventure. Denver's second horse-drawn streetcar line was about to open, running northwest across the railroad tracks over South Platte Road to a dirt path in vacant highland. The land east of Broadway was prairie, though speculators were buying and selling lots around the barren crest of Capitol Hill. A telegraph line to the East Coast had been in operation for a decade, construction gangs were installing another along the Colorado territorial line and the Porter and Stebbins Telegraph Company was in the process of linking Denver north to Cheyenne and south to Santa Fe. That week's *Rocky Mountain News* led with the story that "Denver was thrown in to a violent state of excitement on Saturday night by the statement that a large band of Indians in war paint and fully bent on mischief were in possession of several stock ranches on and near the line of the Kansas Pacific." A lengthy report followed on the management of the water supply, preceding a list of winners at the annual Territorial Fair, which included awards for the best celery. The smelting works at Golden were turning out a thousand dollars' worth of silver bullion a day and the small ads offered English breech-loading double guns, steam pumps and cattle, and under the heading "Obstacles To Marriage," a doctor offered, "Happy relief for young men from the effects of Errors and Abuses in early life. Manhood restored, impediments to marriage removed." In short, the white man was getting on and there was no longer room for the indigenous peoples who had hunted the plains for generations. In 1864, a force of Colorado Territory militia had massacred Cheyenne and Arapaho women and children at Sand Creek, and under the terms of the Treaty of Medicine Lodge three years later, settlers had forced the survivors to relocate to Oklahoma. Only the Ute clung on, riding into Denver to trade from encampments on the plains—land nobody yet needed to steal. Isabella spoke out in support of the Ute, whom she saw degraded and exploited by the Indian Department. "To get rid of the Injuns," she noted, "is the phrase used everywhere."

Isabella called Denver "that great braggart city." It was too sophisticated for her taste. "One no longer sees," she wrote with regret, "men dangling from the lamp-posts when one looks out in the morning." Only fifteen years earlier, the treeless Denver amounted to a scattering of cabins resting on posts in the sand spits of Cherry Creek and Colorado had not even been designated a Territory. Everything changed when a veteran of the California Gold Rush sieved up placer metal in the South Platte River near Pike's Peak. Fifty-eighters and fifty-niners poured in by the thousand and Denver became the hub around which the West evolved. On the crowded dirt streets:

> There were men in every rig: hunters and trappers in buckskin clothing; men of the Plains with belts and revolvers, in great blue cloaks, relics of the war; teamsters in leathern suits; horsemen in fur coats and caps and buffalo-hide boots with the hair outside, and camping blankets behind their huge Mexican saddles; Broadway dandies in light kid gloves; rich English sporting tourists, clean, comely, and supercilious-looking; and hundreds of Indians on their small ponies, the men wearing buckskin suits sewn with beads, and red blankets, with faces painted vermilion, and hair hanging lank and straight, and squaws much bundled up, riding astride with furs over their saddles.

Denver might have civilized itself, but most of the West had not yet been won. While Isabella was trotting through pine forests on Birdie, a brilliant one-armed ethnologist and army major called John Wesley Powell was capsizing in the rapids of Canyon County, dreaming he could float all the way from Colorado's western slope to the Pacific. The week Isabella rode into Denver,

Powell and his team were squatting around a campfire eating ran-
cid bacon and moldy flour cakes while speculating how many miles
lay ahead before the wide blue ocean appeared round a bend.
Shivwit Indians had already arrowed three of Powell's men to
death, yet he carried on to run the cocoa-colored Colorado and
became the first white man to traverse the Grand Canyon. Imagine going into that when you didn't know it was there. "We are
now ready to start on our way down the Great Unknown," Powell
reported to his journal. "We are three-quarters of a mile in the
depths of the earth, and the great river shrinks into insignifi-
cance . . ." Powell's work in Colorado reveals how little was known
of the region when Isabella was capering in her free-legged air. As
for Powell himself—he returned to Washington a celebrity and
spent the rest of his career surveying the Colorado River for the
federal government while names filled the map like a rising tide,
even though the Pacific was still a long way off. That dazzling region beyond the 100th meridian was turning from myth to fact in
the national imagination, and in Denver Isabella became close to
one of its most devoted apostles. William Byers was a land surveyor from Ohio, and he had hauled a printing press by horse
from Omaha, Nebraska, and founded Colorado's first newspaper,
the *Rocky Mountain News*. It was hard without the telegraph, and
for eighteen months Byers relied on the Pony Express for stories
and filled in the gaps with Indian-bashing. He typified the energetic, resourceful frontiersman who forged the West. As leader of
the Colorado Territorial Board of Immigration, Byers promoted
agriculture and tourism as a way of diversifying the fledgling
economy. The board printed tens of thousands of pamphlets and
appointed immigration agents in England and Germany. Byers
and his peers had a vision of the West. They believed that as its
mines and fields "poured forth golden harvests," the region would
prove the success of the national experiment in democracy. With
nothing to check people's inventive and moral energies in a region
barely invested with laws, the new West would be the most Amer-

ican part of America. When the Union Pacific Railroad bypassed Denver and went through southern Wyoming—a potentially fatal blow to the territorial capital—the pioneers set to and constructed spur lines to the railhead. The first locomotive puffed into Denver in 1870 and the *Rocky Mountain News* expanded to a nine-column format. Besides hobos, speculators and tourists, the trains brought the English sparrow to Denver, nesting in the boxcars. Rapid development had dispersed the tensions of the Civil War. (Many Southerners had settled in Denver before the conflict—mostly attracted by the mines—and a Confederate flag once flapped over the big outfitting store on Larimer Street.) But in 1873 Denver's bright prosperity dimmed when financial panic spread inward from the coasts following an international drop in the demand for silver. Isabella was unable to withdraw money from Denver banks. Evidence of a recessionary national economy recurs throughout *A Lady's Life*, revealing that the West was not isolated after all. While Isabella continued her love affair with America and Americans, she noted their obsession with wealth, just as Fanny Trollope had forty-five years earlier. Endorsing the adage, "There is no God west of the Missouri," she added to it, "The almighty dollar is the true divinity, and its worship is universal." Unlike Fanny, Isabella did not disapprove. She understood that American cash was replacing British class.

The 600,000-strong twenty-first century metropolis still had its unfettered charm. Denver might be isolated in the context of modern America, but the city is the hub of a region bigger than Great Britain. Spread out, not stacked, it is *sui generis*, a confection of monumental architecture from its booms: the post-Panic 1870s, the 1920s and 1950s. The silver barons' sandstone homes have colonised the Capitol Hill district and its crest is no longer bleak. Some of the mansions are inns now. At a mine, the owner wore a cowboy hat at breakfast. In the alleys and small roads behind, the overhead electricity cables and telephone poles spoke of another age, somewhere between Isabella's and my own. At night, penitential Hopper-like beams fell from casements, casting pools of light on to the sidewalk, where they joined pools of water from a flux of summer rain.

Isabella rode for fourteen hours with only raisins to sustain her, and both boots and stockings froze to her feet. She frequently lost the path and was obliged to beat through dense bush. Yet despite bouts of altitude sickness, she felt healthy and vigorous, and up-lifted spirits brought on flights of rhetoric. "Lord what is man?" she wondered as Birdie labored through snow and splinters of ice showered down from the willows. One night in Perry Park she lay alongside two pedlars in a cabin wallpapered with copies of the *Phrenological Journal*. The country there was cold and hard and beautiful. When she left the pedlars, she suffered snowblindness and sunburn, and had to walk up to her shoulders in snow while Birdie fell down thirty times in one day. She was transcendently happy, and sorry when she saw the goal of her journey, the peaks of the Continental Divide. She crossed through the Breckenridge pass with a gunslinger who turned out to be Comanche Bill, one of the most notorious mountain men and the biggest Indian exter-minator on the frontier. When he left her she rode into lightless silver towns at night and dossed in boardinghouse kitchens with "freighters"—men who carried supplies to the mines from the point where horses and wagons could go no further. Talk in the morn-ing still concerned bodies swinging from gibbets. "At the mining towns above this," Isabella noted, "nobody is thought anything of who has not kicked a man." She met a British Guards Officer, a central-casting aristocrat on a four-month furlough hunting elk and buffalo. She found him repulsive, presiding over the natives, "with a Lord Dundreary drawl and a general execration of every-thing; while I sat in the chimney corner, speculating on the reason why many of the upper class of my countryman . . . make them-selves ludicrously absurd . . ." She warmed to the absence of class consciousness in America and tolerated the prevailing insistence that the former colonies had leapfrogged their imperial master. "An American," she concluded the Lord Dundreary section of *A Lady's Life*, "is nationally assumptive, a Briton personally so." Tocqueville couldn't have put it better.

Her exploits featured in the *Rocky Mountain News*: "She travels almost altogether on horseback," the organ reported on October 23, 1873, "and has laid out a pretty good winter's work in Colorado." At Georgetown, famous for its silver lodes, Isabella inquired about hiring a fresh horse to get up to Green Lake. It was a perilous ride through five feet of snow and everyone advised her against the ascent. Her landlord nonetheless agreed to send a messenger to a stable. "If it's the English lady traveling in the mountains," the reply came back, "she can have a horse. But not anybody else."

"Mining," wrote Isabella, "turns the earth inside out." In the Black Hawk valley, casinos have filled the adit holes blasted into the mountainsides, a modern symbol of failed hope and spent endeavor. Lurid strips bulged out from the foot of the cliffs. The flat tops of the mesas glowered and an early-morning desolation prevailed until dusk. My only companions on the highway were bikers without helmets or silencers. With nothing to replace silver and gold except gambling, the region had stagnated since frontiersmen shipped pamphlets to Europe promising golden harvests. Georgetown, the Silver Queen, was quietly dying, like much of small-town America in the foothills of the twenty-first century. A few retail outlets of the Silver Shoppe variety battled on, but one sensed that the war had been lost. I crossed the Continental Divide, like Isabella, at Breckenridge, now a ski resort crowded with river rafters. Eastward, buffalo herds grazed an attenuated landscape, bleached of color; a place where the fabled drifters of the Southwest might roam to a Ry Cooder soundtrack. Fairplay and the other gold towns looked bleak, but on the small roads through Pike Forest the air smelled sweet with juniper. Following a track up to Turkey Rock at Westcreek, I lost the GPS by

Deckers. I was off the map, like her—where I like to be. The creeks were running hard and the Rockies sharp against a milky sky. A waxwing trilled in the pines, clear and high-pitched. It was not in the hardly bearable league, but something in one unclenched.

Colorado Springs spooked her. She considered herself inured to the presence in every rooming house of consumptives taking "the camp cure" in the allegedly health-giving Colorado climate. ("There were eight boarders," she wrote of one flophouse, "each looking nearer the grave than the other.") The Territory had earned a reputation on the East Coast as a sanatorium, but it can't have been a very effective one, as men seemed to be spouting blood and expiring wherever Isabella went. But "medicinal" waters attracted the worst cases. From the parlor of her lodgings in Colorado Springs, she noticed, through the open door of an adjacent bedroom, "two large white feet sticking up at the end of the bed." She watched as the landlady chattered on, hoping the feet would move. But they seemed to grow stiffer and whiter. Then a tubercular young man left the bedroom sobbing, and announced the death of his only brother. Nobody took any notice. "It turns the house upside down when they just come here and die," the landlady told Isabella later. "We shall be half the night laying him out."

Isabella returned to Estes Park. "It is uninteresting down here," she wrote before setting off again for the cabin under the mountain, this time charged with the mailbag. "I long for the rushing winds, the piled-up peaks, the great pines, the wild night noises, the poetry and the prose of the free, jolly life of my unrivalled eyrie." The Welsh families had left for the winter, leaving a pair of Byronic law students to look after the livestock. Isabella introduced herself to the two baffled men, and ended up keeping house for them for a month, dusting the cabin with a buffalo's tail and frying venison steaks in home-churned butter. She had the same small carpet bag of clothes that she had carried from Hawaii and resembled at that time more of a troll than a duck. Later—much later—one of the young men, by then an eminent lawyer and mayor of Denver, recalled those days, and reflected on *A Lady's Life*, a book which impressed him. "Her physical unattractiveness," he wrote of Isabella, "which so influenced us when we first met her, was really more than compensated for by a fluent and graphic pen, which made the mountains as romantic and beautiful as doubtless were her own thoughts." Isabella and Nugent were reunited. He evidently did not find her unattractive. He told her that after her departure, "he had discovered he was attached to me and it was killing him." A few days after the encounter she confided in Henrietta. "I miss him very much. He is so charming and can talk on all subjects and has real genius." When he left, the colors went too. "It takes peace away," she wrote. At night, she lay awake listening to fine snow hissing through chinks in the walls. In November her hair froze in its plaits and when she poured boiling water from the kettle it hardened to ice before striking the tin basin. Isabella said that in the Rockies she realized how little one really needs. One learns that lesson so often, and so often forgets it again when immersed in what Isabella called the tyranny of "things." She was lucky to see the park in the last moments of its isolation. Speculators were about to invade the fertile bottomland, along with squatters looking to stake a claim. In a single month, May 1874, twenty-five claims were filed on 4,000 acres.

At the beginning of December 1873, she began the long journey home to Scotland. Nugent rode with her for the first leg, out of the mountains to the milling hamlet of St. Louis on the Big Thompson. It was seven degrees below, but her heart was colder. The little moisture in the air aggregated into the feathers and fern leaves of frostfall. "It was still and cloudless," she observed, "and the shapes of violet mountains were softened by a veil of the tenderest blue." When Nugent turned back, heading for his wild beast's den, she watched him until he melted into the snowy plain, leading the horse on which she had ridden 800 miles.

Trail Ridge Road is the highest continuous paved highway in the U.S., hairpinning so deeply into the interior of the Front Range that it is closed for six months of the year. At one end, the head-waters of the Colorado River rise in Grand Lake, which the Ute called "Spirit Lake." I hiked along the inundated banks of the Colorado in Kawuneeche Valley. A ribbon of cloud hung parallel to the ground halfway up the outer edge of the pines on the lateral moraine, and gophers fished in warps of water next to the col-lapsed walls of a dude ranch. Five feet of snow lay on the side of Trail Ridge Road. It was Arctic up there: ptarmigan, snow but-tercups and furry animals that turn white in winter. At the highest point, prairie falcon butterflies hovered on the tuff. A kind of peace came down, and there it was again—that sense that these jour-neys were more than the sum of their parts.

In Colorado, Isabella had chipped away at her fears and anxi-eties, many towing debilitating physical symptoms, to find herself finally "uplifted above love and hate and storms of passion, calm amidst the eternal silences." She had worked at it. And that's what I had to do. Even the beauty of the Front Range landscape was an agent of liberation. One had to set the struggle free.

I was sorry Isabella had not been to that spot. She would have loved it. But at a lookout near Desolation Peaks, the National Parks people had erected a metal sign quoting her. It said, "Every valley ends in mystery." It was she who was following me.

There is in the departure of every train the faintest echo of death. The following year, the bibulous Evans shot Nugent dead over a land dispute. Isabella, meanwhile, published a book on the Sand-wich Islands. The magazine *Leisure Hour* serialized the letters she had written to Henrietta from Colorado and readers received them so warmly that Isabella turned them into a book, "as a rec-ord of a phase of pioneer life which is rapidly passing away." *A Lady's Life in the Rocky Mountains* appeared in 1879 and established its author as a traveler of national renown and an intelligent, insightful commentator. When she wrote, she was fighting the fight to be truly herself, and in *A Lady's Life*, she got as near as she ever would. If you could cut her words, they would bleed. Isabella always insisted that she had reproduced the letters without changes. It was untrue. She catered to the proprieties of home, excising passages readers might consider racy and playing down the personal romance with Nugent while building up his general leading-man appeal. He was a figure "any woman might love, but no sane woman would marry," Isabella declared to Henrietta, but she deleted the sentence before publication, along with all the talk of attachment, and how much she missed him when he was not there.

Isabella became a fixture on the publishing list of John Murray, a family-owned firm specialising in eccentrics. Both John Murray III and John Murray IV were her friends for decades, and the former taught her to ride a tricycle outside the Albemarle Street office. When home induced illness, Murray IV dispatched Isabella on another world tour, in the course of which she stopped in New York and San Francisco on the way to Japan, China, Singapore, Malaysia, Egypt and the Holy Land. She was in fine health until the ship back to Britain, where she fell sick. Her life was a poem to the healing powers of travel. Within a year of Isabella's return, Henrietta died of typhoid. Isabella was distraught, and coped with her grief by marrying her sister's doctor, John Bishop. She was fifty, he was forty, and they had the wedding invitations printed on mourning stationery. Isabella even wore a black wedding dress, seeking immolation on the marital bed. Bride and groom were united by their common devotion to the morphology of lichens, and they spent their evenings bending over a microscope. God knows marriage in middle age is hard enough, and in this case the cell structure of composite organisms was not sufficient to maintain it, as Isabella's health again careered downhill. She perked up when Bishop expired of pernicious anaemia in 1886 and, via a spiritual medium, tried to make contact with Rocky Mountain Jim beyond the grave, claiming that at the time of his death years earlier he had appeared to her as a ghost. When she got bored of that, she set off for Asia. In 1892, she became the first woman admitted as a Fellow into the Royal Geographical Society, a reflection of genuine admiration on the part of the walrus-whiskered satraps of that deeply conservative institution. Isabella had joined the immortals. She and Darwin were on first-name terms. Isabella advised Gladstone on the issue of the Armenian Christians, twice speaking on the topic in the House of Commons, had an audience with Queen Victoria, and in her seventies rode a horse alone over the Atlas mountains. She wrote many more books and outlived all her doctors, dying in Edinburgh aged seventy-two, bags packed and labeled for the next journey.

6

NO THERE THERE

Catherine Hubback Goes to California

I discovered Catherine Hubback while leafing through papers at Jane Austen's birthplace in Chawton, Hampshire. The archive staff referred to the novelist among themselves as "Jane," as if she were one of them, just popped out to the photocopier. A loose photograph in a file of correspondence revealed Catherine, one of Austen's army of nieces, a fiftyish woman with hair stowed neatly under a lace-trimmed velvet mobcap, a high forehead, widely spaced eyes and the glimmer of a wry smile, as if she knew that you might as well smile, after all. She wore a starched collar and a

velvet jacket fastened by a brooch. The photograph was taken in 1874 by the San Francisco photographer G. D. Morse. San Francisco? It was a long way from Chawton. Through the window flush by my desk, wintery light silhouetted the skeletons of ash trees, and frost tinged the soil of the flower beds—a kind of anti-California. When I tracked her down, I found that Catherine had arrived in America just months after the railroad joined the country together and shifted the frontier to San Francisco—another middle-aged English writer with a useless husband who went to America to start again: a second act. It was a New World only in the metaphorical sense. People had been planting and hunting and fishing all over it for centuries. It was middle-aged like her; it became itself in middle age. In her modest Oakland home she did housework for the first time and headed out on excursions to the trails of the forty-niners with a bonnet, a picnic and worn-out boots.

Catherine Hubback, née Austen, was the daughter of Jane's brother Francis. Known as Frank, he was the novelist's nearest brother in age, and she was close to him. "God bless you," she ended one letter. "I hope you continue beautiful and brush your hair but not all off. We join in an infinity of love." Catherine, born in 1818, the year after Jane expired, was the eighth of eleven children. Her mother died when she was five. In 1828, when her father remarried, the family moved to Portsdown Lodge on a hill above Portsmouth in Hampshire. The thirty-seven-acre estate overlooked Spithead and the Isle of Wight, and Catherine and her siblings played cricket on their own pitch and had picnic parties in a horse cart. She remembered Lord Palmerston canvasing in Portsdown in the year of the Reform Act, when she was fourteen. He was not called Lord Cupid for his attention to buttered crumpets, and as a precautionary measure the adults ordered Catherine and her sister out of the room just as the great man appeared. In the Jane Austen Archive in Hampshire I had found some of Catherine's leatherbound sketchbooks from that period. She was a fine draughts-woman, inking trees and valleys and disembodied faces. Sketches of crofts and boats and watercolors appended her accounts ("straw-berrys [sic] 2s"), verses of her own poetry and a short story—the contents of a girlhood packed with hopes and dreams, scratched on friable blue paper between leather covers. She had deep-set hazel eyes and fair hair, all her aunt's spirit and some of her intel-ligence. A family member later said her temperament was best described as "*espiègle*," a word which suggests something vivid, mischievous and sparkling. Chawton and the other Austens were only twenty-five miles from Portsdown. The teenage sketchbooks include views from Chawton windows, line drawings of card games, ringlets and bonnets. Aunt Cassandra, Jane's executor, was close to Catherine. The pair sat for hours reading Jane's novels aloud: the foundation of the Janeite cult. Cassandra also read out unpub-lished material, including an incomplete novel later called *The Watsons*, the bleak story of four unmarried sisters desperate to get settled before their impoverished father expires. In 1842 Cathe-rine married John Hubback, a blue-eyed barrister at Lincoln's Inn. John was a north-countryman—his father, a hatter and furrier, served as mayor of Berwick-upon-Tweed in Northumberland. The couple went on honeymoon down the Rhine and into the Low Countries, landscapes Catherine sketched, and afterward set up home in London's Bloomsbury, as Fanny and Thomas Trollope had done two decades earlier. There they lived sociably. John was ambitious and successful. In 1844 he published *Evidence of Succession to Real and Personal Property and Peerages*, a door-stopping volume still consulted at the beginning of the twentieth century. Three sons appeared in short order: John Junior in 1844, Edward in 1846 and Charles in 1847.

Then John experienced a catastrophic mental collapse. He was thirty-seven. In the family, they said it was a consequence of overwork. Whatever the cause, the results were terminal, for him, and for her. She shut up the Bloomsbury house and the couple set off with the children in search of a cure, heading at first to a Worcestershire spa town. But John's behavior grew increasingly erratic. For Catherine it was a draining of hope. In the end she had to put him into an asylum. He wrote her unfathomable letters, lost, in his mind, in some foreign land where nobody spoke his language. Catherine, with three children under six, returned to Portsdown Lodge and spent the next twelve years living with her father and stepmother. Frank, knighted in the last of William IV's investitures and now with a mane of springy white hair, taught the boys chess and took them to Wymering church in the pony carriage on Sunday mornings and on official visits to Portsmouth dockyard to inspect 131-gun lines. In 1860 he was appointed Admiral of the Fleet. But it was a desperate time for Catherine. She had lost the emotional center of her life. "Her husband's collapse," John Junior wrote later, "was the major traumatic event of her life, quenching the springs of gaiety within her." In 1850 she was thirty-two, and had been married eight years. She was still close to Cassandra: the children remembered the pair talking in Jane Austen quotations over the tea table in the inner drawing room at Portsdown. (This sounds uncomfortably like a *Monty Python* sketch.) Now Catherine picked up a pen in a bid to establish a settled life for her children, just as Fanny Trollope had picked up hers eighteen years earlier. What else could they do? Catherine's first effort, *The Younger Sister*, appeared two years after John's collapse. Essentially Catherine reproduced Jane's unpublished story of Emma Watson and her three unmarried sisters, though she had to expand it, as her publisher, Thomas Cautley Newby, would only take the work if she turned it into three volumes to satisfy the circulating libraries. (The sharp-eyed Newby had already published the first novels of Anne and Emily Brontë as well as Anthony Trollope—it was Newby who tried to suggest Anthony was really Mrs. Trollope.) The triple-decker came in at 750 pages, its underlying theme the effect of class distinction and gradations in the social order.* But Catherine's characters are dead on the page. As a critic wrote much later, "She looked at people and their behaviour through Jane's eyes, but she had not got that touch." Catherine published under her married name. She dedicated the book to Jane, but did not reveal that she had lifted the story wholesale. Various Austens disapproved, fretting that Catherine might turn her attentions to another unpublished work by the Hampshire sphinx, the fragment known in the family as "Sanditon." "The Copy [of *Sanditon*] which was taken, not given," another niece, Anna Austen Leigh, sniped to her brother, "is now at the mercy of Mrs. Hubback, and she will be pretty sure to make use of it as soon as she thinks she safely may." But she didn't. She had ideas of her own. Nine more three-volume novels followed in thirteen years, an output that makes Anthony Trollope look like a part-timer. The books teem with Austen staples: visits from long-lost cousins, the consequences of 40,000 pounds a year, interminable dialogue in the drawing room and emotions shifting in slow arcs, like ocean-going ships. Unmarried rectors arrive in a carriage for tea, servants ferry supper trays and blushing orphaned girls like Kate Penrose in *Life and Its Lessons*—a story "Founded on Fact," according to the title page—meet rotters while eclipsed by London belles in Regency designer frocks. The plots give a clue to the author's inner life: grooms jilt brides, men commit bigamy, women have marriages annulled against their will. The prolix sagas throb with "passionate grief" and the hooves of a postman's horse toll—like the ping of an incoming email—"the knell of lost happiness." One sees Hubback reflecting on the choices women make while weeping silently in the sunny parlor of her father's

---

*Jane Austen's original version of the story was published later as *The Watsons*. Sixty-eight pages of the heavily corrected manuscript sold for $1.6 million in 2011. A dozen more pages reside at the Morgan Library & Museum in New York. Parts of the text are vintage Austen: "Female economy will do a great deal, my lord, but it cannot turn a small income into a large one."

home. "How odd it was," Kate Penrose says of her grandmother, "to think that women were made for nothing better than to order dinners, cast up accounts, mend clothes, and such like employments." As memoir, the novels speak volumes. As literature, they ring hollow. The stories are complex and melodramatic, the prose strains for effect, and the notion that Jesus redeems in the long run is as plausible as the prediction from a gypsy in a booth at Vauxhall Gardens. Catherine's tedious Christian moralizing is a long way from Austen's subtle skewering of human foibles. While she can hint at the truth, Catherine couldn't write what was in her heart, and as a result the novels fail. They are hard to get hold of these days. I read them under supervision in the Rare Books Room of the British Library, the marbled spines cracked with age rather than use. Catherine earned a little money from them, so her characters did not suffer in vain. Henry James' English-born grandmother devoured the stories. "What she liked, dear gentle lady of many cares and anxieties," Henry wrote of his gran in his autobiography, "was 'the fiction of the day,' the novels, at that time promptly pirated, of Mrs. Trollope and Mrs. Gore, of Mrs. Marsh, Mrs. Hubback and the Misses Kavanagh and Aguillar, whose very names are forgotten now [not entirely], but which used to drive her away to quiet corners whence her figure comes back to me bent forward on a table with the book held out at a distance and a tall single candle placed . . . straight between the page and her eyes."

The curtain rose on the second act when the children left school. John Junior moved to Liverpool and completed a five-year apprenticeship in the grain trade, working for a paternal uncle. Edward did the same. When Charlie left school, Catherine was no longer tied to Portsdown. The grain-trading brother-in-law paid for her to set up home across the river Mersey from Liverpool, in Birkenhead on the Wirral peninsula, close to the two elder boys. The day she arrived, September 28, 1862, the working men of

Birkenhead took to the streets and rioted. Motivated largely by anti-Catholic protest, they were demonstrating in support of Garibaldi and against papal authority and Napoleon III's occupation of Rome. When Birkenhead's large Irish Catholic community joined in, the event, which became known as the Garibaldi Riots, turned violent. Irish families in England endured some of the worst social deprivation in the country—as the anti-abolitionists used to say, they lived like slaves. The "leveling" tendencies Trollope deplored in Cincinnati were not in evidence on Merseyside, even thirty years later. The sight of brawling riots was a poor start for Catherine. She had strong anti-Catholic feelings herself, and no sympathy for the benighted Liverpudlian Irish.

Her middle son, Edward, a restless spirit, failed to find a berth in England. The golden opportunities of California glittered, and he sailed out in 1868, writing home with enthusiasm from San Francisco, where, following the family trade, he found work at a wheat brokerage. Meanwhile Catherine visited her husband in the asylum. She had lost hope that John would recover. But her status was obscure while he was still alive: neither a spinster nor a widow nor a married woman in any meaningful sense. Even widows had a stake in society. She didn't. Her life reiterated Jane Austen's central theme—the universal truth that women need a husband. After John Junior married in 1870, Charlie, unsuited to the grain trade, replied to a newspaper advertisement for a job at a mill in Prince William County, Virginia. Catherine was free to make a fresh start in a country where she had no past, and in the autumn of 1870 she sailed to America with Charlie. She was almost obsessively close to the children. John said she had a telepathic connection with him and was able to recount, in letters, visions of what he was doing. "My mother's disposition was certainly what is now known as psychic," he wrote. "She had the faculty of sensing what was going on at a distance."

On arrival in New York, she continued west on the rails, planning to keep house for Edward. She had not left England since her honeymoon, and there she was clattering alone through Iowa and Nebraska and Wyoming, embroidering a handkerchief on a small wooden frame and listening to the rhythmic pounding of pistons and the wail of a steam whistle while mesas and desert chimneys sped by. She was fifty-two.

California was not American when Fanny Trollope stepped off the *Edward* in New Orleans, and Yo Semite was less familiar to New Yorkers than the Alps. In 1820 Spaniards still held the entire Southwest. The following year Alta California was absorbed into the independent country of Mexico: *los Californios* were Mexicans who traded hides and tallow with European and American merchants in return for tableware, cloth and chocolate. As the Spanish missions broke up, elite families took over their ranching estates, hiring gangs of *vaqueros* to rope cattle. Few visitors troubled the sweeping bay around the 500-strong fishing village of Yerba Buena. In 1847, Yerba Buena changed its name to San Francisco. Then the U.S. seized all the land from California to New Mexico and southern Colorado, enlarging the nation by a third. Still nothing much would have happened for a long time, as California remained remote and uninteresting to a Yankee. But in January 1848, something very big indeed happened when logger James Marshall spotted a lump of something in the tailrace of a sawmill he was building at Coloma. The Gold Rush forged a kind of headstrong, rootless sense of heroic opportunity and glamour still summed up by the word California. Until recently the Golden State was to the U.S. as the U.S. was to the world: an empire of infinite possibility.

Just two decades after Marshall's strike, on May 10, 1869, laborers of the western Central Pacific Railroad and the eastern Union Pacific Railroad met at Promontory Summit in Utah. There, between the cowcatchers of two locomotives facing each other like bulls in combat, railway magnate Leland Stanford drove in a golden spike that linked both halves of the Transcontinental

Railroad—the spikes (only one was gold) ran 1,000 miles from the east and 700 miles from the west. The hammers and spike were wired to a telegraph line so that each hammer stroke would be heard as a click at telegraph stations nationwide (in fact the strokes could not be heard, so the telegraph operator faked them). Stanford's message to both coasts read "DONE." The linking of the rails was a national event, one of the most significant in the forming of America.

The track drew a line between two periods of history. It reduced travel from coast to coast from six months to ten days and unified the country in ways that were not only geographical. Before the railroad, each city and region kept its own time: noon was when the sun was directly overhead. Shortly after Stanford hammered in his spike, a schoolteacher from Saratoga Springs invented the first uniform standard time system—four time zones, each an hour apart from the next. It took a while to catch on. When Catherine traveled, the dusty railroad stations still had two clocks, one for local solar time, another for railroad time.

In the arid semi-desert, the train stopped for water at lone homestead stations where women in calico dresses pumped at wells and cowboys on silver-pommeled saddles galloped away in clouds of dust. The crouching black hills of Wyoming, the pools of light at night in the long hollow box of the carriage, moonlit pines in a canyon—it was a long way from the damp streets and seething tenements of Birkenhead. A New World indeed—one of freezing dawn chill on the plains, newsboys touting cigars, soap and tinned bacon, and miniature sunflowers growing on the track in Nebraska, where the railway "stretched from horizon to horizon, like a cue across a billiard-board."

At first the line only went west as far as Sacramento, but six months later the Central Pacific reached the Bay Area at Oakland, and it was there, early in 1871, that Catherine stepped off, met at the thronging railroad station by Edward. She arrived in a period of spectacular industrial growth. At the outbreak of the Civil War, California was still so isolated that the state authorities refused to legalize the paper currency of the federal government. A decade later, San Francisco—by far the biggest settlement west of the Mississippi, as well as the most hilly on the continent— enjoyed a fully developed transportation system including ferries, streetcars and both five-horse and steam-powered rail lines, and in 1873 the cable car appeared on the steep streets. Before the railroad, everyone in San Francisco was young and foreign, and Americans who had come of age in the Wild West already regretted urban modernization. An editor of the 1873 *City Directory* moaned, "In these modern days of fashionable effeminacy and flabby feebleness . . . [the population of San Francisco] never walks when it can possibly ride." But the Jeffersonian ideal of meritocracy did not extend to social equality: when Catherine arrived the center of wealthy society had already shifted from Rincon Hill to California Hill, where the plutocrats were building their mansions, and which was shortly to be renamed Nob Hill. Stanford, Collis Huntington, Mark Hopkins and Charles Crocker—the Big Four railroad architects of that civilization—

had all been Sacramento storekeepers and made their first fortunes supplying forty-niners. Huntington cornered the shovel market, which was the one to corner under the circumstances. He went on to control the Southern Pacific and almost the entire transport industry of the West. The desire to open up the country was so intense that Washington lawmakers handed swathes of public land the size of small European countries to railway barons. Contracts were rigged, funds siphoned, specifications fiddled, stock manipulated, Congressmen bribed, auditors inveigled, escrow accounts bled, promises broken. Homesteaders ranching on proposed train routes were helpless in the face of the acquisitive might of the rail companies, as *Once Upon a Time in the West* reveals, and most Jill McBains would not, in real life, have kept their Sweetwaters. Whoever owned the land, the one-house railheads that watered steam engines so trains could scream on toward California grew into the towns and cities that made middle America. By the end of the nineteenth century, America had created itself. According to Matthew Arnold, last seen complaining about Harriet Martineau in Ambleside, the country was "no longer interesting."

Edward had taken a house in Oakland, where rents were lower than in San Francisco, the climate warmer and topography gentler. When it was incorporated in 1852, the settlement among hilly oaks and redwood consisted of a scattering of tents and a couple of Mexican ranches. Since then the iron horse had displaced the wild cattle in the valley and travelers crowding off trains had boosted the population to 10,500. By 1880 Oakland was the second largest city in California with 35,000 residents and no oak trees. But dairy farmers still reported fresh bear tracks on the chaparral at the mouth of Temescal Creek. Catherine liked California straightaway, especially the climate. Both she and Edward said they never knew how much they hated Liverpool till they left it. She listed herself as a widow in the *City Directory*. Oakland was a place almost literally without a past, and Catherine

217

could start over, as everyone else did. "There is no there there," according to Gertrude Stein, who grew up in Oakland. The wood-framed Hubback house was on the northwest corner of Eleventh Street and Grove, close to the forest on the edge of town. Like everyone else on Eleventh Street, Catherine employed a succession of Chinese manservants who sent up beefsteak and omelette for breakfast and failed to put enough lard in the pastry. She threw herself into her new life, becoming an active member of St. John's Episcopal Church on Eighth Street and Grove,* where she made friends and taught at Sunday School. She loved flowers, and in the morning cool set about transforming the garden. American food was so good that she put on weight. She walked along the shore of Lake Merritt and took the horse-drawn streetcar that ran between the estuary and North Oakland, enjoying the weather even when torrential rain pooled in Grove Street in a lake she called the Dead Sea. But downpours never lasted long. In neatly written letters home to John and his wife, Mary, she included ink sketches of ladies in long flowery skirts holding parasols and chattered with excitement about the way she was arranging her new abode. "Our house is very comfortable especially my sitting room which has a charming bay window looking west. It makes a delightful room at this time of year as our drawing room is north. I am going to have a Chinese sofa in it, the *sitting* room—then it will be all complete—it is matted, and has a large table covered with a painted cloth, so that I can *cut out* on it." She loved fixing up this place and making it her own. "I only wish I could show you both my room," she wrote to John and his wife. "It really is so pretty and full of fancies. Mr. Emerson, our landlord's brother, and next-door neighbour rather likes to come in here and pay me a visit, he says he knows nobody who has so much invention—and he

*St. John's moved from Eighth and Grove (now Martin Luther King Way). The site is currently occupied by a Catholic church and the shrine of Our Lady of Fatima—Catherine would have hated that.

wanders about the room admiring all my contrivances." The image of the woman indoors writing letters is a Jane Austen classic, and Catherine's correspondence forms an epistolary novel more vivid than her ten real novels. The pages tell a family saga, the story of the immigrant struggle, and from them Catherine's inner life flares up, just as it had in the Jane Austen Archive when the winter light of Hampshire slanted on to her girlhood sketchbooks. Now I was trying to detect another current of electricity—the one that ran from the innocent teenager to the embattled middle-aged woman. Unlike Oakland, Catherine did have a past. It may have been secret, but it lived within her, as the past always does. In the simple pleasures of her California life, she found some small redemption from its trials. I admired that. What is middle age if not a phase of acceptance before the final curtain?

Pirated editions of her novels had appeared in America but she had no interest in writing further volumes: that part of her life was over. She tried features and short stories. In her first year in California, a piece appeared in *Overland Monthly*, the first literary magazine in the West. "The Stewardess" was a purple, six-page account of a woman on a transatlantic ship who gets involved in a smugglers' plot. But there was no money in literary journalism. So, while Ed commuted to San Francisco on the ferry, Catherine gave lessons in lacemaking and embroidery. She was self-contained as a cat, with an equally feline capacity for condescension. Like Fanny Trollope and Fanny Kemble, Catherine took umbrage at the American obsession with equality. Tocqueville was dead, but Europe had still not caught up, as the Birkenhead riots indicated, and the first line of *Democracy in America* might have come straight from one of Catherine's letters: "Among the new objects that attracted my attention during my stay in the US, none struck me more forcibly that the equality of social conditions." Catherine thought people bad-mannered, the maniacal determination "to get on" undignified, and as for American preoccupation with money—what could be more vulgar? Her neighbor Constance Jordan, who drifts through the letters like a nomadic slattern, "has the brusque unfinished ways of most Americans, who are either extremely affected, or unpleasantly natural." (Poor old Mrs. J. Her four noisy children had dirty pinafores and "rough heads," whatever they were, and had a great many accidents. When one girl broke her arm, it was Catherine who had to apply chloroform, as Constance fainted clean away. Worst of all, the Jordans were "Jewish-looking," or at least had "very large dark eyes.") In general women's liberation had gone much too far. The American female, Catherine wrote, "seems to me like the fisherman's wife who was not satisfied with anything short of the sun and the moon." Servants too were again a menace. A young woman interviewed to look after a friend's baby wanted a room of her own in which to entertain male callers, as well as use of the piano. Worse, "they expect to take their meals with the family," the habit that had enraged Trollope in Cincinnati. Catherine's critical commentary on the ways of Oakland humankind is reminiscent of Austen, but more direct, and the irony of her unshakeable belief in the superiority of everything English would not have been lost on Aunt Jane. Like Tocqueville, Catherine went from optimism to pessimism and back when thinking about the success of the American democratic experiment, but, like him, she loved America. I came to admire her capacity to overcome prejudice. It was a consequence of her trauma: John's tragedy enabled her to look beyond what would otherwise have been limited horizons. So she had salvaged something from the gloom.

Every week she took the ferry to San Francisco to shop at the wharf market, where Pacific halibut lay on slabs like murdered Roman emperors. In many ways she was a natural traveler, and despite the priggish comments, she sucked up the energy of the frontier, its bracing sense of optimism. San Francisco was the capital of the West, and the place where miners still came to spend their money. When Mark Twain lived there five years before the Hubbacks, a tart at the Hotel Nymphomania handed him a calling card advertising *Three hundred pounds of black passion. Fifty cents.* Now, that's cheap. Catherine's city had forty bookstores and sixty hotels as well as gambling houses, saloons, theaters and even an opera. The harbor was so crowded with masts that people compared it with a forest, and land at such a premium that people bought water lots—underwater real estate they filled with the residue from blastings, hauling away sand and flattening hills. Shanties rose between Spanish and Mexican *casitas* while imported machinery and sacks of grain blocked the wooden sidewalks and quays, and behind the reclaimed streets, fine houses and stores stretched up Montgomery Street, the commercial artery between the residential districts of North Beach and South Park.

There was no shortage of fires (the city had already burned down six times), murders, or cardsharps. Twain called San Francisco "a gambling carnival." Bowie knives flashed in the alleys while ruined men hanged themselves in cheap boardinghouses. "Every sun that rose in the morning," Twain wrote, "went down on paupers enriched and rich men beggared." Many of the gambling dens were in Chinatown, a network of tenements with cigar factories in the cellars. Outside, Chinese men treadled sewing machines at night lit by swinging lanterns. Aromas of sandalwood drifted from the temples and smoked duck and sodden pork from the kitchens. Tens of thousands of Chinese men and about 500 women lived in San Francisco in 1871, mostly working as domestic cooks, or street vendors selling soup. They made up 8 percent of the state population. Most came from the southern province of Guangdong, where railroad companies had dispatched gangs of recruiters. Those who signed up were indentured to one of the six companies that paid passage to California—almost slaves. Many came to mine, many more to build the railroads, working for twenty-eight dollars a month and cooking dried oysters and salted cabbage under canvas: 80 percent of the workforce that laid the tracks through the Sierra Nevada were Chinese. They were persecuted—the usual stuff about taking away the white man's job. The authorities levied punitive taxes on their laundries, denied them the right to purchase mining claims and put them in prison for offenses that passed without comment in others. Catherine was fond of her Chinese servants and expressed indignation at their treatment, which she perceived as an affront to Christian morality—and besides, she naturally identified with the dispossessed.

She lent Edward her remaining capital to set up a wheat brokerage with a young English partner at 316 California Street in downtown San Francisco. The firm appeared to make a promising start. Edward, she said, "is worried that he is growing dreadfully American and caring for nothing but money." She was in regular touch with her other two sons ("I like to hear all about the babies very much," she wrote to John). Over in Virginia, the mill had failed, drought had made farming impossible, and Charlie had married and produced a son. He had found work at a vineyard and then as a plowman and woodchopper but the family regularly had nothing to eat but bread. Their struggle was on Catherine's mind all the time, and she mailed what money she could. When, back in Birkenhead, John too had business problems, she wrote phlegmatically of her own situation, "I have lived through so many [difficulties] that I don't seem to mind them so much." Catherine had the élan characteristic of the nineteenth century but a sense of the sad absurdity of life one associates with the twentieth. She looked back ruefully at the first years of her marriage. "That was in my prosperous days," she wrote once, "when I dressed well, and we gave dinner parties." But moans were few. Like Fanny Trollope, Catherine got on with it, relying on feline self-containment and emotional restraint. She looked outward. In Oakland she founded an Improving Society aimed at raising moral standards.

"I am so fond of travelling for its own sake," Catherine wrote to Mary. So was everyone else in San Francisco: tourism was a craze. The railroads had transformed the American perception of landscape. To the pioneers, uncultivated land was space to be conquered, an unknown negative where they might die of thirst, or from buffalo attack, or an Indian arrow. They were afraid of it. John Gast's famous oil *American Progress* is an allegorical representation of the modernization of the West. Columbia, golden-haired personification of the United States, leads civilization westward above the settlers' wagons, stringing telegraph wire as she flies and gripping a schoolbook while Native Americans and wild animals slink away on the plains below. Catherine's California excursions reflected a new realization that "wilderness" could be part of the American narrative, and nature a source of strength and healing. The Alps remained the best-known European landscape, celebrated remorselessly by the Romantics with their cult of the sublime. But the Alps were puny compared with the Sierra Nevada, Yo Semite, Yellowstone. Post-railroad Americans integrated grand wonders and the monumentalism of natural spaces into their national vision, and in 1872 the federal government formalized the notion when President Grant signed Yellowstone on to the statute books as the first national park. Catherine caught this wave. Nobody was interested in the fact that Shoshone sheep eaters had been living off Yellowstone for centuries, or that other Indians had been using the ecosystems of the West for generations in all kinds of different ways. The indigenous peoples' relationship with the landscape was spiritual as well as practical. They did not tame it or harness it: they were part of it. In northern California, after decades of assault on the Modoc and their land, the government deported the whole Modoc people out of their homeland at Tule Lake to the Klamath Reserve in Oregon. The Klamath people refused to share their food and lumber with the Modoc. It was the beginning of the Modoc War, in which braves and U.S. army marksmen faced each other across the lava beds of northeast California. The preservation of wilderness was only a chapter of the story. Those driving through railroad construction projects also had to get inconvenient indigenous populations out of the way (the real ones, not the Fenimore Cooper kind). The Hunkpapa Lakota chief Sitting Bull had already knelt on the banks of the Yellowstone river and faced soldiers protecting Chinese laborers laying the rails of the Northern Pacific, and Sherman, the general who burned his way to Savannah, had used the same armed tactics to clear a belt of the West for the railroad. Between 1848 and 1860, white men's guns killed 120,000 of the 150,000 Indians in California. That was the cost of expansion, of Manifest Destiny, of the USA. Catherine witnessed the most fatal chapter in the indigenous story. It was a kind of turning to the wall: an end. There was nothing uniquely American about it. In account after account of indigenous dispossession, I could have been reading about the Chukchi, the Inuit or any other of the myriad groups dragged into a cash society and separated from the landscape that invested their universe with meaning. A Crow scout once said this in a council meeting when his people were under pressure to sell their land: "The soil you see is not ordinary soil. It is the dust of the blood of the flesh and bones of our ancestors. We fought and bled and died to keep other Indians from taking it and fought and bled and died, helping the whites. You will have to dig through the surface before you can find the earth, as the upper portion is Crow. The land as it is, is my blood, and my dead."

Having dealt with the people, railroad barons set about the destruction of the bison. Eighteen seventy-two was a pivotal year for that doomed species. One of the first trains ran for 120 miles through a single herd. Over the next three years, white hunters converged on Dodge City, Kansas, to ship over a million hides to Europe and the East Coast, where they provided the drive belts of the industrial revolution.

Catherine girlishly longed to paddle in the Pacific, and traveled with a neighbor by rail to Watsonville, where she enjoyed her first experience in a mudwagon, a kind of light stagecoach built to withstand the atrocious California roads. The vehicle was so jammed with passengers that it was impossible for any of them to be thrown out (a regular occurrence). Santa Cruz, Catherine wrote home, "is not much of a town but the country round it is lovely, canyons with clear running streams that never dry." Yellow violets, columbine and pink mallow bloomed on the forest floor and one of the redwoods was so big that a family lived in it. On the journey up the coast to Pescadero, one passenger was obliged to lie on the luggage stowed at the back. It took nine hours, the north wind blew in their faces and one woman wouldn't stop talking to the driver, who continually twisted round to reply, at which point the horses stopped. ("I am sure," wrote Catherine, "that if her tongue had been as cold as my feet, she would not have said a word.") The party inspected a newly erected lighthouse at Pigeon Point. The Fresnel lens had been installed, and the keeper and his three assistants were preparing to light the lard-oil lantern for the first time. Beyond a Chinese fishing camp on the bay, Portuguese shore whalers had opened a trading center and rigged up a boom and cable to load lumber, as well as a wharf with a grain chute. Catherine loved it all, even the freezing hotel in Pescadero with hard beds and a broken window. It was fresh and new and had no associations. She spent the next day on Pescadero beach, paddling at last, and sent for lunch to be brought down from the San Gregorio House in Half Moon Bay. The tourists rushed off to clamber over the rock formations at the northern end of the beach and pick up sand-polished bits of topaz and jasper. Geology was the science that mattered most, like climate studies now: people believed it would unlock the future. After Martineau's visitor Charles Lyell published his multi-volume *Principles of Geology* in 1830, popularizing the idea that the earth was shaped by slow-moving forces, rocks had taken on tremendous significance in the public imagination and the fascination continued into the Edwardian era, as one observes in the case of Captain Scott, who dragged hundreds of pounds of specimens across Antarctica while dying of cold.

At the head of every tourist trail, a photographer lay in wait. In 1872, most people, including Catherine, had never seen their own image, except in a looking glass. The telephone and phonograph had reached Eleventh Street but the framed photograph remained a novelty. Spotting an opportunity, more than a dozen portrait photographers had opened studios on San Francisco's Montgomery Street, and Catherine was one of many who made a pilgrimage to experience the remarkable phenomenon of appearing on paper. (So had Isabella Bird.) The new art form fascinated Catherine. She learned to tint photographs, earning extra money by selling the prints at Carleton Watkins' Yosemite Gallery on the same street as the studios. Portraiture was the photographers' main source of income, but the most skilled began to experiment with a new form: landscape. The technical challenges were immense, the market initially uncertain. But there was an opportunity to be brilliant. A few were, and Englishman Eadweard Muybridge was the most brilliant of all. He had a studio at 429 Montgomery and had just received the Medal of Progress at the Vienna Exhibition for his pictures of Modoc warriors at the lava beds. Like Catherine, he chose California as the place to reinvent himself. She changed her status—he even changed his name.

Muybridge is remembered for his sequence of photographs of a galloping horse. He was the first man to capture motion, and he did it by inventing a way of making exposures at a fraction of a second. Whichever way you trace the history of cinema, a techno-

logical revolution still then in the future, it always comes back to Muybridge. He remains one of the most influential photographers of all time. His was a peculiarly California story. Born in Kingston upon Thames in 1830, just as photography was invented, Muybridge emigrated to America in his twenties. His initial whereabouts are lost in the fog of the past, but at one point he was in New Orleans photographing steamboats discharging cotton from the Mississippi plantations. By 1855 he had set up as a bookseller in San Francisco, touting new editions of Audubon's birds from 113 Montgomery Street. In 1860 he handed the business over to his brother, and headed east on the Butterfield Overland Stage. Just north of Fort Worth in Texas, the six mustangs drawing the stage bolted, smashing the coach into a tree. Two people died, and Muybridge suffered an orbitofrontal cortex brain injury. He was under treatment for a year and had double vision, among other things. He returned to England to recover. In 1866 he went back to California "a different man" and reinvented himself as a landscape photographer. He lodged near Catherine in a boardinghouse in Oakland, wore an unruly beard and was known to be kindly, eccentric and highly strung. Like all frontiers, San Francisco was a place of new beginnings where one could obliterate the past, and Muybridge changed his surname twice, as well as the spelling of his first name.

In the 1860s and 1870s the Civil War photographer Timothy O'Sullivan worked for two government-sponsored surveys west of the 100th meridian. The images, when they appeared in galleries and magazines from New York to Savannah, inspired a craze for wilderness photography and cemented the image of the untamed American West, still one of America's most enduring cultural myths. There are no operatics or stage-settings in an O'Sullivan picture, just aridity, hard clarity and emptiness. You can't look at his photographs of Yampah Canon in Colorado or the California sierras without hearing eternal silence. Like most of his contemporaries, O'Sullivan was based on the East Coast. It was California photographers like Muybridge who popularized Yosemite as a landscape of epic grandeur. When that happened, Yosemite took over from Niagara Falls as the epitome of majestic America, and elided its name at the same time. Stereoscopic landscape photography flourished in San Francisco in Catherine's period and she loved looking through the special glasses, and for a time it was Muybridge's medium: seen through a viewer, two pictures of a mountain scene taken from different positions merge into one three-dimensional image. It was a poignant choice for a man suffering double vision. He sold hundreds of thousands. Muybridge, like O'Sullivan, used wet plate collodion negatives and albumen prints. He pioneered the mammoth plate, a twenty-by-twenty-four-inch glass negative that had to be carted around, as the photographer had to develop the image before the collodion dried. You had ten minutes. In the northern California sierras Muybridge often had four assistants and a mule train, and when the others refused to follow him up some vertiginous path, he carried the gear himself in relay, including the portable darkroom. Muybridge went for the drama of the cliff face, the fury of the turbulent river and the romance of a streak of cirrus cloud. He was among the first artists to produce exultantly monumental depictions of the natural world of the United States. He liked shadows, exploding waterfalls and chaotic rocks, chopping down trees by the score and including the wreckage of their dismembered trunks and branches in the frame. Muybridge sought to express the fragility and smallness of humanity, regularly inserting a tiny man somewhere in the background, almost swallowed by a vast rockscape. Sometimes he posed himself, sitting perilously on an overhang, looking absurdly vulnerable.

Commissions multiplied. The U.S. Lighthouse Board engaged him to photograph their new Pacific creations. The classically composed Pigeon Point prints depict the solid new lighthouse rearing into a huge sky scudded with cloud, a pair of tiny figures at the base, the wickies' house, the whalers' loading boom and a swirl of

dark rocks that burst from the foam like tectonic waves. The lumi-
nous water animates the picture. While working on this commission, Muybridge met Flora, a glamorous photographic retoucher
half his age. She was married, and he paid for her divorce. The
couple wed and had a son they called Floredo. Flora enjoyed
the company of a wealthy surveyor called Harry Larkyns. Muybridge had warned her off him. When Floredo was three, Muybridge found a snapshot of the child on the sideboard at his nurse's
house. Flora had written on the back, "Little Harry." It was ironic
that a photograph, of all things, destroyed Muybridge's happiness.
Larkyns was surveying at the Yellow Jacket silver mine in the
Sierra Nevada at the time. The afternoon of the day Muybridge
found the photograph, he put a pistol in his pocket and ran to
catch the Vallejo ferry. From there, he took the new train up Napa
Valley to Calistoga. It was already dark when he got there, but he
hired a man with a horse and buggy to drive him up Knights Valley to Yellow Jacket, and practiced firing his pistol on the way. At
the mine manager's house, Muybridge asked for Larkyns. When he

appeared, lit by a full moon, Muybridge shot him dead. At the trial, the mix of celebrity, adultery and assassination caused a sensation. The penalty for murder was death. Muybridge's defense team pleaded insanity. Muybridge remained in a cell, more isolated and fragile in a crowded jail than any of the figures in his titanic rockscapes. Like actors, lawyers had more scope to ham it up then. "Let him take up the thread of his broken life," the lead defense lawyer pleaded with the jury, "and resume that profession upon which his genius has shed so much luster . . . let him go forth into the green fields, by the bright waters . . . and in the active work of securing shadows of their beauty by the magic of his art . . ." They did. The members of the jury were all married men who felt certain they would have done the same had their wives betrayed them, and they acquitted without finding the plaintiff insane. Muybridge therefore got off a murder he admitted. His hair had turned white in three months. But it was Flora, not Muybridge, who paid the highest price. Abandoned by her husband, her lover dead, she went into a decline, and was dead herself at twenty-four. Floredo entered an orphanage.

Muybridge continued his restless inquiry. After the trial, he turned to the panorama—a sequence of plates of San Francisco taken on the same day and joined together. His famous thirteen-plate, seventeen-foot production hangs in the private banqueting room of The Big Four restaurant in the Huntingdon Hotel. When I was in San Francisco I telephoned, and the maître d' invited me in to have a look. The dining rooms were full, the piano was tinkling, and a rich, meaty aroma floated from the kitchen. The banqueting room, however, was empty, and I had half an hour alone with Muybridge.

Three things struck me as I looked at the sequence of images. First, how extraordinarily developed the city was in 1878. Second, how beautiful the bay seemed with its forest of masts, and Alcatraz, and washing flapping on flat roofs in the foreground. Third, how steep that topography was and is: at the left end of the

panorama, stepladders reached down from homes to the level below. I already knew it, as I was still blotting sweat from the hike up
to California Street. But the stepladders brought it home. This
was a city built by resourceful people. And who was more resourceful than Muybridge? His next obsessional project required
every skill he had, at least in the mental resource department. It
was the galloping horse. Leland Stanford kept thoroughbreds on
an estate forty miles south of the city, now the site of Stanford
University. The stable had won eighteen world records, and Stanford had already commissioned Muybridge to find out whether,
when a horse ran, all four hooves were ever in the air at the
same time. Muybridge had photographed his racehorse Occi-
dent galloping round the Bay District Track. After months of
experimentation, Muybridge created a superfast shutter that he
installed on a bank of cameras at Stanford's racetrack, which then

photographed a jockey galloping past on another thoroughbred, Sallie Gardner. Trip wires on the track activated the camera batteries. The flickering, shifting results were dazzling. It was the first time anyone had ever seen pictures of motion.*

In 1874, Catherine visited Coloma. Twenty-five years had passed since the first gold rush. Some forty-niners had settled, and Coloma enjoyed liveries, breweries, the Sierra Nevada House hotel and a branch of Wells Fargo bank in Bill McConnell's general store. An express wagon shuttled to and from Sacramento every day. The wooden jail had burned down, but its stone replacement was in constant use, and out on the diggings beyond the exfoliated hills and commercial mines lone speculators still panned the creeks. The following year, Catherine took her most adventurous trip, north to what was known as "The Geysers," actually a region of volcanic terrain in the Mayacamas Mountains. Proceeding by boat and rail to Cloverdale, where she spent the night, Catherine took a brightly painted mudwagon through Red Bluff and up into the mountains. At the Toll House Hotel in the elbow of a glen the wind poured into Napa Valley and a cuckoo clock hooted for its far-off country. Red Bluff was an ocean-going port then, and ships came up on the Sacramento River to unload goods that could then be sent by road to the Nevada mines (the China Rapids blocked further riverine progress). On the four-and-a-half-hour drive up to the volcanic plateaux the track teetered on narrow hilltop ridges with "3 inches of road to spare" before the cliff fell into the peaceful ravine. Jonestown was empty, yet only a few years earlier 2,000 silver miners slept under canvas there alongside a single roofed house which sold whiskey. "Canon grand, geysers rather a humbug," Catherine noted, but the journey back out was

---

*Muybridge took stills which, ran together, looked like cine film. My iPhone Muybridge app does the reverse: it films in video, then chops the images down into stills. So I have a sequence of my son leaping across my bedroom transformed into a set of Muybridge stills. Thus technology marches on.

"never to be forgotten." The mudwagon carried nine passengers in three rows, and Catherine was seated at the end of a row. "If I had stretched out my arm," she wrote, "I could have dropped a stone straight down into the river two thousand feet below us." From Pine Tree Flat they ran to Calistoga, where Clark Foss took the reins outside Cheeseborough's Hotel. Six feet two and over two hundred pounds, sporting sideburns and a ten-gallon hat, Foss was the leading whip on the route and renowned throughout northern California—Robert Louis Stevenson, who rode with him, described him as "glorified with legend." A younger stage driver reported in awe that Foss "could handle six horses like you'd handle that many cats. He would lift them right off their feet and swing them around corners so fast you couldn't see the lead team," and the local newspaper wrote that Foss "drove his six-in-hand as though four fiends were after him, directing them by his thundering voice as much as with his huge fists, and at the same time snapping his long whip with a shot like a pistol, echoing through the hills." As Catherine knew, "He upset last year and killed a lady, and since he has been more cautious." Some of the men in her party said he was nowhere near cautious enough, and that they would not do it again for a hundred dollars. But as the stage hurtled down with Foss in full throat and red tassels streaming from the silver bridles, Catherine lost herself in the moment. All the pain and misery and struggle flew away with the whoosh of the wind. She told John she couldn't wait to do it again.

That year, which was 1874, their landlord announced that he wanted the Eleventh Street house back. The Hubbacks moved half a mile to 959 Seventh Street, a run-down area past the market and toward West Oakland. Seventh was a wide road that followed the railway, and the new garden looked up at the railroad embankment. It was not as good an area, and they could hear the shunting yards. Oakland had mushroomed since Catherine arrived. "We have to walk a long way now to reach anything like country," she wrote home from Seventh Street. She never complained on her own account and only worried about the financial security of Edward and Charlie. Rampant speculation on railroads and real estate had brought disaster and when, in 1873, financier Jay Cooke closed his Philadelphia bank after reckless capital investment, he set off panic and depression that dragged on till the late 1870s, as Isabella Bird discovered when she could not draw money out of any bank in Denver. Catherine wrote to ask John if he could make Edward a loan, so that she could give what little she earned lacemaking, tinting photographs and teaching to Charlie. In 1875 she returned to England on a visit in order to obtain funds from a small inheritance she had received in trust from her stepmother. In the Wirral, staying with John and his expanding family, she visited her husband in the asylum. He did not recognize her.

That year, the Bank of California failed. Edward's business went bankrupt and he fell out with his partner. When Catherine returned to Oakland they had to move house again, this time to 1128 Myrtle Street, three blocks from the first house. She blamed the banks. So did John Steinbeck when he documented the next economic collapse sixty-four years later in *The Grapes of Wrath*. So did we when we faced the next one seventy years after that. Again, one wonders how much we have learned. Meanwhile Edward found a job as an agent for the Stockton Transportation company. He was courting, and in 1876 announced his engagement. Catherine had never intended to remain in California once he settled, and it was time for a change. She longed to know her new grandchildren in Virginia and to see another part of her adopted land, and that November moved to Charlie and Dina's farm in Gainesville. Her American reinvention had been more successful than she could have hoped. It was an ongoing process. In the course of Catherine's California adventure the Bay Area had developed at breakneck speed even by the standards of the American frontier: San Francisco was now the ninth city in the country. But on the other coast Charlie was still eking out a homesteaders' existence, his farm unconnected to the turnpike by road. It was a bitterly cold winter. Within six months of arrival, Catherine was dead. Aged fifty-eight, she had succumbed to pneumonia. There were no regrets. "I don't think," she had written home, "you need pity me for any part of my California life unless it is that stockings will wear out so fast."

EPILOGUE

I had finished a book publicity tour with an event in Marin County—a plane a day for two weeks, and lots of room service. I needed open space and an escape route. The morning after the event I picked up a small Toyota in downtown San Francisco, crossed the Bay Bridge to Oakland and plowed along a ten-lane highway to Sacramento and beyond until the traffic and the high-rises and the projects thinned, and I turned on to Highway 49, the road furrowed by the wagon trails of the forty-niners. Catherine had been there. The rails brought maps, because engineers and surveyors had made them, and like her I used W. J. Keeler's 1867 chart, splintered with creeks and dotted with mining camps but showing, almost complete, the dark crosshatching of a train line. It was to be the last of my American journeys, at least for the time being. I felt sad—it had been a wonderful time in every way—but there was too a sense of completion.

Coloma and El Dorado County lie on the South Fork of the American River around the sawmill where Marshall found his nuggets. It was a warm day in early spring but at the Sierra Nevada Hotel a wood-burning stove was batting out heat. Polaroids of happy visitors covered one of the end walls, and on the other a huge screen was showing pop videos under a buffalo head. A row of men sat at the bar drinking beer. They were technology entrepreneurs from Silicon Valley, on a kayaking trip—"getting drugged up on nature," one of them said. Californians have trailblazed since landscape photography exploded from Montgomery Street studios in the 1870s, and the extravagant wilderness around them remains an integral part of the process—a connection made when Catherine trundled along the new tourist trails in a mudwagon. Later, on the top of a hill, I photographed a statue of Marshall peering from a column and pointing to the spot where the first nugget gleamed. The discovery might have launched a California dream that the kayakers were still pursuing, but for Marshall the dream died, and so did he, in poverty in a broken-down Coloma cabin. Now, his boyhood home in New Jersey is a national monument. On Coloma green, they had preserved the miners' jail. Every gold town on the 120-mile Mother Lode had its jail, along with a saloon and a brothel. There was no official currency, how-

ever, and between 1849 and 1855 fifteen private mints operated in California. At first, most miners were either *Californios* or indigenous Americans. Within a year, prospectors had shipped in from all over the Union. When the economy tanked in Chile, 5,000 Chileans arrived. Like Mexicans, Chilean miners were skilled at coyote mining, which was the most dangerous kind: men dug precarious narrow tunnels like coyote to reach the buried river channels that held gold deposits. In 1850—the year California entered the Union as the thirty-first state—15,000 more Mexicans showed up at the diggings, in flight from Apache raids in Sonora. Thousands of Irish came at the same time, during the potato famine. Two years later, 25,000 Chinese fled starvation and war in Guangdong and headed to the California diggings. Twenty-eight thousand French appeared after their crops and their government failed at the same time. The weak died of disease or bad whiskey and the losers went home, leaving an instant state of strong, first-generation Americans making it up as they went along. The population of California was disproportionately young and male before Catherine arrived, and geographical isolation allowed the immigrants to develop a unique society. The suggestion persisted—persists still—that on the Pacific coast Americans might find new and alternative ways of living. California was a psychological frontier as well as a geographical one. Homesteaders like Rebecca plowing up the Midwest and wagon trains trundling across the Plains were already expanding America, and the Gold Rush accelerated the process. The push west was a truly American business. In the eighteenth century the British government had decided that the line of the Allegheny Mountains would mark the limit of their American empire. What could be less American than stopping halfway? In 1846 British politicians had simply ceded the whole of Oregon because there were no beaver left (their representatives had killed them all). Tocqueville was of the opinion that a "restless spirit" was the defining American characteristic—forward movement, progress, conquering. American society reconfigured itself as the frontier steadily advanced: the Atlantic, the Alleghenies, the Mississippi, the 99th meridian, the Rockies, the Pacific—each forward thrust won by a succession of Indian wars. In the far West, the last frontier, an abundance of land promoted the most equal equality. For 300 years, the dominant feature of American life was expansion. The first period of national history ended with the frontier gone—though many, including Teddy Roosevelt, went on to believe that the disappearance of a domestic border triggered the start of an imperial adventure, taking the frontier overseas, and JFK took up the idea as a metaphor for social progress when he called space "the new frontier." And so it goes on. One hundred and sixty-one years separated the Gold Rush from the Deepwater spill off New Orleans—the one in which 5 billion barrels of oil spewed into the Gulf of Mexico. The period had been shaped by the quest for minerals and hydrocarbons and it had been a hard-fought journey from shovels and sieves to wells seven miles deep. But one wondered where the next leg would end—and what had been learned.

Before Columbia, the land opened up and cows grazed in meadows flecked with flowers. Angel's Camp, Fourth Crossing, Chinese Camp—those names had appeared after Keeler's map, marking the diggings of the 1850s. After Moccasin Creek, the road began to sashay, and the green hills on either side wore misty turbans. Valley quails dotted and dashed down the creeks. At Coulterville, I had a fried-egg sandwich on processed white bread and slept in a simple hotel. In 1850 George Coulter pitched his tent in the foothills of the Sierra Nevada, and 161 years on, Coulterville (population 200) had made slow progress. Even the Sun Sun Wo Company was still standing, the store that serviced the men working the placers in Black, Boneyard and Maxwell Creeks. When I turned off Highway 49 late the next afternoon and headed west, it was twilight—the time of cow dust—and swallows were returning to the nests. Far ahead, the coastal mountains fretted the horizon. A sense of space and peace descended, like a benediction. The valley widened to agricultural flatlands and the sky filled the windscreen, a blue cupola streaked with white wisps. The ratio of people to land increased a little; posters advertised a rodeo; I passed cattle ranches, sheep ranches, a llama ranch, intensive fruit farming. After Los Banos the road climbed through dry oak woodlands of interior chaparral, cresting the Diablo Range before Gilroy, where a sign welcomed me to the Garlic Capital of the World. But it wasn't garlic growing in the fields: it was artichokes. Miles and miles of them— 95 percent of America's artichokes grow around Castroville in the Salinas Valley. I could smell them. Each year the town elects an Artichoke Queen. The first was crowned in 1948. Her name was Norma Jean Baker, soon better known as Marilyn Monroe.

Left to right — Edward Modena, Randy Barsotti, Marilyn Monroe, Enrico Bellone.

No novelist has conjured the ambiguity of the American dream more effectively than John Steinbeck. He grew up in Salinas, in the valley between the Santa Lucia and Gabilan mountains, a lush and fertile region where he set most of his books. The limestone of the mountains runs through the stories like a seam. I recognized the landscape George and Lennie trudged through in *Of Mice and Men* on their way to find bindlestiff work, dreaming of settling in their own place, petting rabbits and living "off the fatta the lan'." In Salinas, a team of volunteers run the Steinbeck family home as a period restaurant. The white-haired waitresses—the youngest was seventy-two—wore Victorian rig. They brought mushroom bisque where there should have been grilled chicken, and ice cream where there ought to have been mushroom bisque, bustling back and forth underneath a portrait of John Ernst, Steinbeck's father, a dark, Hanoverian figure with a moustache that meant business. Steinbeck had a happy childhood in that house, but people turned against him later because he was frank about the poverty he witnessed. They especially hated *Cannery Row* and its Monterey derelicts. For a period, all America turned against Steinbeck. The day before he went to Stockholm to collect his Nobel Prize, the *New York Times* published a vitriolic attack, and after *The Grapes of Wrath* many had called him a Communist. Steinbeck was always on the side of the workers, the marginalized, the dispossessed. In *Grapes* he showed California—the promised land—as a place of violence, labor camps, exploitation and starvation; the sequel to Catherine and Edward's experience of a California Golden Age. The author said it was a nasty book, and that he would have made it nastier if he could. In the thirties, when the novel is set, California actually tried to seal its borders from the rest of the U.S. to keep the Okies out. It was already no longer quite such an empire of infinite possibility.

At Carmel I joined the Pacific Coast Highway, the über-route that shadows the ocean for 660 miles from the canyons of Orange County to the grasslands of the Mendocino Coast. Carmel was,

according to Steinbeck, founded "by starveling writers and un-
wanted painters." Little evidence remained of starveling. The
town has evolved into an exclusive enclave of swept wide streets
that fall precipitously to the ocean and art galleries hung with terrible art. In a grotesque irony, one of the tricksy shops, an emporium flogging fake English furniture, had called itself Jane Austen
at Home (*New In: Cath Kidston!*). On the white sand beach, men
pounded along behind jogging buggies with customised tires. As
Steinbeck said, "If Carmel's founders should return . . . they would
be instantly picked up as suspicious characters and deported over
the city line." I stayed one night in a faux-Normandy inn, ate in an
expensive Italian restaurant, and the next morning, headed around
Monterey Bay, where prevailing north-westerlies had twisted cy-
presses on the granite headlands into fugitive ghosts. At Monterey
itself, the fish guts and flies were gone from the beaches and the
sardine canneries no longer lined the wharf, but the tide pools still
smelled of iodine and death. They were Steinbeck's central metaphor in *Cannery Row*—moist microcosms of life. I ate *chicharrónes*,
albóndigas and corn tortillas, and visited San Carlos de Borromeo
de Carmelo, one of the first missions in Alta California, and for
the Hispanic period the most powerful. Between 1770 and 1836,
Spanish Fathers baptized 4,000 Eslene Indians under the cate-
nary arch of the mission church, regrettably not the only thing
they did to them. The pinkish-yellow, bell-shaped flowers of
mission manzanita still bloomed against the sandstone. A couple
emerged from Mass and dipped their hands in the fountain. The
silence was heavy. Out of town and across the Salinas River estuary, I hung around in Santa Cruz, mostly on the beach where a
pair of Hawaiian princes once stood on the first American surf-
boards. The wind was gusting in from the ocean, bending the
long grass double. Homely Santa Cruz had none of the urbane
glamour of the coastal towns of Southern California. The board-
walk, the municipal wharf, the Coney Island–style funfair—little
had changed since the 1950s, an era that represents California's

best, compared with the bankruptcy of the 2011 administration, which I heard relentlessly picked over on the car radio. The Golden State had come to represent everything wrong with the U.S., its ongoing carnival of plebiscites a symbol of a nation haunted by decline. Fifty years ago, I heard a commentator drawl, the U.S. made half the shoes on the planet. Now there are only two firms producing shoes in the whole country.

The dimpled hills drew close to the coast, spliced with gulches and saltwater tidal creeks. The sun had burned off the clouds, the wind had subsided, and the ocean glittered an intense deep blue, as if it had been painted. Not long after Davenport, the blink of Pigeon Point Lighthouse glanced off the water. In the first half of the nineteenth century, on this, among the foggiest coastlines of the world, with submerged rocks to boot, clippers heading for the Gold Rush regularly foundered. Faced with mounting disasters, the California authorities erected fifty-nine lighthouses up and down the coast. At 115 feet, Pigeon Point is the second tallest and the oldest still functioning. The tower flashes every ten seconds, just as it did when a lard-oil lamp lit the 8,000-pound Fresnel lens in 1872. I booked myself into Pigeon Point Lighthouse Hostel, four bungalows on the site of the former keepers' house. My bungalow, called Pelican, had three bedrooms, a bunkroom and a kitchen with a fridge the size of a garden shed containing a Tupperware marked, "Free! Vegan organic curry!" In the morning a grey whale fluked beyond the lighthouse. Its spume dissolved into the dawn air, the polished back sank, and the sun levered itself above the cordillera to beam rays of light on the beach. When apocalyptic weather came in, I was pleased, as it meant I had to stay longer. The yellow skies distended with thunder and I ate the vegan curry. On the radio, I heard that heavy snowfall had closed Yosemite and landfalls had cut off Big Sur on both sides—helicopters were delivering medical supplies. Twenty-foot waves crashed on to the lighthouse, and driving rain turned the world silver. Was there not some relief that the *Sturm und Drang* of youth had ceased, or most of it, and that one could at

last enjoy serenity freed from the shackles of the past—or at least with the chains loosened? In order to go forward, one has to leave so much behind. Let's face it, I look crap in shorts. And now for the first time in half a century I could also, to some small degree, accept my brother's indignity. There would be further flares of rage on that topic, but seeing through a glass darkly is still seeing, and acceptance arrives in drops, not cupfuls. Journey's end approached, and I faced a longer voyage when I got home—a trip that would take years. But I faced it with a degree of serenity I had not experienced for a very long time. I was leaving America preparing to come to rest on flatter ground. But I would never leave my girls.

When the storm ended, California emerged newly minted. Coyote brush and blackberry nodded with droplets and changing light reconfigured the view north to Pescadero State Beach and

Half Moon Bay. Harbor seals played on the rocks. Inland from the lighthouse, dark creeks ran fast through the old-growth redwoods. What the live oak is to Georgia, so is *sequoia sempervirens* to California: trees that Steinbeck called "ambassadors from another time." In *Travels with Charley: In Search of America* he wrote of the redwoods' "warm monster bodies," and the "cathedral hush" he experienced when walking in the sequoia groves of Northern California. Again and again Steinbeck reaches for sacred vocabulary to describe the vast trees with their flat, bright green leaves and soft, fibrous bark. In *Travels with Charley* they are "godlike" and "holy." He said that in that book, the story of a road trip across America, he was "trying to rediscover this monster land," and it was as if he found something of its essence in the trees of his childhood home. The first decades of the twentieth century were fertile ones for American letters. After the closing of Manifest Destiny and the events described in this book, other writers sought to make sense of what they had inherited, as Steinbeck had. Dos Passos, Fitzgerald, Faulkner, Hemingway, Wolfe, Steinbeck himself and Caldwell—all were born within seven years of one another. But what did Steinbeck discover in his search for America? According to *Travels with Charley*, he found lassitude and indifference and an absence of the thrusting frontier spirit that forged his country. He cited boredom and material desires as the manifestation of social rot. He found a diminution of regional identity and an increase in Americanization. All that is still true, and more so, yet for all the talk of plummeting shoe production I couldn't help thinking that although I had been reading about American decline all my life, the country seemed robust enough. The neurotic nationalism Fanny Trollope noticed almost two centuries ago persists within the freakery of Republican politics, but on the whole I had found joy amid the shards of disillusion almost everywhere I went in America. Unlike memoir, fiction never lies, and in his novels Steinbeck brought to the American dream of self-improvement a message of tolerance and compassion. He found something he

246

called a universal American identity which turned out to be a *good* thing. "We are a nation," he wrote, "a new breed. Americans are much more American than they are northerners, southerners . . . more alike than the Welsh are like the English." Whitman said, "The United States themselves are essentially the greatest poem," and in book after book Steinbeck showed he believed it. I believe it too, especially now, when the American century is over. The country has had to redefine itself, just as my girls had. And it is so much more likeable as a result.

When I headed north across the Golden Gate Bridge two days later, a flash shower engulfed the forest of cranes and container ships on the Oakland shore in a gray cloud. The bay spouted with a million geysers. North of San Francisco, tucked into the narrow strip of land west of the coastal range, the highway coiled around Sausalito and through Marin County, a fuzzy landscape of galleries, organic coffee shops and joggers. The eucalyptus were shedding, and their smell infused the Toyota. But then, after a thin spreading of poorer settlements, the cabins and trailers dissolved, and Point Reyes National Seashore blazed away across Drakes Bay. The seismic nature of the California landscape revealed itself in literal terms at Point Reyes: rolls and rolls of once liquid rock. Inland, cattle and sheep grazed, and offshore central-casting California surf rolled in for a hundred miles. Black oyster catchers looped overhead and the sun emerged intermittently, between mild rain. In the afternoon I turned inland on Highway 36, away from the ocean. There was no other traffic at all there. Moist grasslands merged into redwood forest and the South Fork Mountains, a landscape of towering firs drooping with snow. Taking a break to walk in the muffled snowy silence, I experienced a vague sense of relief. I had made it to the half-century mark more or less intact, and the prospects ahead no longer seemed gloomy. I had learned, from my six characters, that there were many ways of tackling the hurdles of late middle age. Accept what can't be changed, like Fanny Trollope, and forswear anger, bitterness and self-pity. Sail into decrepitude with dignity, like Fanny Kemble, and carry on washing in milk pans with Harriet's vigor and Isabella's élan. Submit to hard work like Rebecca. Salvage joy in the daily detail, like Catherine.

People say all the journeys have been made, and all the adventures covered. I no longer believe that; it is never too late. And the past lives on. You often only understand what a journey means years after it's over. The stories in this book reveal the importance of continual reinvention. Never give up. America and the trailblazing women in these pages have helped me think of myself as a single person again, rather than two, as I had hoped at the outset they would. There did seem to be something to celebrate. Reinvention is not necessarily a conscious process. Sometimes it happens reflexively.

I bought supplies at Red Bluff, where the ocean-going vessels once disgorged whiskey and whores. Then I headed east toward the percolating ground of the Mayacamas Mountains. Volcanoes and cinder cones lay straight ahead, blunt in the lowering sky. I had booked a motel at Mineral, a settlement at 4,750 feet. It was dark when I arrived, and three feet of snow lay on the ground. A scent of resin hung on the air. A neon motel sign depicted a cocktail glass with a cherry. Mineral was on the first road ever cut to Nevada, a supply route to the mines, and now it supplies the Reno casinos. A note on the locked reception door gave a phone number. When I rang, the friendly proprietor said he had left room five open. I crunched around the back to find room five toasty. The man had even left the light on. The next day was my fiftieth birthday. After a lazy start I dunked stale bread in a Styrofoam cup of instant coffee and looked out of the window on to a serrated ridge of the Mayacamas, gleaming hopefully in bright spring sunshine.

NOTES

LIST OF ABBREVIATIONS

CH—Catherine Hubback
FK—Fanny Kemble
FT—Fanny Trollope
HM—Harriet Martineau
IB—Isabella Bird

ALL—Isabella Bird, *A Lady's Life in the Rocky Mountains*, 1879.
AT—Anthony Trollope, *An Autobiography*, 2 vols, 1883.
ATP—Rebecca Burlend & Edward Burlend, *A True Picture of Emigration: or Fourteen Years in the Interior of North America*, 1848.
DMA—Frances Trollope, *Domestic Manners of the Americans*, 1832; page numbers refer to ed. Donald Smalley, New York, 1949.
EiC—*An Englishwoman in California: The Letters of Catherine Hubback, 1871–76*, ed. Zoe Klippert, Oxford, 2010.
HMA—Harriet Martineau, *Harriet Martineau's Autobiography*, 3 vols, 1877.
Journal—Fanny Kemble, *Journal*, 2 vols, London, Philadelphia & Boston, 1835.
JRGP—Fanny Kemble, *Journal of a Residence on a Georgian Plantation in 1838–9*, 1863; page numbers refer to ed. John A. Scott, Athens, Georgia, 1984.
Retrospect—Harriet Martineau, *Retrospect of Western Travel*, 3 vols, 1838.
RG—Fanny Kemble, *Record of a Girlhood*, 3 vols, 1878; page numbers refer to www.archive.org
RLL—Fanny Kemble, *Records of Later Life*, 3 vols, 1882.
SiA—Harriet Martineau, *Society in America*, 2 vols, Paris, 1837.
TAT—Thomas Adolphus Trollope, *What I Remember*, 3 vols, 1887–9.

All books published in London unless otherwise indicated.

INTRODUCTION

6 **I am afraid she** *RLL*, vol. 1, p. 4.

7 **Travellers are privileged to** Pat Barr, *A Curious Life for a Lady: The Story of Isabella Bird*, 1970, p. 54.

8 **America . . . is hardly better** *DMA*, p. 99.

8 **Old Woman** *ibid.*, p. 100.

11 **the complete sympathy of** Michael Holroyd, *Bernard Shaw*, 1997 (1-vol. edn), p. xiv.

CHAPTER I: MERELY TELLING THE TRUTH

13 **to hatch golden eggs** *The Friendships of Mary Russell Mitford*, A. G. L'Estrange, 1882, vol. 1, p. 191.

13 **The Tariff and Bank Bill** *A Subaltern's Furlough: Descriptive of Scenes in Various Parts of the United States . . . During the Summer and Autumn of 1832*, E. T. Coke, 1833, pp. 167–8.

14 **an exact likeness of** anon., *Bentley's Miscellany*, 1839, vol. 4, p. 40.

14 **No other author of** *New Monthly Magazine*, vol. 55, issue: 219, Mar. 1839, p. 417.

15 **Of all these tourists** from suppressed passages in Mark Twain, *Life on the Mississippi*; *DMA*, Smalley intro., p. v.

15 **Lady Louisa Stewart told** Frances Eleanor Trollope, *Frances Trollope: Her Life and Literary Work from George III to Victoria*, 1895, vol. 1, p. 161.

15 **I am convinced that** *The Letters of Charles Dickens*, eds. Madeline House, Graham Storey & Kathleen Tillotson, Oxford, 1974, vol. 3, p. 395.

15 **The man looked like** Anthony Trollope, *Is He Popenjoy?*, 1878.

15 **So that there might** AT, vol. 1, p. 45.

16 **Of all the people** *ibid.*, p. 33.

17 **dingy, almost suicidal chambers** *ibid.*, p. 3.

17 **My father was a** TAT, vol. 1, p. 4.

17 **He is a good, honourable** FT to Julia Garnett Pertz, May 17, 1827, Letters, Garnett-Pertz Collection, Houghton Library, Harvard University.

17 **a highly respected but** *TAT*, vol. 1, p. 58.

17 **carried sunshine** *ibid.*, p. 228.

19 **always seemed to be** AT, vol. 1, pp. 15–16.

19 **Fanny Wright is at** FT to Harriet Garnett, Oct. 7, 1827, Letters, Garnett-Pertz Collection, Houghton Library, Harvard University.

19 **I can scarcely believe** Margaret Lane, *Frances Wright and the Great Experiment*, Manchester, 1972, p. 25.

19 **Will wonders never cease** Helen Heineman, *Mrs Trollope: The Triumphant Feminine in the Nineteenth Century*, Athens, Ohio, 1979, p. 47.

20 **among the many young** FT to Mary Russell Mitford, 22 Apr. 1827, Cincinnati Historical Society Archive.

20 **The first indication of** *DMA*, p. 3.

20 **like the fragment of** *ibid.*, p. 5.

20 **Only one object rears** *ibid.*, p. 4.

20 **looking so mighty, and** *ibid.*, p. 5.

21 **the first symptom of** *ibid.*, p. 9.

21 **two distinct sets of** *ibid.*, p. 13.

21 **exquisitely beautiful, graceful, gentle** *ibid.*, p. 13.

21 **with those Colossian strides** Monique Parent Frazee, *Mrs Trollope and America*, Caen, 1969, p. 32.

22 **where the firm ground** Richard Ford, *Observer*, 4 Sep. 2005.

22 **the fragment of a** *DMA*, p. 5.

25 **The total want of** *ibid.*, p. 18.

25 **Let no one who** *ibid.*, p. 16.

26 **that wearisome level line** *ibid.*, p. 19.

27–28 **I believe that man** see www.nobelprize.org

28 **The past is never dead** William Faulkner, *Requiem for a Nun*, 1950, act 1, scene 3, p. 85.

29 **The house was new** *DMA*, p. 24.

30 **It required some miles** *ibid.*, p. 27.

30 **a new world** *ibid.*, p. 26.

30 ***Amerika, du hast es*** Johann Wolfgang von Goethe, "*Den Vereinigten Staaten*" ("To the United States"), 1827.

31–32 **Desolation was the only** *DMA*, p. 27.

32 **The Fanny Wright of** *ibid.*, Smalley intro., p. xvii.

32 **the brain fever which . . . I can never forget** FT to Charles Wilkes, Feb. 14, 1828, Cincinnati Historical Society Archive.

32 **the nature of true** *DMA*, p. 71.

32 **the advocate of opinions** *ibid.*, p. 14.

33 **the metropolis of the** *ibid.*, p. 30.

33 **on every side, that** *ibid.*, p. 48.

33 **Louisville is a considerable** *ibid.*, p. 34.

34 **I have seen fifteen** *ibid.*, p. 36.

34 **Are any of you** *ibid.*, p. 37.

34 **with an air of** *ibid.*, p. 38.

34 **American weakness on the . . . thin-skinned, but the** *ibid.*, p. 355.

35 **the chances were five** *ibid.*, p. 88.

35 **if the people had** *ibid.*

35 **Though I do not** *DMA*, p. 43.

36 **I am delighted with** FT to Charles Wilkes, Feb. 14, 1828, Cincinnati Historical Society Archive.

36 **The "simple" manner of** *DMA*, pp. 44–5.

36 **Is your father ill** Frances Eleanor Trollope, *Frances Trollope: Her Life and Literary Work from George III to Victoria*, 1895, vol. 1, p. 112.

36 **for it is more** *DMA*, p. 52.

36 **because I refused to** *ibid.*, p. 53.

36 **By an improved method** *Cincinnati Gazette*, Mar. 28, 1828.

37 **It is more than** *DMA*, Smalley intro., p. xxi.

37 **Our manner of life** *DMA*, pp. 95–6.

37 **crunching knee deep through** *ibid.*, p. 96.

37 **as an extra drawing-room** *ibid.*

37 **Shakespeare, madam, is obscene** *DMA*, p. 92.

37–38 **The want of warmth** *ibid.*, pp. 278–9.

38 **a cardinal article of** TAT, vol. 1, p. 183.

38 **I must not venture** *DMA*, pp. 127–8.

40 **voluble as a French . . . a person of uncommon** *ibid.*, Smalley intro., p. xl.

41 **singularly unladylike in her** *ibid.*, p. xxxix.

41 **universal pursuit of money** *DMA*, p. 301.

41 **that most un-American phrase** *ibid.*, p. 120.

41 **Ours is a ready** William Makepeace Thackeray, *Vanity Fair*, 1847–8, p. 99.

41 **You will see them** *DMA*, p. 222.

41 **She had a burn** *Courier de la Louisiane*, New Orleans, Dec. 27, 1827.

41 **She had arched toes** *ibid.*, Jan. 10, 1828.

41 **She was in the** *L'Abeille*, New Orleans, Jan. 8, 1828.

42 **When she found she** *DMA*, p. 54.

42 **Queer effect of hearing** *ibid.*, Smalley intro., p. lvii.

42 **This adventure frightened me** *DMA*, p. 57.

42 **In Winesburg servants were** Sherwood Anderson, *Winesburg, Ohio*, New York, 1919, p. 212.

43 **wild and lonely farm** *DMA*, p. 48.

43 **I think it the** *ibid.*, pp. 49–50.

43 **appeared to live so** *ibid.*, p. 74.

43 **Cincinnati has not many** *ibid.*, p. 62.

44 **Horrid groans and terrible** *Cincinnati Enquirer*, Jan. 20, 1830.

44 **Perhaps they are right** *DMA*, p. 69.

45 **We do these things** *ibid.*, p. 67.

45 **To me the dreary** *ibid.*, p. 86.

46 **My boyhood was, I** AT, vol. 1, p. 2.

46 **I feel convinced in** *ibid.*, p. 24.

46 **Looking back at those** TAT, vol. 1, p. 168.

47 **a wilderness of lamps** William Wordsworth, *The Prelude, Book Seventh, Residence In London*, in *The Complete Poetical Works*, 1888.

47 **This frightened me, as** FT to Julia Garnett Pertz, Aug. 22, 1831, Letters, Garnett-Pertz Collection, Houghton Library, Harvard University.

47 **The touch of his** AT, vol. 1, p. 42.

48 **4,000 dollars['] worth of** FT to Julia Garnett Pertz, Aug. 22, 1831, Letters, Garnett-Pertz Collection, Houghton Library, Harvard University.

48 **could scarcely have been** Thomas Hamilton, *Men and Manners in America*, Philadelphia, 1833, p. 293.

49 **These species of amusement** *Cincinnati Gazette*, Nov. 20, 1829.

53 **Were I an English** *DMA*, pp. 43–4.

53 **In the social system** *ibid.*, p. 316.

54–55 **This is a society** Alexis de Tocqueville to his mother, Dec. 6, 1831, *Oeuvres complètes*, Paris, 1954, vol. 14, p. 153, trans. Leo Damrosch.

55 **The entire society** Alexis de Tocqueville, *Voyage en Amérique*, Paris, 1831, vol. 1, p. 279, trans. Leo Damrosch.

55 **The more deeply one** Alexis de Tocqueville to Ernest de Chabrol, Jun. 9, 1831, *Lettres choisies*, Paris, 2003, p. 186, trans. Leo Damrosch.

55 **How much money did** Bill Bryson, *Notes from a Small Island*, 1997, p. 193.

55 **The people here seem** Alexis de Tocqueville to his mother, May 14, 1831, *Lettres choisies*, Paris, 2003, p. 170, trans. Leo Damrosch.

55 **the only religious, enlightened . . . a distinct species of** Alexis de Tocqueville, *Democracy in America*, Paris, 1835, vol. 1, ch. 17.

56 **We Trollopes are far** T. H. S. Escott, *Anthony Trollope, His Work Associates and Literary Originals*, 1913, p. 32.

57 **Oh . . . that ladies would** Teresa Ransom, *Fanny Trollope*, Stroud, Gloucestershire, 1995, p. 119.

57 **A bluestocking who travels** *New Monthly Magazine*, no. 96, 1852.

57 **A sadder household was** AT, vol. 1, p. 45.

58 **The doctor's vials and** *ibid.*, p. 38.

59–60 **How few women there** Anthony Trollope, *The Way We Live Now*, 1875, p. 4.

60 **She was an unselfish** AT, vol. 1, p. 27.

60 **an Italian marquis who** *ibid.*, p. 28.

60 **With her politics were** *ibid.*, p. 29.

60 **We were inseparable companions** TAT, vol. 2, p. 329.

60 **She was the happiest** *ibid.*, pp. 330–31.

60 **one of the most** John Doran, *Athenaeum*, Oct. 10, 1863.

60 *fn* **one huge dismal wet** cited in *Literary Review*, Mar. 2012.

CHAPTER II: BRAVE NEW WORLD

62 **the heiress of Mrs** Una Pope-Hennessy, *Three Englishwomen in America*, 1929, p. 163.

63 **We have never seen** *The Diary of Philip Hone 1828–51*, ed. Allan Nevins, New York, 1927, vol. 1, pp. 77–8.

63 **This is a brave** *RG*, vol. 3, p. 299.

63 **influenced England against the** Georgia Historical Society, sign, Butler Island, Georgia.

63–64 **Rose at half-past four** *Journal*, vol. 2, p. 14.

64 **My going on the stage** *RG*, vol. 1, p. 191.

64 **Insignificant** Dorothy Marshall, *Fanny Kemble*, 1977, p. 54.

64 **Well my dear, they** Ann Blainey, *Fanny and Adelaide: The Lives of the Remarkable Kemble Sisters*, 2001, p. 29.

64 **A vision to the** *New Monthly Magazine*, vol. 27, Nov. 1, 1829.

65 **The divine Fanny! I** Arthur Henry Hallam to Richard Monckton Milnes, Jan. 9, 1830, *The Letters of Arthur Henry Hallam*, ed. Jack Kolb, Columbus, Ohio, 1981, p. 348.

65 **Hallam had an opera** *ibid.*, p. 350.

65 **Ellen Tree lacks the** Arthur Henry Hallam to Emily Tennyson, Oct. 30, 1832, *The Letters of Arthur Henry Hallam*, ed. Jack Kolb, Columbus, Ohio, 1981, p. 675.

65 **I do not care** *RG*, vol. 3, p. 185.

65 **Such shoals of partners!** *ibid.*, p. 35.

65–66 **We were all of** Una Pope-Hennessy, *Three Englishwomen in America*, 1929, p. 135.

66 **horribly in love** *JRGP*, Scott intro., p. xxiv.

67 **You cannot imagine how** Dorothy Marshall, *Fanny Kemble*, 1977, p. 57.

67 **ringing grooves of change** Alfred, Lord Tennyson, "Locksley Hall," 1842.

67 **The streets are thronged** *RG*, vol. 3, p. 7.

68 **Society is becoming a** Dorothy Marshall, *Fanny Kemble*, 1977, p. 65.

68 **I am weary and . . . It rains** *Journal*, vol. 1, p. 3.

68 **I have left my** *ibid.*, p. 8.

68 **Ah! One can tell** *RG*, vol. 3, p. 246.

68 **I danced myself half** *Journal*, vol. 2, p. 10.

69 **In the early evening** *ibid.*, vol. 1, p. 76.

69 **an aquatic Vauxhall** *ibid.*, p. 80.

69–70 **Mercy on me how** *ibid.*, p. 67.

70 **Even though I had** Dorothy Marshall, *Fanny Kemble*, 1977, p. 81.

70 **As the day fell** *Journal*, vol. 1, pp. 276–7.

70 **not so new and** *ibid.*, p. 174.

70 **saw anything more lovely** *Journal*, vol. 2, p. 24.

70 **Came home: found a** *ibid.*, p. 15.

70–71 **Came down and found** *Journal*, vol. 1, p. 192.

71 **I never saw anything** *ibid.*, vol. 2, p. 51.

71 **I love Philadelphia for** *ibid.*, p. 149.

71 **a good specimen of** Dorothy Marshall, *Fanny Kemble*, 1977, p. 91.

71–72 **So Old Hickory means** *Journal*, vol. 2, p. 38.

72 **the Athens of our** John James Audubon, *Ornithological Biography*, Edinburgh & elsewhere, 1831–9, vol. 2, p. 17.

72 **My spirits seemed like** *Journal*, vol. 2, p. 188.

72 **Oh God! Who can** *ibid.*, p. 287.

72 **What a savage he** *ibid.*, p. 237.

73 **the universal kindness which** *RG*, vol. 3, p. 299.

73 **Of all the portions** *Journal*, vol. 2, p. 196.

73 **a very just judgement . . . realise Shakespeare's finest conceptions** *JRGP*, p. 121.

74 **the most beautiful cemetery** *Retrospect*, vol. 3, p. 273.

74 **a pleasure garden instead** *Journal*, vol. 2, p. 176.

74 **I'm sick of the** *ibid.*, p. 11.

75 **between 5 and 6** *RLL*, vol. 1, p. 24.

75 **I found that my** *ibid.*, p. 7.

75 **I have had so** *ibid.*, pp. 17–18.

76 **too *prononcée*** George Fisher's diary, cited in E. Dudden, *Women in the American Theatre: Actresses & Audiences, 1790–1870*, Yale, 1994.

76 **The fact is that** *JRGP*, pp. 37–8.

76 **I acted like a** *Journal*, vol. 2, p. 26.

77 **Nov. 30, 1832, sat** *ibid.*, p. 9.

77 **as a race incomparably** *ibid.*, p. 196.

77 **I visited Boston several . . . I saw more pictures . . . its charitable and literary** *ibid.*, pp. 197–8.

77 **Oh! What a breaking** *ibid.*, p. 36.

77 **the authoress has unsexed** *Niles' Weekly Register*, Baltimore, Washington & Philadelphia, Aug. 8, 1835.

77–78 **My conscience! Who'd have** *My Conscience! Fanny Thimble Cutler's Journal of a Residence in America Whilst Performing a Profitable Theatrical Engagement: Beating the Nonsensical Fanny Kemble Journal All Hollow!!!*, anon., Philadelphia, 1835, p. 3.

78 **the heiress of Mrs** Una Pope-Hennessy, *Three Englishwomen in America*, 1929, p. 163.

78 **It is like herself** Dorothy Marshall, *Fanny Kemble*, 1977, p. 111.

78 **By her way of** *HMA*, vol. 1, pp. 365–6.

78–79 **My heart still answers** Constance Wright, *Fanny Kemble and the Lovely Land*, 1974, p. 101.

79 **I am weary of** Dorothy Marshall, *Fanny Kemble*, 1977, p. 115.

79 **as long as you** *ibid.*

79 **You cannot make me** Pierce Butler, *Mr. Butler's Statement, originally prepared in aid of his professional counsel*, Philadelphia, 1850, p. 46.

79 **Since my marriage to** Dorothy Marshall, *Fanny Kemble*, 1977, p. 158.

79 **What need of intellectual** *ibid.*, p. 114.

80–81 **even aged females apparently** David E. Stannard, *American Holocaust: The Conquest of the New World*, Oxford, 1992, p. 124.

81 **There your white brother** Jon Meacham, *American Lion: Andrew Jackson in the White House*, New York, 2008, p. 91.

81 **For census purposes a** The 1798 Constitution, Article 1, Section 2.

81 **Few families can have** Malcolm Bell Jr., *Major Butler's Legacy: Five Generations of a Slaveholding Family*, Athens, Georgia, 1987, p. xix.

82 **We travelled all night** *JRGP*, p. 33.

82 **that all but universal** *ibid.*, p. 46.

82 **a most ominous tolling** *ibid.*, p. 39.

83 **rattling their brittle canes** *ibid.*, p. 47.

83 **savage** *ibid.*, p. 48.

83 **to hail us like** *ibid.*, p. 48.

83 **It seemed to me** *ibid.*, p. 47.

84 **quite the most amphibious** Malcolm Bell Jr., *Major Butler's Legacy: Five Generations of a Slaveholding Family*, Athens, Georgia, 1987, p. 271.

84 **Every shade of green** *JRGP*, p. 56.

84 **I do not weary** *ibid.*, p. 114.

84 **from glittering graceful branch** *ibid.*, p. 56.

84 **O missis!** *ibid.*, p. 256.

85 **It is too dreadful** *ibid.*, p. 190.

85 **these dreadful possessions of** *ibid.*, p. 138.

86 **It seems to me** *ibid.*, p. 154.

86 **great barnlike** *ibid.*, p. 216.

86 **Well, what do you . . . Me come say ha . . . a procession of sable** *ibid.*, p. 217.

87 **And here in their** *ibid.*, p. 70.

87 **almost universal** *ibid.*, p. 76.

87 **Oh God, Thou surely** *ibid.*, p. 70.

87 **the childish excitability of** *ibid.*, p. 224.

87 **edged with an exquisite** *ibid.*

87 **I sometimes despise myself** *ibid.*

88 **I pity them for** *ibid.*, p. 192.

88 **Oh what a shocking** *ibid.*, p. 108.

88 **three times as dear as** *ibid.*, p. 118.

89 **these heaven-blinded negro** *ibid.*, p. 126.

89 **like most southern men** *ibid.*, p. 93.

89–90 **Why do you listen** *ibid.*, p. 210.

90 **This is no place** *ibid.*, p. 211.

90 **surrounded by all this** *ibid.*, p. 241.

90 **I must, for their** *ibid.*, p. 214.

91 **in this land of . . . In my country, ruins** *ibid.*, p. 331.

95 **the whole town lies** *ibid.*, p. 115.

96 **a few happy negroes** *Transatlantic Crossing: American Visitors to Britain and British Visitors to America*, ed. Walter Allen, New York, 1971.

96 **that gently mannered city** Margaret Mitchell, *Gone with the Wind*, 1936, p. 55.

97 **When I'm asked** Brad Gooch, *Flannery*, 2009, p. 373.

99 **If you will govern** Pierce Butler, *Mr. Butler's Statement, originally prepared in aid of his professional counsel*, Philadelphia, 1850, p. 69.

99 **I consider that it** *ibid.*, p. 70.

99 **She has discovered that** Charles Greville, *The Greville Diary*, ed. Philip Whitwell Wilson, 1927, vol. 2, pp. 546–7.

100 **For God's sake and** *JRGP*, Scott intro., p. xlv.

101 **I feel as if** Dorothy Marshall, *Fanny Kemble*, 1977, p. 196.

101 **as formerly stagecoach horses** *ibid.*, p. 208.

102 **She held that marriage** Pierce Butler, *Mr. Butler's Statement, originally prepared in aid of his professional counsel*, Philadelphia, 1850, p. 9.

102 **The Lord help Butler** Hershel Parker, *Herman Melville: A Biography*, Baltimore, 1996, vol. 1, p. 617.

102 **Delicate women, grave gentlemen** *The Diary of Philip Hone 1828–51*, ed. Allan Nevins, New York, 1927, vol. 1, p. 357.

102 **She has half a . . . a deep sullen brute** Cornelia Brooke Gilder with Julia Conklin Peters, *Hawthorne's Lenox: The Tanglewood Circle*, Charleston, South Carolina, 2008.

102 **Both are now free** Constance Wright, *Fanny Kemble and the Lovely Land*, 1974, p. 137.

103 **from which nothing short** Edward FitzGerald, *Letters of Edward FitzGerald to Fanny Kemble 1871–1883*, ed. William Aldies Wright, 1895, p. 2.

104 **Mrs Kemble possessed to** Lady Anne Ritchie, *From Friend to Friend*, 1920, p. 92.

104 **Slavery is our king** S. Preston, *Charleston Daily Courier*, Jun. 4, 1860.

104 **At that time it** James F. Rhodes, *History of the United States*, 1996, vol. 3, p. 435.

104 ***Though with the North** Punch*, Mar. 30, 1861.

105 **When the day of** David Hepburn Milton, *Lincoln's Spymaster: Thomas Haines Dudley and the Liverpool Network*, Mechanicsburg, Pennsylvania, 2003, p. 121.

106 **two friendly Unions of** *The Times*, Mar. 15, 1862.

106 **It was the first** Amanda Foreman, *A World on Fire: An Epic History of Two Nations Divided*, 2010, p. 209.

106 **lay thick as the** *ibid.*, p. 242.

106 **It was not a** *ibid.*, p. 342.

109 **The men dropped here** Stephen Crane, *The Red Badge of Courage*, New York, 1895, p. 28.

109 **murder red** *ibid.*, p. 76.

109 **We are now witnessing** Hansard, clxiii, May 27, 1861, pp. 131–6.

109 *fn* **The good writers are** Ernest Hemingway, *Green Hills of Africa*, 1935, p. 16.

109 *fn* **The cold passed reluctantly** Stephen Crane, *The Red Badge of Courage*, New York, 1895, p. 1.

110 **I don't mind you** Mrs Gaskell to Charles Eliot Norton, Jun. 10, 1861, *The Letters of Mrs Gaskell*, eds J. A. V. Chapple & Arthur Pollard, Manchester, 1966, pp. 654–5.

112 **maudlin middle-age romanticism** Mark Twain, *Life on the Mississippi*, New York, 1883, p. 268.

112 **A sort of dreamy** *JRGP*, p. 96.

113 **With this sauce I** *ibid.*, p. 86.

113 **twilight after glare** *ibid.*, p. 205.

113 **painful conversations** *ibid.*, p. 210.

113 **the most powerful anti-slavery** *New Monthly Magazine*, vol. 27, issue: 159, Aug. 1863, p. 417.

113 **the most valuable account** Henry James, *Essays in London and Elsewhere*, 1893, p. 107.

113 **free from care** Charles Lyell, *Travels In North America, Canada and Nova Scotia With Geological Observations*, 1885, p. 169.

113 **Mrs. Trollope and Mrs.** Nil Admirari (F. W. Shelton), *The Trolliopiad; or, Travelling Gentlemen in America; a Satire*, New York, 1837, p. xiv.

113 *fn* **The London *Times* is** Amanda Foreman, *A World on Fire: An Epic History of Two Nations Divided*, 2010, p. 74.

114 **I beg to present** William T. Sherman to Abraham Lincoln, 22 Dec. 1864, Robert Todd Lincoln Papers, Manuscript Division, Library of Congress (196).

114 **Hell is empty, and** Amanda Foreman, *A World on Fire: An Epic History of Two Nations Divided*, 2010, p. 766 (from *The Tempest*).

115 **The white population was** Frances Butler Leigh, *Ten Years on a Georgia Plantation Since the War*, 1883, pp. 1–2.

115 **Gallantry took its last** Introduction to the film *Gone with the Wind*, 1939, written by Sidney Howard et al.

116 **There was a mean** Erskine Caldwell, *God's Little Acre*, New York, 1933, p. 214.

117 **The slaves received him** Frances Butler Leigh, *Ten Years on a Georgia Plantation Since the War*, 1883, p. 14.

117–18 **The South was still** *ibid.*, p. 2.

118 **The baneful leaven of . . . Shall I not go** *ibid.*, pp. 79–80.

118 **Do you wonder we** *ibid.*, pp. 70–71.

118 **Love for, and belief** *ibid.*, p. 77.

119 **Savannah is our Leamington** *ibid.*, p. 255.

119 **The country is no** Dorothy Marshall, *Fanny Kemble*, 1977, p. 242.

119 **twilight after glare** *JRGP*, p. 205.

119 **I do not care** Lady Anne Ritchie, *From Friend to Friend*, 1920, p. 86.

120 **that evil name uttered** MS letter, Henry W. and Albert A. Berg Collection of English and American Literature, New York Public Library.

120 **what Mrs. Kemble did** Lady Anne Ritchie, *From Friend to Friend*, 1920, p. 86.

120 **friend of many lonely** Henry James, *Essays in London and Elsewhere*, 1893, p. 119.

121 **The terrific Kemble herself** Leon Edel, *Henry James: The Conquest of London 1870–1883*, 1962, p. 86.

121–22 **had so fine a** T. S. Eliot, *The Little Review*, v, Aug. 1918, New York.

122 **Good heavens, she's touched** Michael Holroyd, *A Strange Eventful History*, 2008, p. 153.

122 **Your Old Gossip . . . Catherine the Great** Constance Wright, *Fanny Kemble and the Lovely Land*, 1974, p. 204.

122 **the air she lived** Leon Edel, *Henry James: The Master*, 1975, p. 150.

122 **Mrs. Kemble told me** February 21, 1879, *The Notebooks of Henry James*, eds F. O. Matthiessen & K. B. Murdock, New York, 1947, p. 12.

122 **agitated** Henry James, *Essays in London and Elsewhere*, 1893, p. 86.

122 **There was no handy** *ibid.*

122 **always the tragedienne** Leon Edel, *Henry James: The Middle Years*, 1962, p. 53.

122 **the first woman in . . . one of the consolations** Leon Edel, *Henry James: The Conquest of London 1870–1883*, 1962, p. 230.

122 **A prouder nature than** Henry James, *Essays in London and Elsewhere*, 1893, p. 83.

122 **the beauty of her** *ibid.*, p. 100.

123 **The Terrific Kemble** Leon Edel, *Henry James: The Conquest of London 1870–1883*, 1962, p. 86.

123 **she had abundantly lived** Henry James, *Essays in London and Elsewhere*, 1893, p. 85.

CHAPTER III: A GREAT EMBRYO POET

124 **grimly bent on the** Charles Dickens to William Henry Wills, Oct. 14, 1854, *Charles Dickens as Editor, Being Letters Written by Him to William Henry Mills, His Sub-Editor*, ed. R. C. Lehmann, 1912, p. 154.

124 **How very fortunate it** Charles Darwin to S. E. Darwin, Apr. 1, 1838, Letter 407, Darwin Correspondence Project, www.darwinproject.ac.uk

125 **The best happiness in** *Retrospect of Western Travel*, 1-vol. selection, ed. Daniel Feller, New York, 2000, intro., p. ix.

125 **I am more democratic** *ibid.*, p. xvi.

126 **I was astonished to** Charles Darwin to C. S. Darwin, Dec. 7, 1836, Letter 325, Darwin Correspondence Project, www.darwinpro ject.ac.uk

127 **I believe myself possessed** *Retrospect of Western Travel*, 1-vol. selection, ed. Daniel Feller, New York, 2000, intro., pp. xix–xx.

127 **a national instructor** *ibid.*, p. xi.

128 **Do you know that** R. K. Webb, *Harriet Martineau: A Radical Victorian*, 1960, p. 14.

128 **She is one of** *The Correspondence of Thomas Carlyle and Ralph Waldo Emerson, 1834–1872*, Cambridge, 1883, vol. 1, p. 121.

128 *fn* **If I was not** *RLL*, vol. 1, p. 4.

129 **Oh, do not go** *HMA*, vol. 1, p. 270.

129 **chiefly because I felt . . . partly** *SiA*, vol. 1, p. xi.

129 **All that I had heard** *Retrospect*, vol. 1, p. 36.

130 **O the speculations and** *ibid.*, p. 39.

130 **We had wintry hearts** Una Pope-Hennessy, *Three Englishwomen in America*, 1929, p. 278.

130 **She made us all** *ibid.*, p. 284.

130 **No nation can pretend** *ibid.*, p. 299.

130 **extraordinary woman who found** *Retrospect of Western Travel*, 1-vol. selection, ed. Daniel Feller, New York, 2000, intro., p. xiv.

131 **of so dazzling a . . . a private race of** *Retrospect*, vol. 3, p. 120.

131 **The gay birds of . . . We were alone with . . . Here and there was . . . Never was the world** *ibid.*, pp. 141–5.

132–33 **seems to exert some** *SiA*, vol. 1, p. xv.

133 **Her deafness is a** *RLL*, vol. 1, p. 11.

133 **the person questioned seemed** *SiA*, vol. 2, pp. 141–2.

133 **I was even told** *ibid.*, p. 95.

133 **I am afraid she** *RLL*, vol. 1, p. 4.

133 **great disparity of intellect** *ibid.*

134 **very much indeed, in** *RLL*, vol. 1, p. 17.

134 **I really strove hard** *HMA*, vol. 1, p. 365.

134 **a green-room cast of** *ibid.*

134 **regenerate some self respect** *SiA*, vol. 2, p. 197.

134 **The insane in Pennsylvania** *ibid.*, p. 201.

134 **The fault in general** *ibid.*, p. 202.

134–35 **society basking in one . . . a sweet temper and** *Retrospect*, vol. 1, p. 228.

135 **I had rather suffer** *SiA*, vol. 2, p. 175.

135 **She is gone to** *RLL*, vol. 1, p. 27.

135 **There was no bearing . . . every laugh had lost** *Retrospect*, vol. 2, pp. 85–6.

136 **The crescent streak is** *SiA*, vol. 1, p. 102.

136 **It is an absorbing** *ibid.*, p. 108.

136 **The nursery, the boudoir** *ibid.*, p. xiv.

136 **with his bundle . . . without attracting particular notice** *Retrospect*, vol. 2, p. 164.

136–37 **I was privately told** *ibid.*, pp. 167–8.

137 **If any of us** *SiA*, vol. 1, p. 121.

138 **Everything appears alive, the** *ibid.*, p. 118.

138 **that Rembrandt light on** *ibid.*

138 **Whether the singularity of** *SiA*, vol. 1, p. 119.

138 **perhaps the most remarkable** *ibid.*, p. 121.

138 **a magnificent sepulchre** *ibid.*, p. 119.

142 **a glorious place** *SiA*, vol. 1, p. 96.

142 **This Bazaar is the** *Retrospect*, vol. 2, p. 249.

142 **Thrice-precious tube!** James Flint, *Verses on Many Occasions*, Lynn, Massachusetts, 1851, p. 93.

142 **Buckeyes were superior to** *Retrospect*, vol. 2, pp. 223–4.

142 **We should foster Western** *ibid.*, p. 230.

142 **Many a time in** *SiA*, vol. 1, p. 95.

143 **I suppose, while Luther** *Retrospect*, vol. 3, p. 148.

143 **an ugly, deaf, sour** *Retrospect of Western Travel*, 1-vol. selection, ed. Daniel Feller, New York, 2000, intro., p. xix.

143 **a poor flimsy tool** *ibid.*

143 **Why, surely madam, you** *Retrospect*, vol. 3, p. 219.

143 **I am sure no traveller** *HMA*, vol. 2, p. 3.

144 **If there is any** *SiA*, vol. 2, p. 163.

144 **I regard the American** *ibid.*, vol. 1, p. 20.

145 **In the crucible of** Frederick Jackson Turner, *The Frontier in American History*, New York, 1920; page numbers refer to 2008 Penguin selection, *The Significance of the Frontier in American History*, p. 22.

145 **it is too soon** *SiA*, vol. 2, p. 254.

146 **Every factory child carries** *ibid.*, vol. 1, p. 8.

146 **mutual injury of every** *The Chartist Circular*, no. 27, 28 Mar. 1840.

146 **The details of her** *RLL*, vol. 1, p. 131.

146 **There is something infinitely** *The Times*, 30 May 1837.

146 **They have realised many** *SiA*, vol. 2, p. 254.

146 **is deficiency of moral** HM, *How to Observe: Morals and Manners*, 1838, p. 28.

146–47 **When Spurzheim was in** *Retrospect*, vol. 2, p. 188.

147 **detestably so—the restraint** Una Pope-Hennessy, *Three Englishwomen in America*, 1929, p. 293.

147 **as remarkable as licentiousness** *SiA*, vol. 2, p. 204.

147–48 **Seeing what I have** *ibid.*, p. 246.

148 **Is it to be** *ibid.*, p. 179.

148 **The principle of the** *SiA*, vol. 1, p. 106.

149 **in as bad odor** Una Pope-Hennessy, *Three Englishwomen in America*, 1929, p. 303.

149 **But what has she** Charles Dickens to William Macready, Mar. 22, 1842, *The Selected Letters of Charles Dickens*, ed. Jenny Hartley, Oxford, 2012, p. 97.

149 **It is Martineau with** Michael Slater, *Charles Dickens: A Life Defined by Writing*, 2009, p. 177.

149 **vomit of conceit** Charles Dickens, *Household Words*, Jan. 19, 1856.

150 **the cast-iron man, who** *Retrospect*, vol. 1, p. 243.

150 **There are glimpses of** HM, *Deerbrook*, 1838, ch. 46.

150 **a sour apple crushed** R. H. Horne, cited in *The Times Literary Supplement*, 9 Jun. 1950.

150 **So much for Monkey** Charles Darwin to S. E. Darwin, Apr. 1, 1838, Letter 407, Darwin Correspondence Project, www.darwinproject.ac.uk

150 **Erasmus has been with** *ibid.*

150 **an occasional annoyance, presently** *HMA*, vol. 1, p. 131.

151 **Oh, horrid, horrid, my** *RLL*, vol. 1, p. 107.

151 **the quality of the** *Harriet Martineau: Selected Letters*, ed. Valerie Sanders, 1990.

151 **There is no God** Peter Ackroyd, *Dickens*, 1990, p. 758.

154 **What an unpleasant life** Matthew Arnold to D. G. Boyle, Mar. 11, 1877, *Letters of Matthew Arnold 1848 to 1888*, ed. George W. E. Russell, part 2, 1895, p. 137.

154 **Miss Martineau I relish** *HMA*, vol. 3, p. 290.

154 **It is the first** Charlotte Brontë to James Taylor, Feb. 11, 1851, *The Brontës: A Life in Letters*, ed. Juliet Barker, 1997, p. 312.

155 **not a touch of** *Daily News*, Feb. 3, 1853.

155 **the happiest single woman** *HMA*, vol. 1, p. 133.

155 **the most manlike woman** Elizabeth Barrett Browning to Mrs. James Martin, *c.* Sep. 1844, *The Letters of Elizabeth Barrett Browning*, ed. Sir Frederic [sic] George Kenyon, 1897, vol. 1, p. 117.

155 **My mind has been** *HMA*, vol. 1, p. 132.

155 **as a born lecturer** Margaret Oliphant, "Harriet Martineau," *Blackwood's Magazine*, no. 121, 1877, p. 479.

158 **I am not afraid** *HMA*, vol. 2, p. 37.

158 **I must and will** *ibid.*

158 **From week to week** privately owned letter, cited *The Times Literary Supplement*, Nov. 30, 2001.

158 *fn* **one of the best** Victoria Glendinning, *The Times Literary Supplement*, Apr. 4, 1975.

159 **So *very* mediocre,—neither** *The Collected Letters of Harriet Martineau: Letters 1863–1876*, eds Deborah Anna Logan & Valerie Sanders, 2007, vol. 5, p. 78.

159 **renewal of the soul** HM to Florence Nightingale, n.d. May 1861, *ibid.*, vol. 4, p. 276.

159 **He is *awful* at** Peter Ackroyd, *Dickens*, 1990, p. 874.

CHAPTER IV: IS THIS AMERICA?

160 **A little boat was** *ATP*, p. 18.

162 **The gradual diminution of** *ibid.*, p. 5.

162 **flowing with milk and** *ibid.*, p. 21.

162 **I gave up the** *ibid.*, p. 5.

163 **the immense forests of** *ibid.*, p. 8.

163 **in North America pauperism** *The Times*, Aug. 2, 1831.

163 **You might have seen** *ATP*, p. 10.

163 **I shall never forget** *ibid.*

163 **At breakfast we had** Robert Louis Stevenson, *The Amateur Emigrant*, 1895, p. 4.

163 **We were a company** *ibid.*, p. 12.

164 **all now belonging to** *ibid.*, p. 10.

164 **All's well! I know** *ibid.*, pp. 14–15.

164 **The captain and cabin passengers** *ATP*, p. 16.

164 **Its appearance was really** *ibid.*, p. 14.

164 **and streets thronged with** *ibid.*, p. 15.

164 **Our unsettled condition was** *ibid.*, p. 17.

165 **Our enquiries of the** *ibid.*, p. 18.

165 **No person, however slender** *ibid.*, p. 19.

166 **his appearance would have** *ibid.*, p. 21.

167 **a village of Pike** anon., *History of Pike County, Illinois*, Chicago, 1880, vol. 1, p. 198.

168 **The nights in winter** *ATP*, p. 28.

168–69 **brought home his game . . . We accordingly dressed our** *ibid.*, p. 30.

169 **I could not but** *ibid.*, p. 36.

170 **We had indeed some** *ibid.*, p. 29.

170–71 **The great fact was** Willa Cather, *O Pioneers!*, Boston, 1913, p. 5.

171 **burning summers when the** Willa Cather, *My Ántonia*, Boston, 1918, p. 1.

171 **We come and go** Willa Cather, *O Pioneers!*, Boston, 1913, p. 122.

171 **It does not matter** Willa Cather, "A Gold Slipper," *Harper's Monthly Magazine*, 134, Jan. 1917, p. 174.

172 **in the atomic conditions** Frederick Jackson Turner, *The Frontier in American History*, New York, 1920; page numbers refer to 2008 Penguin selection, *The Significance of the Frontier in American History*, p. 48.

172 **Remorse the most pungent** *ATP*, p. 47.

173 **This was one of** *ibid.*, p. 45.

173 **On the farm the** Willa Cather, *My Ántonia*, Boston, 1918, p. 88.

173 **a large full-grown rattlesnake** *ATP*, p. 49.

173 **a moderately comfortable existence** *ibid.*, p. 51.

174 **It was most uncomfortable** *ibid.*, p. 54.

174 **A sort of circle** *ibid.*, p. 57.

175 **I have no right** *ibid.*

175 **some of the most** *ibid.*

176 **There are after all** *ATP*, p. 59.

176 **We have seen a** *ibid.*, p. 60.

176 **In the crucible of** Frederick Jackson Turner, *The Frontier in American History*, New York, 1920; page numbers refer to 2008 Penguin selection, *The Significance of the Frontier in American History*, p. 22.

CHAPTER V: ABOUT LOVE AND HATE

179 *A lady an explorer?* *Punch*, June 1893.

179 **up-to-anything free-legged air** Jane Robinson, *Wayward Women*, 1990, p. 83.

179 **your frugiferous bat** IB to Henrietta Bird, Feb. 13–25, 1879, *Letters to Henrietta: Isabella Bird*, ed. Kay Chubbuck, 2002, p. 305.

180 **where the boar frost** *ALL*, p. 96.

180 **that indomitable original** Jan Morris, *The Times Literary Supplement*, Nov. 18, 1977.

180 **I have found a** *ALL*, p. 1.

180 **written without the remotest** *ibid.*, p. vii.

180 **a hardly bearable joy** *ibid.*, p. 23.

180 **You can form no** *ibid.*, p. 299.

181 **the great revival** IB, *The Aspects of Religion in the United States of America*, 1859, p. 1.

182 **It is a matter** *ibid.*, p. 4.

182 **I have wine at** IB to Henrietta Bird, Oct. 13, 1872, *Letters to Henrietta: Isabella Bird*, ed. Kay Chubbuck, 2002, p. 37.

183 **No bills . . . no conventionalities** IB to Henrietta Bird, Mar. 24, 1872, *ibid.*, p. 32.

183 **a small slice of** *ALL*, p. 8.

183–84 **I dreamt of bears** *ibid.*, p. 18.

184 **for the benefit of** *ibid.*, p. vii.

184 **As night came on** *ibid.*, p. 17.

184 **True democratic equality prevails** *ibid.*, p. 137.

184 **Womanly dignity and manly** *ibid.*, p. 19.

184 **I have met nothing** *ibid.*, p. 279.

184 **Five distinct ranges of . . . They are gradually gaining** *ibid.*, p. 34.

185 **Plains, plains everywhere . . . like** *ibid.*

185 **I sat down and** *ALL*, pp. 44–5.

185 **Except for love, which** *ibid.*, p. 77.

185 **This is another world** *ibid.*, p. 73.

185 **rude, black log cabin** *ibid.*, p. 90.

186 **apologising gracefully for not** *ibid.*, p. 92.

186 **there no lumberer's axe** *ibid.*, p. 102.

187 **mean everything that is** *ibid.*, p. 84.

187–88 **Somewhat dazed by the** *ibid.*, p. 133.

188 **There is health in** *ibid.*, p. 84.

189 **In one's imagination it** *ibid.*, p. 98.

190 **It was something, at** *ibid.*, p. 114.

190 **He has pathos, he . . . His conversation is brilliant** *ibid.*, pp. 144–5.

190 **Breezy mountain recklessness** *ibid.*, p. 144.

190 **You're the first man** *ibid.*, p. 239.

190 **The handsome, even superbly** *ibid.*, p. 241.

190 **after giving him a** *ibid.*, p. 92.

191 **because of the altitude** George Kingsley, *Notes on Sport and Travel*, 1900, p. 179.

191 **hardly bearable joy** *ALL*, p. 23.

192–93 **It is often said** Bobby Bridger, *Buffalo Bill and Sitting Bull: Inventing the Wild West*, Austin, Texas, 2002, p. 323.

193–94 **The Earl of Dunraven** *Rocky Mountain News*, Denver, Jul. 22, 1874.

195 **steer south, and keep** *ALL*, p. 158.

197 **To get rid of** *ibid.*, p. 215.

197 **that great braggart city** *ibid.*, p. 159.

197 **One no longer sees** *ibid.*, p. 161.

198 **We are now ready . . . We are three-quarters of** Wallace Stegner, *Beyond the Hundredth Meridian: John Wesley Powell and the Second Opening of the West*, Boston, 1954, p. 95.

199 **There is no God . . . The almighty dollar is** *ALL*, p. 213.

200 **Lord what is man?** *ibid.*, p. 195.

200 **At the mining towns** *ibid.*, p. 208.

200 **with a Lord Dundreary . . . An American is nationally** *ibid.*, p. 206.

201 **She travels almost altogether** *Rocky Mountain News*, Denver, Oct. 23, 1873.

201 **If it's the English** *ALL*, p. 223.

201 **Mining turns the earth** *ibid.*, p. 225.

202 **There were eight boarders** *ibid.*, p. 177.

202 **two large white feet . . . It turns the house** *ibid.*, p. 179.

202 **It is uninteresting down** *ibid.*, p. 280.

203 **Her physical unattractiveness which** James H. Pickering, *"This Blue Hollow": Estes Park, the Early Years, 1859–1915*, Boulder, Colorado, 1999, p. 281.

203 **he had discovered he** IB to Henrietta Bird, Nov. 18–20, 1873, *Letters to Henrietta: Isabella Bird*, ed. Kay Chubbuck, 2002, p. 175.

203 **I miss him very . . . It takes peace away** *ibid.*, p. 176.

203 **It was still and** *ALL*, p. 295.

204 **as a record of** *ibid.*, p. vii.

205 **any woman might love** IB to Henrietta Bird, Nov. 18–20, 1873, *Letters to Henrietta: Isabella Bird*, ed. Kay Chubbuck, 2002, p. 175.

CHAPTER VI: NO THERE THERE

208 **God bless you. I** David & Diana Hopkinson, *Niece of Miss Austen*, unpublished ts, n.d., Hopkinson Deposit, Jane Austen's House Museum, Chawton, Hampshire, p. 16.

209 **strawberrys 2s** Catherine Austen, later Hubback, Journal/Sketchbook 1837, Jane Austen's House Museum, Chawton, Hampshire.

210 **Her husband's collapse was** David & Diana Hopkinson, *Niece of Miss Austen*, unpublished ts, n.d., Hopkinson Deposit, Jane Austen's House Museum, Chawton, Hampshire, n.p.

211 **She looked at people** David & Diana Hopkinson, *Niece of Miss Austen*, unpublished ts, n.d., Hopkinson Deposit, Jane Austen's House Museum, Chawton, Hampshire, n.p.

211 **The Copy that was** cited by Kathryn Sutherland, *The Times Literary Supplement*, Dec. 6, 2002.

211 **the knell of lost** Catherine Hubback, *Life and its Lessons*, 1851, vol. 2, p. 146.

211 *fn* **Female economy will do** Jane Austen, *The Watsons*, 1871, p. 114.

212 **How odd it was** Catherine Hubback, *Life and its Lessons*, 1851, vol. 1, p. 8.

212 **What she liked, dear** Henry James, *A Small Boy and Others*, 1913, pp. 4–5.

213 **My mother's disposition was** John H. Hubback, *Cross Currents in a Long Life*, privately printed, 1935, p. 14.

216 **stretched from horizon to** Robert Louis Stevenson, *Across the Plains*, 1892, p. 12.

216 **In these modern days** Peter R. Decker, *Fortunes and Failures: White-Collar Mobility in Nineteenth-Century San Francisco*, Cambridge, Massachusetts, 1978, p. 212.

217 **no longer interesting** Matthew Arnold, *Civilization in the United States*, 1888.

218 **There is no there** Gertrude Stein, *Everybody's Autobiography*, 1937, p. 208.

219 **Among the new objects** Alexis de Tocqueville, *Democracy in America*, Paris, 1835, vol. 1, p. 1.

220 **has the brusque unfinished** CH to Mary Hubback, Jun. 2, 1872, *EiC*, p. 54.

220 **rough heads** *ibid.*

220 **Jewish-looking . . . very large dark eyes** CH to Mary Hubback, Jun. 23, 1872, *EiC*, p. 56.

220 **seems to me like** CH to John Hubback, Dec. 1, 1872, *ibid.*, p. 80.

220 **they expect to take** CH to Mary Hubback, Jun. 23, 1872, *ibid.*, p. 57.

221 ***Three hundred pounds of*** Roy Morris Jr., *Lighting Out for the Territory: How Samuel Clemens Headed West and Became Mark Twain*, New York, 2010, p. 144.

221 **a gambling carnival** Mark Twain, *Roughing It*, Hartford, Connecticut, 1872, p. 420.

221 **Every sun that rose** *ibid.*

222 **is worried that he** CH to John Hubback, Oct. 6, 1872, *EiC*, p. 73.

222 **I have lived through** CH to John Hubback, n.d. Apr. 1872, *ibid.*, p. 47.

222 **That was in my** *ibid.*

222 **I am so fond of** CH to Mary Hubback, Nov. 5, 1876, *EiC*, p. 168.

224 **The soil you see** http://lastrealindians.tumblr.com

225 **is not much of** CH to John Hubback, n.d. Apr. 1872, *EiC*, p. 43.

225 **I am sure that** *ibid.*, p. 45.

230 **Let him take up . . . let him go forth** Rebecca Solnit, *River of Shadows: Eadweard Muybridge and the Technological Wild West*, 2003, p. 143.

232 **Canon grand, geysers rather** CH to John Hubback, Apr. 4, 1875, *EiC*, p. 134.

233 **never to be forgotten** *ibid.*

233 **If I had stretched** CH to John Hubback, Apr. 4, 1875, *EiC*, p. 135.

233 **glorified with legend** Robert Louis Stevenson, *The Silverado Squatters*, 1883, p. 10.

233 **could handle six horses** Bill Spiers, www.OurHealdsburg.com

233 **drove his six-in-hand as** *The Independent Calistogan*, n.d. 1879, OurHealdsburg.com

233 **He upset last year** CH to John Hubback, Apr. 4, 1875, *EiC*, p. 136.

233 **We have to walk** CH to Mary Hubback, Oct. 29, 1876, *ibid.*, pp. 166–7.

235 **I don't think you** CH to John Hubback, Apr. 27, 1873, *ibid.*, p. 96.

EPILOGUE

240 **the new frontier** John F. Kennedy, Democratic National Convention Nomination Acceptance Address, Jul. 15, 1960.

242 **off the fatta the lan'** John Steinbeck, *Of Mice and Men*, 1937, p. 16 and elsewhere.

243 **by starveling writers and . . . If Carmel's founders should** John Steinbeck, *Travels with Charley: In Search of America*, 1962, p. 156.

246 **ambassadors from another time . . . warm monster bodies** *ibid.*, p. 143.

246 **cathedral hush** *ibid.*, p. 146.

246 **godlike . . . holy** *ibid.*, p. 144.

246 **trying to rediscover this** *ibid.*, p. 5.

247 **We are a nation** *ibid.*, p. 159.

247 **The United States themselves** Walt Whitman, *Leaves of Grass*, New York, 1855, preface.

SELECT BIBLIOGRAPHY

All books published in London unless otherwise indicated.

FANNY TROLLOPE

Glendinning, Victoria, *Trollope*, 1992
Heineman, Helen, *Mrs. Trollope: The Triumphant Feminine in the Nineteenth Century*, Athens, Ohio, 1979
Ransom, Teresa, *Fanny Trollope*, Stroud, Gloucestershire, 1995
Trollope, Anthony, *An Autobiography*, 2 vols, 1883
Trollope, Frances, *Domestic Manners of the Americans*, 1832
Trollope, Thomas Adolphus, *What I Remember*, 3 vols, 1887

FANNY KEMBLE

Bell Jr., Malcolm, *Major Butler's Legacy: Five Generations of a Slaveholding Family*, Athens, Georgia, 1987
FitzGerald, Edward, *Letters of Edward FitzGerald to Fanny Kemble, 1871–1883*, ed. William Aldies Wright, 1895
Kemble, Fanny, *Journal*, 2 vols, London, Philadelphia & Boston, 1835
———, *Journal of a Residence on a Georgian Plantation in 1838–9*, 1863
———, *Record of a Girlhood*, 3 vols, 1878
———, *Records of Later Life*, 3 vols, 1882
Leigh, Frances Butler, *Ten Years on a Georgia Plantation Since the War*, 1883
Marshall, Dorothy, *Fanny Kemble*, 1977
Olmsted, F. L., *The Cotton Kingdom*, New York, 1861
Ritchie, Anne, Lady, *From Friend to Friend*, 1920
Wright, Constance, *Fanny Kemble and the Lovely Land*, 1974

SELECT BIBLIOGRAPHY

HARRIET MARTINEAU

Arbuckle, Elisabeth Sanders, ed., *Harriet Martineau's Letters to Fanny Wedgwood*, Stanford, 1983

Dzelzainis, Ella, & Kaplan, Cora, *Harriet Martineau: Authorship, Society and Empire*, Manchester, 2010

Hoecker-Drysdale, Susan, *Harriet Martineau: First Woman Sociologist*, New York, 1992

Martineau, Harriet, *Society in America*, 2 vols, 1837

———, *Retrospect of Western Travel*, 3 vols, 1838

———, *Life in the Sick Room*, 1844

———, *Harriet Martineau's Autobiography*, 3 vols, 1877

Pichanick, Valerie Kossew, *Harriet Martineau: The Woman and Her Work, 1802–76*, Ann Arbor, 1980

Saunders, Valerie, ed., *Harriet Martineau: Selected Letters*, Oxford, 1990

Webb, R. K., *Harriet Martineau: A Radical Victorian*, 1960

REBECCA BURLEND

Burlend, Rebecca, & Burlend, Edward, *A True Picture of Emigration: or Fourteen Years in the Interior of North America; Being a Full and Impartial Account of the Various Difficulties and Ultimate Success of an English Family Who Emigrated from Barwick-in-Elmet, Near Leeds, in the Year 1831*, 1848

ISABELLA BIRD

Barr, Pat, *A Curious Life for a Lady: The Story of Isabella Bird*, 1970

Bird, Isabella, *The Englishwoman in America*, 1856

———, *Six Months in the Sandwich Islands*, 1875

———, *A Lady's Life in the Rocky Mountains*, 1879

Chubbuck, Kay, ed., *Letters to Henrietta: Isabella Bird*, 2002

Pickering, James H., *"This Blue Hollow": Estes Park, the Early Years, 1859–1915*, Boulder, Colorado, 1999

Stoddart, Anna M., *The Life of Isabella Bird*, 1906

CATHERINE HUBBACK

Hubback, John H., *Cross Currents in a Long Life*, privately printed, 1935

Klippert, Zoë, ed. *An Englishwoman in California: The Letters of Catherine Hubback, 1871–76*, Oxford, 2010

SELECT BIBLIOGRAPHY

GENERAL

Abbott, Carl, Leonard, Stephen J., & McComb, David, *Colorado: A History of the Centennial State*, Colorado, 1982 & 1994

Blackett, R. J. M., *Divided Hearts: Britain and the American Civil War*, Baton Rouge, 2001

Brookman, Philip, *Eadweard Muybridge*, 2010

Brooks, Van Wyck, *The World of Washington Irving*, New York, 1947

Cobb, James C., *The Most Southern Place on Earth: The Mississippi Delta and the Roots of Regional Identity*, New York & Oxford, 1992

Damrosch, Leo, *Tocqueville's Discovery of America*, New York, 2010

Foreman, Amanda, *A World on Fire: An Epic History of Two Nations Divided*, 2010

Leonard, Stephen J. & Noel, Thomas J., *Denver: Mining Camp to Metropolis*, Colorado, 1990

Meacham, Jon, *American Lion: Andrew Jackson in the White House*, New York, 2008

Rhodes, Richard, *John James Audubon: The Making of an American*, New York, 2004

Roosevelt, Theodore, *The Winning of the West: From the Alleghenies to the Mississippi, 1769–1776*, 4 vols, 1889

Schama, Simon, *The American Future: A History from the Founding Fathers to Barack Obama*, 2008

Solnit, Rebecca, *River of Shadows: Eadweard Muybridge and the Technological Wild West*, 2003

Starr, Kevin, *Americans and the California Dream 1850–1915*, New York, 1973

Stegner, Wallace, *Beyond the Hundredth Meridian: John Wesley Powell and the Second Opening of the West*, Boston, 1954

Tocqueville, Alexis de, *Democracy in America*, Paris, 1835 (vol. 1), 1840 (vol. 11); trans. Henry Reeve & Francis Bowen, 1835, 1840 & 1862, corrected Phillips Bradley, 1945

Turner, Frederick Jackson, *The Frontier in American History*, New York, 1920

Wilson, Edmund, *Patriotic Gore: Studies in the Literature of the American Civil War*, New York, 1962

WPA, *Cincinnati, 1788–1943: American Guide Series*, Cincinnati, 1943

SELECTED ARCHIVE SOURCES

The British Library
Cincinnati History Library and Archives
Cincinnati Public Library
The Historic New Orleans Collection
The Hopkinson Bequest, Jane Austen's House Museum, Chawton, Hampshire
New Orleans Public Library Newspaper Collection, 1787–1974

ACKNOWLEDGMENTS

I wish to acknowledge the help, advice and expertise of the following, with sincere gratitude. In America: William Burlend, Mark Collins, Leslie and Mark Handler, Dee Ratterree, Scott Ratterree, Eric Strachan and Buddy Sullivan. In Britain: Richard Cohen, who introduced me to Fanny Trollope; Michael Goldfarb, Angela Hart, Ceri Hutton, Harry Parker, and Chris Phipps for another index.

Like all nonfiction writers, I would be lost without the cooperation of librarians, archivists and curators. Sincere thanks go to those at Cincinnati Public Library, especially Beth in Books and Newspapers, Susan in Local History and Chris Smith in the Cincinnati Room; to Louise West at Jane Austen's House Museum and, as ever, to the indefatigable staff of the London Library. Thanks also to Ann Brown and Darlene Dawson at the Pardee House in Oakland.

Several editors commissioned pieces that helped *O My America!* grow into a book, among them Ellah Allfrey at *Granta*, Graham Boynton at the *Daily Telegraph*, Jane Knight at *The Times*, Wendy Driver and Frank Barrett at the *Mail on Sunday* and Dan Linstead at *Wanderlust*.

I am deeply grateful to my loyal editors Dan Franklin in London and Courtney Hodell in New York. Thanks are also due to their assistants Steven Messer and Mark Krotov, both now moved on, and to Ellie Steel, most diligent of copy editors. I owe tremendous gratitude to my agents in London and New York, respectively Gillon Aitken and Kathy Robbins. Thanks to their assistants, Imogen Pelham and Micah Hauser, too.

And, of course and as always, thanks to my very best readers: Peter Graham, Jeremy Lewis and Lucinda Riches.

INDEX

Page numbers in *italics* refer to illustrations.

Adams, John Quincy, 45, 73
Alcott, Amos Bronson, 31
Amis, Martin, 194–95
Andersen, Hans Christian, 128
Anderson, Sherwood, 42–43, 116
Arnold, Matthew, 128, 154, 217
Auden, W. H., 30
Audubon, John James, 10, 38–40, *40*, 227
Audubon, Lucy, 39
Austen, Cassandra, 209, 210
Austen, Francis (father of Catherine
    Hubback), 208, 210
Austen, Jane, 7, 207–13, 211*n*, 219, 220

Beaumont, Gustave de, 54
Bell, Alexander Graham, 93
Bermuda, 31
Bethel Methodist Episcopal Pioneer
    Church, 175, *175*
Biblical Mini-Golf, *141*
Bickerdike, George, 162, 165, 166,
    168–69, 172
Bird, Edward (father of Isabella), 181
Bird, Henrietta (sister of Isabella), 182,
    185, 190, 203–205; death of, 205
Bird, Isabella, 7, 8, 179–206, 226, 234,
    248; on American tour, 183; birth of,
    181; in California, 183; in Colorado, 7,
    179, 184–204; death of, 206; at Estes
    Park, 185–91, *188*, 202–203; family

migration to Scotland, 182; first visit
    to America, 181; horseback riding of,
    183–84, 189, 200, 201, 203, 206; ill
    health of, 179, 181, 182, 204, 205;
    marriage proposal received by, 182;
    marriage to Bishop, 205; physical
    appearance and photograph of, 182,
    183, 203; Queen Anne Mansion of,
    187–88, *188*, 195; relationship with
    "Rocky Mountain Jim" Nugent, 179,
    185–86, 189–91, 203, 205–206;
    religious faith of, 189; return to
    Scotland, 203; Rocky Mountains and,
    180, 184–85; world tours of, 182–83,
    205
Bird, Isabella, writing of, 204, 206; *The
    Aspects of Religion in the United States of
    America*, 181–82; *The Englishwoman in
    America*, 181; *A Lady's Life in the Rocky
    Mountains*, 180, 184, 199, 201,
    203–205
Birkenhead, 212–13, 219
Bishop, John, 205
bison, 192, 193, 224
Black Hawk, Colo., 201
Boston, Mass., 72, 77
Brady, Mathew, 107–108, *108*
Bristol, 4, 16, 20, 26, 35*n*, 46, 53–54
Brontë, Anne, 210
Brontë, Charlotte, 154–55
Brontë, Emily, 210

Brougham, Henry, 1st Baron Brougham and Vaux, 128
Browning, Elizabeth Barrett, 155
Browning, Robert, 15
Bryson, Bill, 55
buffalo, 192, 193, 224
Burlend, Edward (son of Rebecca), 161, 162, 169, 176–77
Burlend, John (husband of Rebecca), 161–62, 164, 172; death of, 178; decision to emigrate, 162; grave of, 178, *178*; in Illinois, 165–75; injury suffered by, 169–70
Burlend, Mary (daughter of Rebecca), 162, 176, 178
Burlend, Rebecca, 7, 160–78, 239, 248; arrival in America, 7, 164; birth of, 161; children of, 161–62, 173, 175–76; decision to emigrate, 162, 170; grave of, 178, *178*; in Illinois, 160, 164–78; marriage of, 161–62; photograph of, *177*; religious faith of, 174–75; summer visit to England, 176
Burlend, William "Butch" (great-great-great-grandson of Rebecca), 178, *178*
Butler, Frances "Fan," *see* Leigh, Frances Butler
Butler, Pierce, 75, 76, 81–82, 110, 115, 118; arrest of, 104; character of, 71, 90; death of, 118; family background of, 81; infidelities of, 99–100, 102; Kemble's courtship with, 70–74; Kemble's letters to, 78–79, 100, 102; Kemble's marriage to, 74–76, 78–80, 85, 90, 99–100, 143; Kemble's separation and divorce from, 100–102; physical appearance and photograph of, 71, 98–99, *98*; slaves of, 85–87, 89–90, 99, 104, 113, 117, 118
Butler, Sarah "Sally," *see* Wister, Sarah Butler
Butler Island, 62, 81–87, *86*, 113–14, 119
Byers, William, 198
Byron, George Gordon, Lord, 72

Caldwell, Erskine, 115–16, 246
Calhoun, John C., 150
California, 214, 216–17, 239, 242; author in, 230, *231*, 237, *238*, 240–48; Bird in, 183; Carmel, 242–43; Coloma,

232, 237–38, *238*; Coulterville, 240; Gold Rush in, 197, 214, 232, 237–40, 244; Hubback in, 216–26, 232–34; Oakland, 217–18, 220, 222, 233, 234; Pigeon Point Lighthouse, 9, 244, *245*; removal of Native Americans from, 223; San Francisco, *see* San Francisco, Calif.; Yosemite, 228
Capp, Al, 116, *117*
Carlyle, Jane, 158
Carlyle, Thomas, 128
Carmel, Calif., 242–43
Carnegie, Lucy, 93–94
Carnegie, Thomas, 93–94
Cather, Willa, 170–71, 173
Channing, William, 73, 85, 130, 149
Chicago, Ill., 144, 167
Cincinnati, Ohio, 8, 43, 51–52, 54–55; Audubon in, 38–39; author in, 51–52; growth of, 35; industry in, 35–36; Martineau in, 142; pigs and pork industry in, 13, 35; slavery and, 41; Trollope in, 8, 13, 33–37, 40–50, 142, 147; Trollope's Bazaar in, 47–50, *49*, 69, 142; Trollope's talking panoramas in, 43–44, 46
Civil War, 71–72, 92, 106–10, 115, 159, 187, 199, 216; battles in, 106, 108–109, 114; Britain and, 106, 107, 109–10; Kemble and, 63, 95, 107–10; photography and, 107–108, *108*; Trollope and, 109
Cody, Buffalo Bill, 192–93, *193*
Coleridge, Samuel Taylor, 30
Coloma, Calif., 232, 237–38, *238*
Colorado, 193, 194, 197, 214; author in, 7, 191–92, 194–95, 201–202, 204; Bird in, 179, 184–204; Black Hawk, 201; Byers in, 198; Colorado Springs, 202; Denver, 195–200; Estes Park, 185–94, *188*, 202–203; Longs Peak, 180, 187, 189–92; Masonville, 194; Platte Canyon, 195; Powell in, 197–98; removal of Native Americans from, 196–97
Colorado Springs, Colo., 202
Comanche Bill, 200
Cooke, Jay, 234
cotton, 80, 83, 84, 88–89, 104–105, 107, 114, 118, 136
Coulter, George, 240
Coulterville, Calif., 240

crabs, horseshoe, 94, *94*
Crane, Stephen, 109
cricket, 147, *147*
Crocker, Charles, 216–17
Crockett, Davy, 30
Cromwell, Joe, 34
Cumberland Island, Ga., 93–94

Dante Alighieri, 44
Darien, Ga., 87–89, 95, 117, 118, 147
Darwin, Charles, 39, 206; on
    Martineau, 124, 126, 150
Davis, Jefferson, 104
democracy, 18, 33, 41, 45, 47, 53–55, 73,
    76, 109, 125, 145
Denver, Colo., 195–200
Dickens, Charles, 10, 15, 31, 41, 56, 82,
    149, 149*n*, 158; Martineau and, 124,
    125, 128, 149, 159; mesmerism and,
    151–52
Dickinson, Emily, 107–108
Disraeli, Benjamin, 146, 148
Donne, John, vii
Dorfeuille, Joseph, 44
Dos Passos, John, 246
Dunraven, Windham Wyndham-Quin,
    4th Earl of, 192–94

Economy, Pa., 18
Edwards, Sam, 187, 189
Eliot, George, 128
Eliot, T. S., 121–22
Emerson, Ralph Waldo, 128, 130
Ernest, John, 242
Estes, Joel, 186–87
Estes Park, Colo., 185–94, *188*, 202–203
Evans, Griff, 187–89, 195, 204

Faulkner, William, 10, 27–29, *28*, 43, 58,
    116, 246
FitzGerald, Edward, 103
Fitzgerald, F. Scott, 8, 246
Flint, Timothy, 40–41
Ford, Richard, 22
Foss, Clark, 233

Garibaldi Riots, 213, 219
Gaskell, Elizabeth, 110

Gast, John, 223
George III, King, 16, 81
Georgia, 80, 111, 118, 187; author in,
    90–98; Butler Island, 62, 81–87,
    86, 113–14, 119; Cumberland
    Island, 93–94; Darien, 87–89, 95,
    117, 118, 147; removal of Cherokee
    from, 80–81; St. Simon's Island,
    80, 81, 88–89, 91, 92, 113–14, 118;
    Savannah, 83, 90, 93, 114, 117,
    119; Sea Islands, 5–6, 62, 80, 88,
    90–92, 111
Germantown, Tenn., 29
Geysers, The, 232–33
Gissing, George, 41
Gladstone, William Ewart, 206
Glendinning, Victoria, 158*n*
Goethe, Johann Wolfgang von, 30
Grand Canyon, 198
Grant, Ulysses S., 109, 114, 223
Greville, Charles, 99
Griffith, D. W., 112

Hall, Basil, 53
Hallam, Arthur Henry, 65
Hart, Angela, *153*
Hemings, Sally, 53
Hemingway, Ernest, 42–43, 109*n*, 246
Henly, Robert, Lord, 129
Hervieu, Auguste-Jean-Jacques, 19–20,
    36–37, 44, 48, 50, 65
homesteaders, 43, 80, 160–61, 165, 168,
    176, 185, 217, 239
Hopkins, Mark, 216–17
Hubback, Catherine, 7, 9, 207–35,
    237–39, 242, 248; arrival in America,
    213; in Birkenhead, 212–13; birth of,
    208; in California, 216–26, 232–34;
    death of, 235; family background of,
    208; and husband's mental collapse, 7,
    209–10, 213, 220, 234; marriage of, 7,
    209; move to Virginia, 234; physical
    appearance and photograph of,
    207–209, *207*; return visit to England,
    234; servants as viewed by, 220, 222;
    sketching of, 208–209, 218
Hubback, Catherine, writing of, 7,
    210–12, 218–20; *Life and Its Lessons*,
    211–12; *The Younger Sister*, 210–11
Hubback, Charles (son of Catherine),
    209, 212, 213, 222, 234–35

Hubback, Edward (son of Catherine), 209, 212, 213, 216, 217, 219, 222, 234, 242

Hubback, John (husband of Catherine), 209; mental collapse of, 7, 209–10, 213, 220, 234

Hubback, John, Jr. (son of Catherine), 210–13, 218, 222, 233, 234

Hubback, Mary (daughter-in-law of Catherine), 218, 222

Huntington, Collis, 216–17

Hurricane Katrina, 22, 23

Huskisson, William, 67

Illinois, 166; Burlend in, 160, 164–78; Chicago, 144, 167; Phillip's Ferry, 160, 165; Pike County, 167, 173–74, 177, 178; removal of Native Americans from, 166; Vandalia, 166

Indiana, 31; New Harmony, 18

Indians, *see* Native Americans

Jackson, Andrew, 30, 45, 53, 71–72, 81, 143

James, Henry, 10, 55, 109*n*, 155, 212; Kemble and, 102, 113, 120–23

Jefferson, Thomas, 34, 53, 80, 81

Jeffrey, Francis, 150

Jekyll Island Club, 92

Jerrold, Douglas, 151

John Murray (publisher), 205

Jonestown, Tenn., 28–29, 52

Jordan, Constance, 219–20

Keats, George, 33, 39

Keats, John, 46–47

Keeler, W. J., 237

Kemble, Charles (father of Fanny), 63, 64, 68, 70, 72, 74–75, 101

Kemble, Fanny, 5–6, 62–123, 128*n*, 129–31, 150, 161, 248; acting career of, 5–6, 63–66, 68, 68, 70–73, 75, 76, 101, 104; on American theater tour, 68–74, 76; birth of, 63; in Boston, 72, 77; on Butler Island, 83–87, *86*; Butler's courtship of, 70–74; Butler's letters from, 78–79, 100, 102; Butler's marriage to, 74–76, 78–80, 85, 90, 99–100, 143; Butler's separation and

divorce from, 100–102; character of, 103–104; Civil War and, 63, 95, 107–10; in Darien, 87–89, 95, 147; death of, 122; family background of, 63; James and, 102, 113, 120–23; marriage of, 5; Martineau and, 75, 77, 78, 133–35, 146, 149, 159; in New York, 68–70; "The Perch" house of, 102–103, *103*; in Philadelphia, 70–71, 75–76, 95, 99–100, 119; physical appearance and portraits of, *6*, 64, 66, *66*, 98–99, *98*, 104, *121*; return to England, 100–101; return to U.S., 119; on St. Simon's Island, 88–89; on Sea Islands, 62; second return to England, 119; Sedgwick and, 73, 78, 100, 102; servants and shopgirls as viewed by, 70, 135; sign commemorating, 95, *96*; slavery and, 6, 10, 63, 73, 77, 79, 83–91, 111–15, 135; Stephenson and, 66–67; Trollope and, 62, 64, 70, 73, 75–78, 82, 114; in Washington, D.C., 71–72

Kemble, Fanny, writing of, 63–65, 68, 101, 110–12, 120; *Journal of a Residence in America*, 76–78; *Journal of a Residence on a Georgian Plantation*, 10, 112–14, 120, 159; *A Year of Consolation*, 101

Kemble, Henry, 122

Kennedy, John F., 240

Kentucky: author in, 138–42; Laurel Lake, 103, 139, *140*; Louisville, 33; Mammoth Caves of, 9, 137–38, 140–42, *141*; Martineau in, 137–38; Pleasureville, 50–51, *51*

King, Roswell, Jr., 86–87, 89, 91

King, Roswell, Sr., 86

Lafayette, Gilbert du Motier, Marquis de, 18

Larkin, Philip, 60*n*

Larkyns, Harry, 229–30

Laurel Lake, Ky., 103, 139, *140*

Lawrence, Thomas, 65–66

Lee, Robert E., 117

Leigh, Anna Austen, 211

Leigh, Frances Butler ("Fan"; daughter of Fanny Kemble), 79, 82, 100–102, 104, 110, 117–20, 123; *Ten Years on a Georgia Plantation Since the War*, 115, 117

Leigh, James, 118–19
Leigh, Pierce Butler, 120
Lewis and Clark Expedition, 34
Li'l Abner, 116–17, *117*
Lincoln, Abraham, 104, 109, 111, 113*n*, 114, 115, 166, 174
Longs Peak, Colo., 180, 187, 189–92
Louisiana, 26; New Orleans, *see* New Orleans, La.
Louis Philippe, King, 15, 124
Louisville, Ky., 33
Lyell, Charles, 113–14, 150, 225

Macready, William, 150
Mammoth Caves, 9, 137–38, 140–42, *141*
maps, *xviii–xix*
Marsden, Kate, 179
Marshall, James, 214, 237, 238
Martineau, Harriet, 6–7, 9, 74, 75, 78, 105, 107, 124–59, 217, 248; American tour of, 129–44; atheism of, 151, 154; birth of, 125; Brontë and, 154–55; character of, 124, 126, 127, 154; in Cincinnati, 142; Darwin on, 124, 126, 150; deafness of, 126, 132–33, 146, 154; Dickens and, 124, 125, 128, 149, 159; family background of, 125; fiancé of, 126, 155; health problems of, 151–53, 157, 158; Kemble and, 75, 77, 78, 133–35, 146, 149, 159; in Kentucky, 137–38; The Knoll house of, 153–54, *153*, 157–58; personal life of, 155; physical appearance and portrait of, 126, *126*; slavery and, 135–36, 142–43, 147–48; in South, 135–36; in Washington D.C., 6–7
Martineau, Harriet, writing of, 6, 124, 127–28, 143, 149, 157–59; *Autobiography*, 134, 158; *Deerbrook*, 150; *How to Observe Manners and Morals*, 129; *Illustrations of Political Economy*, 127–28, 135; *Poor Laws and Paupers Illustrated*, 128; *A Retrospect of Western Travel*, 149–50; *Society in America*, 75, 125, 145–49
Masonville, Colo., 194
Melville, Herman, 102
Memphis, Tenn., 29–30
mesmerism, 151–53, *152*
Metternich, Prince Klemens von, 15

Milnes, Richard Monckton, 65
Milwaukee, Wisc., 144
mining, 201, 239
Mississippi, 26; Oxford, 27–28
Mississippi Delta, 26–27, 29
Mitchell, Margaret, 85, 96–97, 116
Monroe, Marilyn, 241, *241*
Moore, George, 58–59
Morgan, J. P., 92, *92*, 93
Morris, Jan, 180
Morse, G. D., 208
Mount Auburn Cemetery, 74, *74*
Murray family (publishers), 205
Muybridge, Eadweard, 226–32; motion studies, 226, *226*, 231–32; San Francisco panorama, 230–31, *231*; self-portrait, *229*
Muybridge, Flora, 229–30
Muybridge, Floredo, 229, 230

Nagin, Ray, 22
Nahant, Mass., 131–32
Napoleon III, 107, 159, 213
Nashoba Commune, Tenn., 18, 19, 30–32, 72
Native Americans, 8–9, 55, 223, 243; Cherokee, 8, 57, 80–81; Choctaw, 30, 80; removal of, 30*n*, 45, 80–81, 166, 196–97, 223–24
Newby, Thomas Cautley, 210
New England, 71, 73, 75, 77, 130, 142, 147
New Harmony, Ind., 18
New Orleans, La., 20–23, 136, 164, 240; author in, 21–24; Hurricane Katrina in, 22, 23; Martineau in, 136; Trollope in, 20–21, 23–24
New York, N.Y., 68–70, 69*n*
Nicholas I, Tsar, 124
Nightingale, Florence, 128, 157
Nugent, "Rocky Mountain Jim," 179, 185–86, 189–91, 203, 205–206

Oakland, Calif., 217–18, 220, 222, 233, 234
O'Connor, Flannery, 97–98
Ohio, 31, 41; Cincinnati, *see* Cincinnati, Ohio
Ohio River, 33
O'Sullivan, Timothy, 227–28

Owen, Robert, 18
Oxford, Miss., 27–28

Palmerston, Henry John Temple, 3rd
    Viscount, 106, 111, 208
Philadelphia, Pa., 70; Kemble in, 70–71,
    75–76, 95, 99–100, 119
Phillip's Ferry, Ill., 160, 165
photography, 226; Civil War and,
    107–108, *108*; landscape, 227–28, 238;
    Muybridge and, *see* Muybridge,
    Eadweard
Pigeon Point Lighthouse, 9, 244, *245*
pigs: in Cincinnati, 13, 35; wild, 94
Platte Canyon, Colo., 195
Pleasureville, Ky., 50–51, *51*
Poe, Edgar Allan, 78
postal services, 35*n*
Powell, John Wesley, 197–98
Powers, Hiram, 44
Punch, 104–5, *105*, 179

Quakers, 75, 131

railroads, 35*n*, 66–67, 82, 93, 119, 199,
    216–17, 221–24, 234; time zones and,
    8, 215; transcontinental, 7, 214–15, *215*
Reform Bill, 53, 67, 127, 162, 208
rice, 84, 95, 117, 119
Ritchie, Anne, Lady, 103–104, 119, 120
Rockefeller, William, *92*, 93
Rocky Mountain National Park, 194
Rocky Mountains, 180, 184–85
Rogers, Samuel, 150
Romanticism, 30, 63–64, 87, 180, 223
Roosevelt, Theodore, 240
Russell, Bertrand, 134*n*
Russell, John, 176

St. John's Episcopal Church, 218
St. Simon's Island, Ga., 80, 81, 88–89,
    91, 92, 113–14, 118
San Francisco, Calif., 208, 213, 214, 216,
    217, 220–23, 234; author in, 230;
    Muybridge's panorama of, 230–31, *231*
Savannah, Ga., 83, 90, 93, 95–97,
    95–97, 114, 117, 119
Sayers, Dorothy L., 110

Scott, Robert Falcon, 225
Sea Islands, Ga., 5–6, 62, 80, 88, 90–92,
    111
Sedgwick, Catharine, 73, 78, 100, 102,
    130
Shakers, 31, 143
Shakespeare, William, 37, 73, 101, 104,
    114, 120, 122
Shelley, Percy Bysshe, 72
Sherman, William Tecumseh, 114, 187,
    189, 224
Shulman, Nickey, 101*n*
Siddons, Sarah, 63, 64, 101
Sitting Bull, 224
slaves, slavery, 4, 8, 10, 41, 55, 76, 81, 85,
    88, 89, 92, 104–105, 107, 111, 166;
    abolitionism and, 71, 73, 79, 85,
    135–36, 142–43; Britain and, 85;
    Butler family and, 81, 83–87, 89–90,
    99, 104, 113, 117, 118; Kemble and, 6,
    10, 63, 73, 77, 79, 83–91, 111–15, 135;
    Martineau and, 135–36, 142–43,
    147–48; Nashoba and, 31, 32; Native
    Americans and, 9; in Sea Islands, 5–6
Smith, Sydney, 151
Stanford, Leland, 214–17, 231
Stanley, Henry Morton, 106
Stein, Gertrude, 218
Steinbeck, John, 234, 242–43, 246–47
Stephenson, George, 66–67, 82, 85
Stevenson, Robert Louis, 163–64, 233
Stewart, Louis, 15
Stowe, Harriet Beecher, 111, 113

telephone, 92–93, *92*, 226
Tennessee, 28, 31; Germantown, 29;
    Jonestown, 28–29, 52; Memphis,
    29–30; Nashoba Commune, 18, 19,
    30–32
Tennyson, Alfred, Lord, 67
Terry, Ellen, 122
Thackeray, William Makepeace,
    41, 57, 66, 96
Thoreau, Henry David, 31
Tocqueville, Alexis de, 10, 54–56, 87,
    134, 145, 201, 219, 220, 239
Trail Ridge Road, 204
Trelawny, Edward, 72
Trollope, Anthony (son of Fanny),
    3, 14–19, 41, 46, 47, 56–60, 108, 123,
    151, 210, 211

Trollope, Arthur (son of Fanny), 17
Trollope, Cecilia (daughter of Fanny), 19, 56, 57
Trollope, Emily (daughter of Fanny), 19, 32, 57
Trollope, Fanny, 3–4, 8, 13–61, 63, 69, 108, 125, 130, 136, 143, 145, 146, 161, 181–82, 199, 209, 210, 222, 246, 247; arrival in America, 4, 20; Bazaar of, 47–50, *49*, 69, 142; birth of, 16; character of, 17–18; in Cincinnati, 8, 13, 33–37, 40–50, 142, 147; Civil War and, 109; death of, 60–61; family background of, 16; Gano Lodge rented by, 37–38, 50; Kemble and, 62, 64, 70, 73, 75–78, 82, 114; leaves New Orleans for Tennessee, 24–26; marriage of, 16; at Nashoba, 32; in New Orleans, 20–21, 23–24; physical appearance and illustrations of, 14, *14*, *16*, 21, 40–41, 48, 59; return to England, 5, 13, 52–53, 62, 67; servants and shopgirls as viewed by, 41–42, 135, 220; talking panoramas organized by, 43–44, 46; in Tennessee, 29–30; travels to Ohio, 4; Wright and, 18–19, 32
Trollope, Fanny, writing of, 56–57, 212; *Domestic Manners of the Americans*, 3–4, 13–15, 53–54, 56, 69–70, 114, 125, 129
Trollope, Frances (wife of Tom), 56
Trollope, Henry (son of Fanny), 19, 33, 36, 37, 44, 46, 50, 57
Trollope, Thomas (husband of Fanny), 16–19, 36, 45–48, 58, 209
Trollope, Tom (son of Fanny), 15, 17, 19, 38, 46, 47, 56, 58, 60
Turner, Frederick Jackson, 144–45, 172, 176
Twain, Mark, 15, 52, 109n, 112, 113, 134n, 167, 192, 220–21

Unitarianism, 73, 125–26, 128n, 130, 133, 149
utopian communities, 18, 30–31, 33; *see also* Nashoba Commune

Vail, Theodore N., *92*, 93
Van Buren, Martin, 174
Vance, David, 22, 29, 33
Vandalia, Ill., 166
Victoria, Queen, 99, 148, 193, 206

Washington, D.C., 45; Kemble in, 71–72; Martineau in, 6–7
Washington, George, 18
Watson, Thomas, 93
Wellington, Arthur Wellesley, Duke of, 67
Wells, H. G., 134n
Welty, Eudora, 10
Wharton, Edith, 155
Whitman, Walt, 114, 247
Whitney, Eli, 80
Wilberforce, William, 181
wilderness, 223–24
wilderness photography, 227–28, 238
Wilson, Woodrow, 93
Wister, Owen, 115
Wister, Sarah Butler ("Sally"; daughter of Fanny Kemble), 78, 82, 87, 100–102, 104, 115, 118–21, 123
Wolfe, Thomas, 43, 246
Wollstonecraft, Mary, 30
Wordsworth, Mary, 154
Wordsworth, William, 47, 154
Wright, Camilla, 18
Wright, Fanny, 18–19, 31, 32

Yellowstone National Park, 223
Yosemite, Calif., 228

A Note About the Author

Sara Wheeler is the author of six books of biography and travel, including *Travels in a Thin Country: A Journey Through Chile*, *Terra Incognita: Travels in Antarctica*, and *The Magnetic North: Notes from the Arctic Circle* (FSG, 2011). She lives in London.